Economics of public
transport

Modern economics
Series editor: David W. Pearce

Economics of public transport

C A Nash

Longman
London and New York

Longman Group Limited
Longman House
Burnt Mill, Harlow, Essex, UK

Published in the United States of America
by Longman Inc., New York

© Longman Group Limited 1982

First published 1982

British Library Cataloguing in Publication Data

Nash, C. A.
   Economics of public transport. – (Modern economics)
   1. Transportation – Great Britain
   I. Title   II. Series
      380.5′90941   HE243   80-42200

ISBN 0-582-44631-7

Printed in Singapore by
Selector Printing Co (Pte) Ltd.

Contents

Preface

The aim of this book is to show how economic analysis may be used as an aid to decision-taking in both the long-run planning and day-to-day management of public transport systems. It concentrates on the conventional road- and rail-based systems which currently form, and for the foreseeable future will continue to form, the bulk of internal public transport throughout the world. Many of the same methods would, however, be applicable to other modes, including air and sea transport. The theme of the book is that a realistic appraisal of the circumstances of public transport shows purely commercial criteria to be grossly inadequate for decision-taking in this sector, but that this in no way negates the need for economic analysis of alternative decisions and for monitoring and financial control. The application of economic analysis to decisions such as fare structures and level, service planning and investment decisions are discussed, case studies and simplified numerical examples being used to illustrate the points at hand. Particular emphasis is placed on the relationship between objectives, external circumstances, organisation and policy.

The need for the book arises for the following reasons:

1. Existing texts on transport economics tend to discuss these issues only at an abstract level, giving the reader little idea of the practical circumstances and constraints which may modify the conclusions in practice, or indeed of how to set about such an implementation.

2. Acceptance of the case for taking objectives other than purely commercial ones into account raises all sorts of issues such as how to formulate those objectives, evaluate alternatives and monitor results, how to finance resulting deficits and how to divide managerial and financial responsibility between central government, local government and the operators concerned. The danger of such an approach is one of blurred responsibilities, with decisions being taken politically without adequate information on their consequences and with financial support taking the form of blanket deficit finance. In those countries where public transport support is of long standing, the viewing of public transport as a social service has tended to discourage the application of economic analysis to its problems.

3. The recent growth of computer-based data collection and analysis systems in public transport operation means that where public transport decision-takers have previously had to rely on judgements based on experience, they are now becoming sufficiently well informed to make use of more scientific decision-taking techniques. However, unless the scope and limitations of these techniques is well understood, there is a danger that their use may worsen, rather than improve, the quality of decision-taking in public transport operations.

Whilst this book is written primarily for advanced undergraduate and postgraduate economics students taking special subjects in transport economics, it is hoped that the book will be accessible to a wider audience, including transport students from other disciplines and students from local government and public transport operators preparing for professional examinations. The level of exposition requires no more than a knowledge of elementary economic theory, and of simple mathematical and statistical techniques such as differentiation and regression analysis, and much of the book will be intelligible without even that.

The book falls essentially into two parts. Chapters 1–6 deal with general issues in the economies of public transport regarding organisation, costing, pricing, service levels, finance and regulation. Chapters 7–10 look at the main sectors of the public transport market – urban, inter-urban and rural passenger and freight. Finally, Chapter 11 draws the threads together in the context of a brief discussion of the future of public transport.

A word is called for on the definition of public transport. Within passenger transport, the definition – including rail, bus and taxi services – is fairly straightforward. In freight, it is less so. We have adopted the standpoint that transport for hire and reward is public transport. However, this distinction is a little artificial, in that much hire and reward work is on behalf of a single operation. It is only where scheduled services and mixed loads are involved that the problems of road haulage become similar to those of other public transport modes. Coverage of the road haulage industry is therefore less comprehensive than that of the bus and coach and railway industries.

Acknowledgements

Sponsorship of my current post by the British Railways Board has enabled me to devote most of my time over the last few years to the problems of public transport, and I am grateful to officers of British Rail and other transport operators for all they have taught me. In particular, Dr J. D. C. A. Prideaux, Mr S. D. Box and Mr R. Edgly have given valuable comments on the first draft of various chapters. I am also indebted to colleagues in the Institute for Transport Studies at Leeds University, especially Mr P. J. Mackie, to Mr M. Kerridge of the Confederation of British Road Passenger Transport and to the students on whom much of the material was tried out. Professor D. W. Pearce, as always, provided valuable advice at all stages. None of the above is in any way responsible for the final version and the views it contains. Without the speed and efficiency of my wife, Diane Petch and Pamela Rammell, who shared the typing, this book would have taken even longer to complete. Thanks are also due to Derek Heathcote for his help with the diagrams.

Chapter 1

The framework of public transport operations

1.1 Decision-taking in public transport

The most fundamental decisions facing any industry are the combination of price and level of output to choose for each product. The principles upon which this choice is based under different market structures are the subject of numerous texts on the theory of the firm, and will not be considered in detail here. Suffice it to say that, from the point of view of the transport sector, we may identify three crucial market structures:

Perfect competition

In most countries, the road haulage industry and in some, road passenger transport is characterised by a large number of small firms supplying similar products with relatively easy entry to the market (except where, as discussed in Ch. 5, the State chooses to restrict entry). This appears to be a sufficiently close approximation to perfect competition for us to expect such industries to be characterised by average cost pricing (but assuming an absence of scale economies, this should equal marginal cost as well) with the scale of output of the industry as a whole determined by demand at that price.

Monopoly

The railway industry is usually characterised by a single national network, plus a number of small specialised companies (for instance, local metros in urban areas), with no competition for the same traffic. (The major exception is, of course, the United States, where preservation of competition between at least two companies to all major points has long been a guiding principle, although recent mergers and bankruptcies have made this increasingly difficult.) In most European countries, bus companies are licensed on the basis of one per route, so that effectively these are also monopolies (and in many cases a single operator covers a wide area).

The general recommendation in the literature for a State-owned or regulated monopoly is a policy of marginal cost pricing. The problem which arises if there are economies of scale is that this implies a failure to cover costs from revenue. Consequently, either subsidies will be needed or departures from marginal cost pricing must be sanctioned. These might take the form of a general shift to average cost pricing, or of departures designed to minimise net loss of benefits by following second-best pricing principles (in simple circumstances, this might mean making proportionate increases of price over marginal cost in inverse proportion to the ratio of own-price demand elasticities (Baumol and Bradford, 1970).

Oligopoly

Oligopoly exists in the transport sector where two or three railways or bus companies provide competing services. It is more common in air transport than in land-based modes. The literature contains a wide variety of solutions to oligopolistic market decisions, according to the degree of collusion and the formation of expectations as to the reactions of the rival. The result may vary from that of pure monopoly where there is complete collusion to that of perfect competition where there is no collusion and no response to price-cutting is expected from the rival.

Given the existence of theoretical models to apply to the principal forms of market structure found in the transport sector, the need to study public transport as a specialism at all may reasonably be questioned. Why not simply apply the models developed for general use? The answer to this question lies in the existence of a number of particular characteristics of public transport which, whilst by no means unique to the sector, make the direct application of the theoretical models less than straightforward.

A very large number of jointly produced products. Although in certain contexts it is reasonable to regard the output of public transport operators as comprising passenger miles and freight ton miles, this is a gross simplification. Customers actually wish to buy trips from a particular origin to a particular destination at a particular time. Thus a bus or rail network of 2,000 stations or stops produces some 4 m. products for each possible journey time, and may thus be involved in setting something greatly in excess of 4 m. fares. Clearly, simplifying formulae are necessary to make the task manageable. Moreover, many of these individual products will use common services for at least part of the journey, so that there is a problem of allocating joint costs. In fact, costing (as shown in Ch. 3) is normally related to services or service groups rather than to the individual trip. There is no obvious or unique way of working out the average cost of each possible distinct trip on the public transport system.

Output is subject to major indivisibilities and cannot be stored. In most simple models, output and sales are taken as synonymous. More sophisticated models may take account of discrepancies between the two as adjustments to stockholding. But in the transport field, production cannot be stored. If unsold, at the time of production, it is lost. Again, this is found in other sectors; services for instances, and virtually in electricity, where storage is possible but very expensive. What makes the problem worse is the importance of indivisibilities. It is not possible to adjust the number of seats in a vehicle rapidly to conform to fluctuations in demand even if these are known in advance. Uncertainty adds to the problem. Thus capacity utilisation in public transport is rarely much above 50 per cent, and frequently much lower. This leads to a puzzle for anyone trying to apply marginal cost pricing, for it appears that marginal cost is always either zero (where there is spare capacity) or very high (where capacity is fully utilised). Nor is this merely true of short-run marginal cost; if demand and supply are steady over time, the position will persist even in the long run.

The consequence of these factors is that a wedge is driven between pricing decisions and output decisions; it is no longer the case that one necessarily determines the other, and indeed most public transport operators consider the two as separate distinct decisions. The most sensible practical approach to pricing decisions is not to base prices on estimates of costs, but to reverse the procedure and to consider the capacity and cost implications of alternative levels of price.

The importance of product quality and its correlation with output. Again, the importance of product quality decisions is by no means confined to transport. What is unusual, however, is the way in which product quality in public transport is correlated with output. Whenever talking about scheduled services, it is the case that an important aspect of quality is the frequency with which the service operates. However, given the existence of economies of vehicle size (Ch. 3), for any given level of traffic, it is only possible to provide an enhanced frequency at increased unit costs. Consequently, increases in traffic levels either produce economies of scale from the use of larger vehicles or improved quality of service from a higher frequency. Either way, the impact is one of increasing returns to scale in terms of the total social cost of the transport facility. This near universality of increasing returns to scale to total output (which may co-exist with increasing, zero or decreasing returns to scale at the level of the individual firm) means that the conflict between marginal cost pricing and breaking even or achieving a given financial target referred to above will always be present to a greater or lesser degree. This, plus the practical impossibility of any close relationship between price and marginal cost for each distinct product, means that public transport is an area ripe for the application of second-best theory even before external costs and benefits are taken into account (section 1.3).

A further complication in the public transport field is the extreme political sensitivity which pricing and output decisions often have. A change in the product line of a public transport operator may leave some sectors of the population unable to get to work, school, shops, doctors, etc. except at greatly increased cost (e.g. taxi) or inconvenience. Freight transport with-drawals may pose similar difficulties for firms, leading in extreme cases to a change in location or liquidation, and thus to unemployment for workers. Similarly, because in many contexts the public transport user feels trapped into using the services of a monopoly producer (frequently the State), fares are always liable to become a contentious issue. Before the development of widespread private and own-account transport these points were, of course, all the more important in the proportion of consumers and firms to which they applied.

A consequence of this is that political authorities have become far more heavily involved in pricing and output decisions in the transport field than in many others, and public transport operators often find themselves taking decisions under constraints which appear totally irrational to the economic theorist. For instance, most railways require government permission to change fares, routes operated and sometimes even quite minor service level changes. Bus companies face similar restrictions through regulatory bodies, or from their ownership or control by local authorities. Fares adjustments to raise fares where marginal costs are high or where demand elasticities are low relative to elsewhere may be forbidden as discrimination, and so forth. Thus a student of public transport needs to study not just the operators themselves, but a whole range of political bodies which may be in a position to influence or to control the decisions of the operator.

1.2 The organisation of public transport operators

There are five main characteristics of transport operators to be taken into account in considering organisational issues:
1. Size and size distribution of competitors.
2. Ownership and control.
3. Types of traffic handled.
4. Mode or modes of transport operated.
5. Geographical area covered.

At one extreme we have the one-man, one vehicle operation, which is still common in road freight, private hire coach and taxi businesses and in the provision of bus services in many countries. Such an operation will almost inevitably be privately owned, restricted to road transport and very limited in terms of type of traffic and geographical area covered. It may deal directly with customers, work through an agency or be entirely contracted out to other operators. The same individual can take responsibility for all decisions with respect to pricing, scheduling, marketing and engineering.

As we turn to bigger firms dealing solely with road transport, the same organisational principles could still be adopted. Each driver could still be responsible for all the functions relating to an individual vehicle, although some form of general management and financial stewardship would obviously be needed, together with a way of providing incentives (bonuses, profit-sharing). In practice, this rarely happens, for two main reasons:
1. It fails to exploit the scale economies and other advantages of specialisation.
2. Competition between individual elements of the same firm may worsen the firm's overall performance by lowering price, leading to poorer utilisation, etc.

Thus, there is usually a division of responsibilities by function. At the simplest level, this may take the form of a split into just two or three departments (e.g.

traffic, engineering and finance) together with some form of co-ordinating mechanism, which may take the form of a quasi-market (with, for instance, the traffic department 'buying' services from the other two) or an administrative procedure involving central planning and/or an inter-departmental committee structure.

In the big transport organisation, be it publicly or privately owned, there are many more alternatives for organisational structure. In general, organisation of the large firm depends on the range of products and markets in which the firm is operating; and on the degree of interdependence (in terms of the technology used or of substitution/complementary relations between goods) between them. A firm producing a number of independent products will be likely to adopt a product-division structure (or even that of a holding company and a number of subsidiaries). If it is operating in a number of separate markets (for instance in different areas), it is likely to adopt a market area structure, at least for marketing and selling (and for production, too, if there are insufficient economies of scale to justify serving all markets from a common pool of resources). A firm producing a single product, or a set of closely related products, is more likely to adopt a functional structure. If the interdependence is solely technological, a functional structure for production may be combined with a product-division structure for marketing and selling; with perhaps the latter divisions actually buying output from the production departments.

As examples, the structures adopted in the late 1970s by three British nationalised operators are illustrated in Figs. 1.1–1.3. The National Bus Company operates throughout England and Wales, with around 17,500 vehicles and whilst certain functions, such as purchasing and finance, and certain types of product, such as some express services and tours, are dealt with at headquarters, there is strong decentralisation on a regional basis, reflecting the fact that it is operating in separate regional markets with no significant economies of scale. The National Freight Corporation, with 24,000 vehicles, on the other hand, divides directly into product groups before decentralising on a regional basis. Railway organisation provides perhaps the greatest problem. Joint use of assets and the need to timetable the use of infrastructure leads to interdependence between seemingly unrelated types of traffic, whilst the fact that much traffic is long-distance means that, if the system is strongly connected geographically, a large proportion of traffic is likely to cross the boundaries of any regional structure and require inter-regional co-ordination. Most railways have a mixture of functional, product and regional decentralisation, as in the organisation chart for BR as in August 1978 (Fig. 1.3) (see Bonavia, 1971).

It may be thought that the internal organisation of the public transport operator is of little concern with respect to the subject-matter of this book. This is far from the truth. In subsequent chapters, we shall be considering how to take the type of decisions faced by all public transport operators on what prices to charge, what services to offer and how to produce them. But the quality of these decisions depends very much on who is

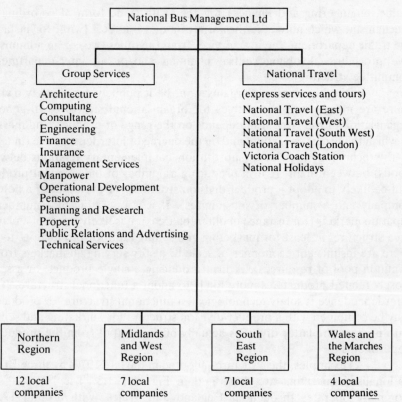

Fig.1.1   National Bus Company as in 1978 (*Source:* Annual Report, 1978).

involved in taking them with what objectives and on the basis of what information. There is much to be said in favour of a decentralisation of transport operations on the basis of products or markets. Such an organisation encourages management to adopt a strongly marketing-orientated approach; that is, to start with the demands of his customers and explore how best to meet them, and enables measurement of achievement to be directly based on market performance. However, correct decisions on the latter depend critically on his being provided with reliable cost data. Where there are significant joint costs, it may be impossible to do this for a particular product in isolation. This is a major problem in rail transport, and has tended to lead to a more centralised organisation, with greater influence being given to the functions providing jointly consumed services. One result of this organisation is the accusation in many countries that railway management is too 'production orientated' (Wyckoff, 1976).

The organisation of the publicly owned transport sector is a particularly difficult problem. A number of central issues emerge.

1. Should separate organisations provide services by the separate transport modes?

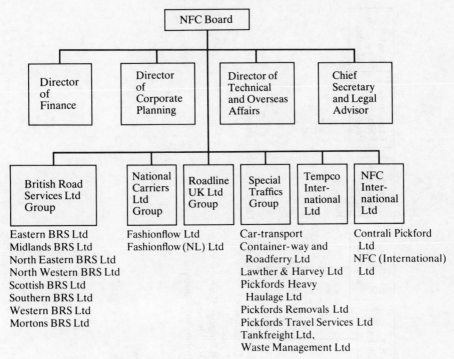

Fig. 1.2 National Freight Corporation as at 31 December 1978 (*Source:* Annual Report, 1978).

This approach has the attraction of separating off operations which are totally independent in terms of production, but leads to other severe difficulties where the different modes do not serve distinct markets. Confining operators to a particular mode means that they will approach markets with a distinct technology in mind, rather than trying to exploit the opportunity in question in the best way possible. Opportunities which require close integration between modes are especially likely to suffer.

2. Should competition be encouraged or suppressed between publicly owned operators themselves and with privately owned operators?

This is clearly a key issue about the organisation of the transport market which will need further consideration (Ch. 5). Some degree of competition may well be desirable as a means of stimulating management and promoting innovation. As a generalisation, however, competition between publicly owned operators leads to inefficient duplication of services and hampers co-operation and integration of services; where more competition than that provided by private transport is deemed desirable, it may be better to allow privately owned operators into the market for specific traffics or services.

3. Should public sector operators be centrally or locally owned and financed?

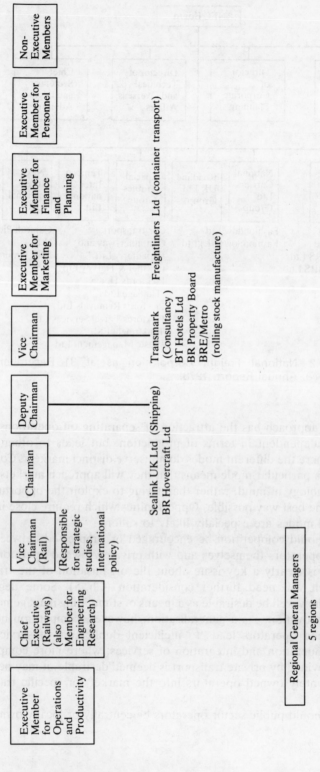

Fig. 1.3 British Railways Board as in August 1978 (*Source:* BRB, private communication).

The answer to this question may seem obvious; where transport facilities are mainly concerned with local transport they should be owned and financed by the local authority in question; where they provide mainly for long-distance trips, they should be State-owned and financed. However, such an approach brings problems. Local authority boundaries do not always coincide with transport catchment areas, so that cross-boundary flows may be large. In the case of rail services, the principle would separate local and national services; yet the two must be planned in close conjunction to secure efficient utilisation of track, rolling-stock and staff. Only where little is to be gained by joint use of assets and staff does complete separation (as exists between many city metro systems and the main line railway) seem desirable. Intermediate solutions, whereby local authorities 'buy' services from the national operators (as is the case in Britain with the National Bus Company and, mainly within the conurbations, BR), have their own problems (see Ch. 4).

1.3 Social and environmental aspects of public transport operations

Reference has already been made to two reasons why public transport operators may not be given a purely commercial remit; the social need for some level of service, and the existence of economies of scale and monopoly power. A third set of reasons is connected with the relative levels of externalities produced by public and private transport. These externalities may be divided into four main categories:

1. Delay to other vehicles and pedestrians.
2. Environmental degradation, of which the most significant factors appear to be noise, air pollution, visual intrusion and the destruction of facilities to provide new transport infrastructure.
3. Accidents.
4. Depletion of non-renewable natural resources.

It is important to realise that, in addition to the direct effects of transport systems, production of inputs for them involves externalities. These require tracing through the economy using a technique such as input–output analysis; for instance, Victor's 16-industry input–output analysis of air, water and solid-waste pollution in the Canadian economy found the petroleum products industry to be that inflicting the greatest 'ecological costs' per dollar's worth of output (Victor, 1972). A particularly difficult effect to deal with is the connection between transport systems and land-use. Yet there is no doubt that patterns of land-use can greatly affect the levels of all the externalities listed above (see Ch. 6).

In terms of these factors there is little doubt that most transport systems, public or private, inflict external costs. There are also some external benefits. In some cases, good transport facilities may directly increase employment and output; private motorists give lifts; good transport facilities may result in the lonely receiving more visitors than otherwise; and the reams of books and films about trains, buses and cars are evidence of a substantial external benefit enjoyed by the transport enthusiast. But the main argument in favour of public transport is that it produces less external disbenefit per unit of output than does private. Now, essentially this is an argument for discouraging private transport rather than for encouraging public. Only if, overall, the demand for transport were totally inelastic would it make no difference, except for distributional factors, whether the optimal mode split were obtained by taxing the one or by subsidising the other (and even in this case, if public expenditure is subject to a binding budget constraint, or if other ways of raising revenue harm resource allocation, one would still favour the tax solution).

The problem with the tax solution is that congestion (whereby each vehicle added to the traffic flow imposes the costs of delay on others) and environmental costs (taking account of the number of people affected, as well as the degree of nuisance) both vary greatly by time and place, being greatest on narrow urban main roads lined with buildings during morning and evening rush hours and least on quiet country roads. A comprehensive system of reflecting these differences in the price charged to motorists would require a meter which recorded the distance travelled, the time of travel and the type of roads used (MOT, 1963). The nearest any city has come to implementing such a scheme is the supplementary licensing system in Singapore, whereby all motorists entering the city in the morning peak must buy and display a supplementary licence (Holland and Watson, 1978).

In planning public transport services, then, one only needs to take into account the external costs of private transport to the extent that they are: (a) not adequately allowed for in taxes and controls on private transport; and (b) the option of adjusting such taxes and controls is not feasible, on political, institutional or economic grounds. The principal difficulty in achieving appropriate discouragement of private transport by other means is one of administrative cost. Petrol tax cannot be varied between location (except for very broad geographical areas) or time of day (except by the accidental method of variations in fuel consumption), but the external costs of road traffic do vary with proximity to people and with degree of congestion. Other methods of charging (tolls, special licences, metering systems) do afford the possibility of variation by time and place, but tend to be much more expensive to administer, except when confined to dense urban areas (such as the Singapore scheme) although the small amount of use made of them may be more due to their political unpopularity. Physical controls may be somewhat more easily administered, but still they cannot readily distinguish between trips according to the benefits they would produce and therefore the suppression of trips is somewhat arbitrary; moreover, the simplest of such controls – parking constraints – will be ineffective against certain types of trip (through trips, or trips to/from private parking spaces).

As long as comprehensive road pricing, whereby motorists are charged directly for the use of congested road space, is regarded as administratively too expensive or politically unacceptable, then, there is likely to be an *a priori* case for 'second-best' policies designed to reduce road traffic in specific areas by the improvement of public transport. Measured in conventional cost–benefit terms as the sum of producer and consumer surpluses, the net social benefit from diverting a trip from car to public transport will be equal to the excess of price over marginal social cost $(P_p - C_p)$ on public transport less the excess of price over marginal social cost on car $(P_c - C_c)$. If we take into account the fact that only a certain proportion (λ) of additional trips attracted to public transport would otherwise have used car, the net social benefit (NSB) of an additional public transport trip may be written:

$$\text{NSB} = (P_p - C_p) - \lambda(P_c - C_c)$$

As long as this remains positive, it is desirable to lower P_p to raise the number of trips on public transport. Therefore, the optimal value of P_p is reached when NSB = 0. If $\lambda = 0$, NSB would be positive only as long as price exceeded marginal social cost on public transport. With $\lambda > 0$, however, an excess of marginal social cost over price on private transport will justify some excess of marginal social cost over price on public (similarly, vice versa). In highly congested conditions, $(P_c - C_c)$ may be such a large negative number that even if λ is low, a large subsidy to public transport is justified in the absence of the introduction of other corrective measures. For instance, evidence suggests that for London commuter rail services, the own-price elasticity of demand may be around 0.3. Lewis (1977) found a cross-price elasticity of road traffic with respect to public transport fares of 0.06. Rewriting the above equation in terms of elasticities and setting equal to zero:

$$\text{NSB} = (P_p - C_p) - \frac{x_c}{x_p} \cdot \frac{P_p}{P_p} \cdot \frac{e_{cp}}{e_{pp}} (P_c - C_c) = 0$$

where x_c, x_p = volumes on car and public transport respectively;

$\quad\quad\quad e_{cp}$ = cross-price elasticity of private transport with respect to public transport fare;

$\quad\quad\quad e_{pp}$ = own-price elasticity of public transport.

Now if on a certain route $x_p = x_c$, the above elasticities would imply a value of λ of 0.2. Suppose that the marginal cost of private car use exceeded price by around 10p per mile. A reduction in rail fares of 2p per mile below marginal cost would then be justified. If the existing volume by car exceeded that by rail $(x_c > x_p)$, other things being equal, a greater reduction than this would be justified; if that by car was less than that by rail $(P_c > P_p)$, a smaller reduction.

However, the main problems in applying such an approach in practice are not difficulties of theory, but of measurement. Application requires knowledge of the following three items:

1. The prices, quantities, own and cross-price elasticities of demand for public transport. Whilst this may not be entirely straightforward (for instance, data may be inadequately disaggregated, and all variables may be so dominated by time trends that patterns of causation are hard to disentangle), it is generally the easiest of the three stages.

2. The physical effects of a change in the volume of traffic on a specific mode at a particular time and location. This poses more problems. The effects on vehicle delay are usually forecast using either a speed–flow relationship (which predicts the traffic speed that will rule on a particular type of road for a given level of flow) or – perhaps more appropriate, particularly in urban areas, where most delays are the result of queueing at junctions – a junction-delay formula. However, even these fundamental relationships show considerable instability, and a great deal of detailed local knowledge of the conditions in question is necessary to produce reliable results. Formulae are also available for predicting the effects on noise, ambient air pollution levels and visual intrusion, measured as the proportion of the field of vision taken up by the object in question (DOE, 1973). Accidents are usually predicted on the basis of a constant rate per vehicle mile on a particular type of road (although other factors, particularly speed, may be important). Little work is available on the matter of forecasting effects on pedestrians, whilst the more intangible items, such as the aesthetic quality of a particular scene, cannot be measured at all except by a subjective 'rating' approach.

3. The money value to be placed upon the effect in question. This is the area in which the greatest problems seem to lie. Some items may be readily valued at the cost of rectifying them (hospital services, repair to vehicle, etc.). Such an approach is adequate only when it is known that the cost will be incurred, and will fully offset the damage done, without any side effects. An example of the difficulty may be seen in the case of estimating the cost of noise nuisance by examining the cost of double-glazing. Double-glazing does not fully offset the nuisance; in particular, it is not effective when windows are open, or when one is outside the house. On the other hand, it may have beneficial heat-insulating and anti-theft properties. Left to his own choice, the victim may choose to have double-glazing or may prefer to suffer the noise and spend the money on something else. It is hard to say in this case even what is the direction of the bias involved in using the cost of double-glazing as an estimate of the value of noise nuisance. Alternatively, one may try to find a market in which the victim reveals the value he places on the externality directly. This is most commonly used in valuing travel time savings, although the results may pose serious difficulties in interpretation (Harrison and Quarmby, 1969). It has been attempted in valuing accident costs (for instance, by examining the speed at which drivers travel on motorways, or the choices pedestrians make between crossing streets on the level and through subways; Ghosh, Lees and Seal, 1975; Melinek, 1974) and environmental costs, usually by comparing houses with similar characteristics except for a particular environmental effect. Its successful use requires thorough knowledge of the consequences of his action by the person doing the choosing, and an absence of other constraints and unquantified influencing factors that is hard to find.

The third, and perhaps most promising, approach to such problems is by survey techniques, in which the respondent indicates how he would react to hypothetical changes in his circumstances. For instance, he may be asked to choose between alternative combinations of changes in property taxes, traffic levels and bus fares (Hoinville, 1971). Even this approach has its drawbacks; the respondent may not fully perceive the situation he is being asked to consider, and even if he attempts to answer truthfully, he may not be able to say how he would react in practice.

Whilst these difficulties may arise with respect to the first three types of adverse effects of transport systems listed above, it may be questioned how far they are a problem with respect to the fourth – depletion of non-renewable natural resources. Although a number of raw materials (including zinc and lead) may be relevant here it is with fossil fuels that most concern has been expressed. Here, the forecasting problem is less acute; the direct fuel requirements of different types of transport systems are well known (Table 1.1), although future changes in these under the pressure of higher fuel prices and the indirect requirements (the energy used in producing the vehicle and infrastructure in question) are less easy to estimate. (In the case of road transport, these indirect requirements amount to around a third of the total energy requirements system. Chapman, 1975, Ch. 4.) Again, the biggest problem is one of valuation. The social cost of using a non-renewable resource may be expressed as the sum of: (a) the marginal cost of its extraction; plus (b) the present value of the net benefit foregone by not having it available at that future date when its value will be highest. Clearly (b) depends critically on the level of future discoveries of reserves, and on the trends in costs of alternative sources of energy (including any environmental costs). Such trends are by no means easy to forecast (Cole *et al.*, 1973, Ch. 8).

Thus there is considerable uncertainty about the weight to be attached to the external effects of public transport services, and even if there were agreement that these issues were to be resolved according to the value judgements underlying the operation of a market economy, economists

Table 1.1 Fuel consumption by transport mode

	Miles/ gallon	Average occupancy	Passenger- miles/ gallon	Maximum occupancy	Passenger- miles/ gallon
Motor car	30	1.3	39	4	120
Rear-engined double-decker bus	7	16	112	75	525
2-car diesel railcar	4	35	140	150	600
3-car electric railcar	1.5	50	75	250	375
London Transport 7-car tube train	0.75	105	79	840	630
Light transit 2-car set	2	50	100	240	480

Source: Harman (1974). The conversion factor of 1 kWh = 0.67 gallon of oil is used. For details see the original.

would be hard put to resolve them. In practice, the question is inevitably at the centre of much public and political controversy and can only be resolved through the working of the political process.

1.4 Conclusion

In this chapter we have suggested a number of reasons why public transport is an industry to which the application of economic theory is far from straightforward. Firstly, most public transport operators produce a very large number of distinct products with a substantial element of joint costs. Secondly, various characteristics of the production process lead to economies of scale and spare capacity being the norm in public transport. Thirdly, public transport decisions very often become the centre of political debate, and there is good reason for this in that they almost inevitably involve external costs and benefits and sometimes extreme hardship. One consequence of these considerations is that neither a purely commercial approach to decision-taking, nor a simple marginal cost pricing approach is likely to provide an appropriate framework for public transport decision-taking. Some alternatives are discussed in Chapter 4; in the meantime we consider in more detail the market for public transport services (Ch. 2) and the structure and measurement of costs (Ch. 3).

Chapter 2

The market for public transport services

2.1 Trends in public transport traffic

There is a widespread view that public transport is a declining industry and that its continued decline is virtually inevitable. Rising income and changing life styles lead to increased car ownership and to the spread of low-density suburban housing that is difficult and expensive to provide with good-quality public transport. The flexibility of using own-account lorries (i.e. lorries owned by the firm to carry its own goods) to carry freight is said to lead to a similar decentralisation in the case of freight transport customers, particularly since the fastest growing sectors tend to be manufactured goods, rather than bulk products. The only field in which rising prosperity clearly leads to growth in the market for public transport is that of international traffic, which lies outside the scope of this book.

Yet Table 2.1 shows that this is not the whole story. Freight traffic on many of the major rail systems shown is growing (albeit much less rapidly than road transport), and where it is not, the decline is generally slow. In most cases, rail passenger traffic is growing. (The principal exception here being, of course, the rapid decline in the US.) The main economic problem of railways has been the failure of revenue to keep pace with rising costs, rather than declining traffic *per se*.

The picture for road public passenger transport is also mixed. Whilst Great Britain has experienced a steady decline over this period, many countries have experienced a growth in traffic, some very rapid. In Great Britain the decline in passenger journeys has been partly offset by a rise in mean journey length. The particularly rapid decline in numbers of journeys in Great Britain may be partly due to the fact that Britain reached an abnormally high level of passenger trips per head, compared with other countries, when public transport was at its peak. Perhaps this was the result of the much greater tendency to live in suburban housing rather than high-density flats in Britain (Webster, 1977).

Turning to road freight, in most countries public hauliers have shared in the rapid growth of this industry, although in many cases not keeping pace

Table 2.1 Percentage change in passenger and freight transport volumes (1967–77)

	Freight ton miles			Passenger miles		
	Road	Rail	Inland Waterway	Private	Bus and coach	Rail
Great Britain	+31	−6‡	−55	+37	−13	+7
Belgium	+64†	+7	+1	+81	+2	−4
Denmark	n.a.	+21	–	+24	n.a.	+7
West Germany	+65	+1	+8	+65	+33	+8
France	+59	+3	−13	n.a.	n.a.	+33
Italy	+42	−1	–	+137*	+72*	+25*
Netherlands	+69	−15	+12	+60	+16	+8
Norway	+61	+22	–	+150*	+22*	+12*
Sweden	+194	+9	–	n.a.	n.a.	+6*
Japan	+76	−28	–	+256	+16	+14
USA	+59†	+33	+16*	+39	+2	−32
USSR	+119	+54	+60	n.a.	+153†	+37

* 1965–75.
† 1966–76.
‡ Excluding National Freight Corporation traffic.
Source: DTp (1979).

with the growth of own-account operation of road goods vehicles. Inland waterways have also enjoyed rapidly growing freight traffic in some countries, albeit of a very specialised nature; Great Britain is the only country in our sample in which inland waterway freight has rapidly declined (from an already very low level).

The use made of public passenger transport depends strongly on the nature of the area concerned; even within Great Britain, there are great differences according to the size of settlement (Table 2.2). Generally, it is the larger cities in which public transport still has a large market share, particularly for the journey to work to the city centre, and it is the realisation that private transport could not possibly cope with a large proportion of such journeys without major disruption and expense in terms of road-building that has led to a worldwide revival of interest in urban public transport. Of other journey purposes, educational and shopping trips show the highest public transport share, since they are most likely to be made by non-licence holders and/or at times when, in a one-car household, the car is in use by another member of the family. It should be noted that figures which show that the public transport share of passenger miles is low (under 20% in Great Britain in 1977) fail to reflect its continuing importance to the sizeable proportion of the population relying on public transport, since members of car-owning households tend to make more trips and longer trips than those in non-car-owning households.

Table 2.2 Percentage of journeys made by different modes in differing types of settlement

Type of settlement and population	British Rail & Underground	Local bus	Long distance bus	Motor cycle	Pedal cycle	Walk	Car/van	Other	Total journeys (thousands)
London built-up area	7	13	0	1	3	37	40	1	54
Birmingham built-up area	1	16	0	1	2	36	44	1	20
Manchester built-up area	1	17	1	1	2	40	38	1	24
Glasgow built-up area	3	24	1	–	2	37	32	2	7
Liverpool built-up area	1	22	0	0	2	35	37	3	7
Urban 250,000 to 1 m.	1	16	–	1	3	38	41	1	63
Urban 100,000 to 250,000	1	14	–	2	4	36	42	1	68
Urban 50,000 to 100,000	2	10	–	1	4	38	43	1	36
Urban 25,000 to 50,000	1	9	–	1	4	38	46	2	46
Urban 3,000 to 25,000	1	7	–	1	4	38	47	3	93
Total urban	2	12	–	1	3	37	43	2	418
Rural (up to 3,000)	1	6	–	1	4	27	57	4	77
TOTAL	1	11	–	1	3	36	45	2	494

Source: Hamer and Potter (1979).
A dash (−) indicates a value of between 0 and 0.49.
Total journeys includes the scaling up to short-walk data to be comparable with the records for the other travel modes.

It is common to distinguish between 'captive' and 'non-captive' public transport users although it should be remembered that even captive public transport users may escape in a variety of ways – by ceasing to travel, which may involve changing job or moving house, walking, cycling or raising the household level of car ownership, and that there is evidence that the quality of public transport services plays a part in the latter decision (Fairhurst, 1975). Captive users are by no means confined to non-car-owning households (currently some 45% of UK households), since many members of car-owning households do not (and for reasons of age or disability often cannot) hold driving licences, and cannot always arrange a lift from another member of the household; in one-car households, the car may be unavailable to most of the household for a large proportion of the time, particularly if it is used by one member for the journey to work (Hillman, 1973). The plight of those without a car available, who have come to depend on public transport for trips to work, school, shopping, social services and recreational facilities (many of which are being centralised on a smaller number of locations to exploit economies of scale) is a major reason for concern about any decline in public transport services. Other captive public transport users are those prevented from using their car by traffic restraint and/or lack of parking facilities. Whilst rising prosperity may reduce the size of the captive public transport population, a considerable proportion will always remain; moreover, in those households where car ownership does not increase, there is good evidence that rising incomes lead to increased spending on public transport. The net effect is that, for households of a given structure, spending on rail transport rises sharply with income despite the depressing effect of increased car ownership; spending on bus and coach remains fairly constant (Table 2.3).

Within the non-captive transport market, public transport will only be used if it offers some advantage in terms of price or quality of service over the private car. That, given favourable circumstances, it is able to do this is shown by the high level of use of inter-city and long-distance commuter services on BR by persons from car-owning households (Table 2.4). By contrast, use of bus falls off dramatically upon acquisition of a car. Further evidence on this is given by Table 2.5, which shows rail passenger miles per head of population, market share, car ownership and real income for a sample of Western European countries. Clearly, the experience of the US and Canada, both very rich countries in which rail passenger travel has all but disappeared, is by no means inevitable. Many of the richer Western European countries have sizeable levels of rail transport despite high levels of car ownership.

In considering the freight market, the great advantage of private (i.e. own-account) operation is its quality of service. Vehicles are dedicated to the manufacturer's own work, and the entire operation is under his direct supervision. Public transport has to strive to equal the standard of service and can only exceptionally better it.

The marketing strength of public transport of freight lies in its ability in certain circumstances to offer reduced costs compared with own-account

Table 2.3 Expenditure on transport and vehicles, 1975
1-man, 1-women, 2-children households

Income	Net purchase of motor vehicles spares, accessories	Maintenance and running of motor vehicles	Railway fares	Bus and coach fares
30–60	1.93	1.93	(0.02)†	0.80
60–80	2.33	3.49†	(0.26)†	0.78
80–90	2.97	4.76	(0.30)	0.67
90–100	3.53	4.03	(0.14)†	0.74
100–120	3.85	5.17	0.21	0.93
120–180	5.81	5.57	0.37	0.91
150–200	7.70	7.04	0.75	0.73
200 or more	10.17	8.88	0.95	0.62
All	5.12	5.43	0.40	0.80

Figures in brackets based on 10 readings or less.
* The upper bound is strictly 59,99,79.99, etc.
† High sampling error
Source: Department of Employment (1979).

Table 2.4 Frequency of travel by mode and car availability

(journeys over 25 miles made by persons aged 16 or more per head per annum)

	Train	Bus	Car or van		Other	Total
			Driver	Passenger		
Households with use of a car	6.7	1.8	28.7	12.6	1.8	51.6
Households without use of a car	5.5	4.3	2.9	4.4	1.3	18.4
All households	6.3	2.7	19.8	9.8	1.4	40.0

Source: DTp (1979).

transport. This it may do in a number of ways. Rail transport may offer much lower costs than road where large volumes and/or long distances are involved (Ch. 10). The professional road haulier may be in a better position than an own-account operator to consolidate traffic from a variety of customers, and thus obtain higher load factors, less empty running and better utilisation of vehicles. These factors are more important in long-distance than in short-distance work, so that it is not surprising to find a mean length of haul in

Table 2.5 Rail passenger traffic, real income and car ownership

Country	Rail market share (%) of passenger miles (1977)	Rail passenger miles per head (1977)	Real GDP per head (£ purchasing power) (1977)	Cars per thousand inhabitants (1975)
West Germany	5.9	378	3,535	267
Sweden	5.7	405	3,450	337
Belgium	10.7	464	3,409	267
Netherlands	6.3	360	3,366	256
France	10.3*	606	3,340	289
Denmark	7.2	366	3,323	256
Norway	5.3	311	3,264	238
Great Britain	6.5	326	2,509	253
Italy	10.3	423	2,125	270

Source: BR/University of Leeds (1980).

public haulage considerably higher than in own-account operation. Another common use of public haulage is to meet temporary or unexpected surges in demand which put pressure on the capacity of an own-account fleet.

Overall, then, there is no reason to assume that the market potential for public transport as a whole must decline over time or as prosperity rises. What is clear is that the market changes, and that if they are to avoid decline in absolute terms, public transport operators must forecast and monitor such change, and adapt their services to exploit new opportunities. This does, of course, raise problems where unchecked the process of adaptation may cause hardship to captive users of the original pattern of services.

2.2 Forecasting the demand for public transport

There are two main approaches to forecasting the demand for public transport. The first involves the use of mathematical modelling techniques of various degrees of sophistication; the second of market research techniques. As we shall see, both have their strengths and weaknesses, and the two approaches may in fact be complementary rather than competitive. In this section, a brief description is given of modelling techniques.

The most commonly used transport demand model in major urban and some inter-urban studies is the four-stage sequential model illustrated in Fig. 2.1. The study area is divided into zones, and for each zone population, job opportunities, location of other attractions such as shopping and re-creational facilities and car ownership are forecast exogenously from land-use plans, income forecasts, etc. Numbers of trips generated by and attracted by each zone for each journey purpose are forecast on the basis of these exogenous variables. Distribution of the trips represents the linking of origins and destinations to produce a pattern of traffic flow consistent with these

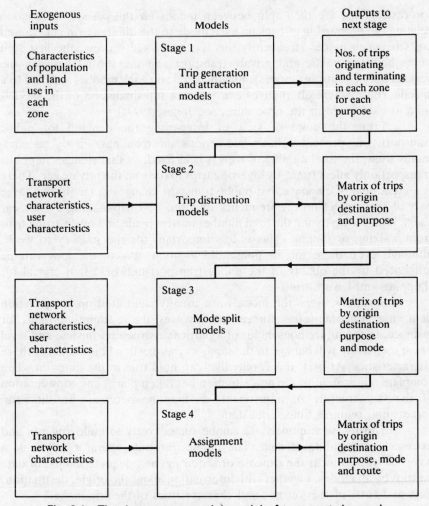

Exogenous inputs	Models	Outputs to next stage

Fig. 2.1 The 4-stage sequential model of transport demand.

generations and attractions, and is usually achieved by some form of gravity model, whereby the number of trips from zone i to zone j (T_{ij}) is directly proportional to the multiple of the numbers of trips generated by (O_i) and attracted to (D_j) the relevant zones, and inversely proportional to the time and/or cost of travelling between them (C_{ij}) raised to some power β. As a way of combining time and cost, the notion of generalised cost is frequently used, whereby time and cost are expressed in common units by attaching a money value to journey time (with usually a higher value for walking and waiting time than for in-vehicle time). The final equation reads:

$$T_{ij} = A_i B_j O_i D_j C_{ji}^{-\beta}$$

where A_i and B_j are constants which are adjusted to ensure that the total trips originating in and terminating in each zone are consistent with the original forecasts. Trips are then split between modes on the basis of a function relating the proportion of trips on each mode to the difference in generalised costs between modes (frequently this is a two-stage process, the first split being between public and private transport and the second between the various public transport modes). Finally, traffic on each mode is assigned to a specific route where alternatives exist. (For a full discussion of the models used at each stage in the procedure, see Jones, 1977.)

From the point of view of forecasting the demand for public transport, this procedure has some serious shortcomings. Firstly, as commonly used, the total number of trips is held fixed, so that changes in public transport only affect traffic by diverting trips to or from the private car. There is a great deal of evidence that public transport changes in fact have a large part of their effect on the frequency of motorised trip-making by non-car users, both by increasing the total number of trips made and by diverting trips from walking or cycling. This is less important for the journey to work, although even there job or household location may in the long run be influenced by the quality of the public transport network. It is crucial for shopping and leisure trips.

Secondly, since the models are usually calibrated on cross-section data, use for time-series forecasting involves the assumption that, for instance, in the future households of a particular structure, income and level of car ownership will behave in the same way as existing households of those characteristics. At best, this is only likely to hold true in the long run when complete adjustment to the new situation has taken place; any consideration of the lag structure of adjustment, as may be necessary in short-run forecasting, requires time series data.

Thirdly, such models are cumbersome, costly to build and run and extremely demanding of data. The public transport operator will seldom have, or wish to incur the expense of acquiring, an adequate sample of data on trips by all modes, together with information about the origin, destination, time and costs of the journey and characteristics of the trip-maker.

An alternative family of models which has attractions for the public transport operator is that known as direct demand models. In this, some or all of the above stages are collapsed, to give an equation in which the number of trips between two zones is related directly to the population of the origin zone and its characteristics, to measures of attraction of the destination zone and to the generalised cost of travel between them. The number of trips in question may relate to all modes, or just to the mode in question. In the latter case, a public transport operator's own ticket sales, or on-vehicle survey data may be adequate to calibrate the model. Such a model allows the total number of trips between all zones to vary with the quality of the transport system, but does not reflect competition between alternative destinations. Thus, if used for work-trips, an improvement on one link may raise the predicted number of work-trips on that link without predicting reductions elsewhere, even though the total employment level is not expected to change. Such models are naturally more use for non-work trips; examples are discussed in Chapter 8.

At a more crude level, demand models may be built which refer to the total number of trips in an area as a whole rather than on specific routes. An example is the simple model used in Chapter 4, in which total passenger miles of travel is treated as a function of an index of average fare levels and an index of average levels of service (in this case, simply total bus miles operated). Such models are useful for strategic planning, but obviously cannot forecast the effects of detailed changes on particular routes, except by assuming that these routes have the same characteristics and responses as the system as a whole.

2.3   The rôle of market research

An alternative to attempting to model the effects of fare and service level changes is to ask customers directly how they will respond. This approach is often criticised on two scores:

1. Customers may not know, or may not give the matter adequate thought to decide, how they would respond to a hypothetical situation.
2. Customers may exaggerate their response to a change if they believe this is likely to give them a better service or lower charges.

Nevertheless, it is extensively used in practice by operators. The dangers of misleading replies may be minimised if the situations postulated are confined to marginal changes from current experience, and respondents are placed in the position of needing to trade off benefits against costs (for instance, they may be asked how they would respond to a given service improvement if it were associated with higher fares).

Market research is, in any case, an essential prerequisite and/or complement to modelling, for instance in discovering what factors customers regard as important and how they perceive these factors (journey time changes, for instance, will be of little impact if they are too small for customers to realise they have occurred). Similarly, the approach may uncover constraints which might be ignored in most models (such as the wish to use a car to shift heavy luggage, or for local journeys at the destination end of a long-distance trip, or the wish to use public transport because of parking problems, or the wish to release the car for use by another member of the family). For many aspects of quality which are difficult to measure (comfort, cleanliness, convenience of exact timings), market research techniques are almost inevitably chosen.

In the freight sector, market research techniques tend to be even more important relative to modelling. This is because of the diversity of the market, which makes successful modelling difficult, and the fact that many freight operators depend for a large share of their traffic on a very small number of customers. It is thus possible to interview all major customers in depth.

Even if models are used for forecasting, surveys will frequently be required before they can be applied in particular circumstances or to particular routes. Ticket sales data frequently do not even provide reliable information on the total amount of traffic between two points. For instance, bus ticket sales data usually at best only provide totals for a route as a whole. Rail data usually do give origins and destinations, but may miss some passengers who receive handwritten tickets (for instance, at travel agents, or as excess fares) or who rebook *en route*. Ticket sales data do not usually record time of travel, journey purpose or any of the characteristics of the trip-maker (income, car ownership, etc.). Thus a model which requires any of these factors as explanatory variables will have to rely on the results of surveys of customers for calibration and for application to specific forecasting tasks.

2.4 Conclusion

This chapter has given some background data on the use of public transport in a number of countries, and has discussed briefly some of the problems involved in forecasting the future demand for public transport. Clearly, both methods and results vary greatly according to the sector of the market with which we are concerned. More detailed consideration of these issues is therefore postponed until Chapters 7 to 10.

Chapter 3

Costs and costing in public transport

3.1 Introduction

The aim of this chapter is to explore two quite different but obviously related subjects – the structure of public transport costs, and the best practical methods of costing for decision-taking. Road freight operations will be considered first, as being in many ways the simplest to understand; then we shall proceed to look at road-based public passenger transport, road infra-structure costs and finally rail services. Examples are given from British experience, and an attempt is made to comment whenever major sources of international differences exist.

At the outset, it is important to appreciate that costing systems are required for a variety of purposes. These fall into two main groups:

1. To evaluate specific changes in service levels, routes operated and traffic levels (perhaps as a result of a fares change). The usual approach to this is to convert these changes into an estimate of a number of key output indicators (vehicle miles, crew hours, etc.) and apply cost parameters to these figures.

2. To monitor performance by route, area or market sector, and to assess subsidy claims. This usually involves an allocation procedure for dividing total cost between the services in question, although it should be noted that if changes in the costs allocated to a particular service over time do not reflect accurately changes in the costs truly attributable to that route, poor decision-taking may result (Ch. 4).

Now neither of these two approaches is necessarily appropriate for examining the structure of public transport costs in broad terms; as a result, a third approach – examination of a cross-section of firms usually using multiple regression analysis – will be discussed. Whilst inappropriate in general as a costing technique for individual companies, reflecting as it does the average position of a sample, none the less the results produced by this technique may have important lessons for the way in which individual companies undertake their own costing.

3.2 Costing road freight operations

The simplest costing system a road haulier or bus company could use is just to add up his costs for the previous year, divide by a suitable measure of output and (for future decision-taking) inflate them by an appropriate index of input price rises. This will be a perfectly adequate approach to costing provided that the following conditions are met:

(a) Output is subject to constant returns to scale and there are no
.   problems of indivisibilities;
(b) Output is homogeneous.

Now studies using cross-section samples of road hauliers of various sizes to estimate cost functions by means of regression analysis have tended to the conclusion that there are no significant economies of fleet size (Edwards and Bayliss, 1971; Chisholm, 1959) – if anything the reverse is the case. If this were not so, it would be surprising if the structure of the industry as described in Chapter 10, with a tremendous diversity of firm sizes, could survive (Harrison, 1965). What was shown quite clearly, however, was the importance of two variables – size of vehicle and level of utilisation. For instance, Edwards and Bayliss found the following variables to explain total cost per vehicle hour for hire and reward operators (the form of equation was double-log, so the coefficients represent cost elasticities):

Variables	Coefficient	Standard error
Constant	−0.8	–
Vehicle weight	0.74	0.02
Vehicle age	−0.23	0.01
Fleet size	0.02	0.006
Proportion night work	−0.01	0.005
B licence = 1, else 0	−0.04	0.017
Tipper body = 1, else 0	−0.06	0.02
Tanker body = 1, else 0	0.15	0.05
Vehicle mileage	0.11	0.01

These coefficients show significant economies with respect to vehicle weight and enormous economies with respect to vehicle mileage (body requirements, depending on the nature of the good carried, also play a part). If large firms do enjoy advantages, it is in their ability to achieve higher utilisation levels, rather than from that size as such.

The conclusion is, then, that one needs to consider separately traffics which, by their characteristics, tend to require different types of vehicle and to yield different levels of utilisation. The former is obvious, although it may pose difficulties where some costs are common to the fleet as a whole. The simplest method of achieving the latter is to divide costs into standing costs (dependent on time) and running costs (dependent on mileage). Usually, this is done on *a priori* grounds along the following lines:

Standing costs	Running costs
Crew wages	Fuel, tyres
Depreciation	Maintenance
Insurance	
Interest	

Now problems immediately appear. For instance, crew wages may be a standing cost inasmuch as labour is paid by the hour (except for mileage bonuses), but the wage bill will vary, at least in the long run, with utilisation in terms of hours in service, whereas other items, such as insurance and interest, will not. Depreciation, too, causes problems. Some firms treat it entirely as a running cost. However, evidence suggests that loss of second-hand value is largely, if not wholly, associated with age and obsolescence, particularly for heavier, longer-lived vehicles (Nash, 1976). But the short answer is that many of these cost categories will be influenced by more than one variable; thus, statistical estimation may be superior to *a priori* allocation.

The importance of the division between standing and running costs is that it enables the dependence of costs on utilisation to be estimated. For example, the 1975 *Commercial Motor* vehicle operating cost tables give the following weekly figures for three vehicle types:

Vehicle	Standing (£ per week)	Running (p per mile)
22-ton capacity articulated	127.75	21.91
14-ton capacity rigid 6-wheel	94.07	15.21
5-ton capacity van	65.65	12.12

Calculating total cost for any given mileage and dividing by ton-mileage gives the following relationship between cost (in pence) per ton mile of capacity offered (c) and miles run (m) for each vehicle type:

$$c = 1.00 + \frac{5.81}{m} \quad \text{(22-ton articulated)}$$

$$c = 1.09 + \frac{6.72}{m} \quad \text{(14-ton rigid)}$$

$$c = 2.42 + \frac{13.13}{m} \quad \text{(5-ton van)}$$

These relationships are plotted in Fig. 3.1. (In 1975, the average mileage per week by goods vehicles of more than $1\frac{1}{2}$ tons unladen weight was 620).

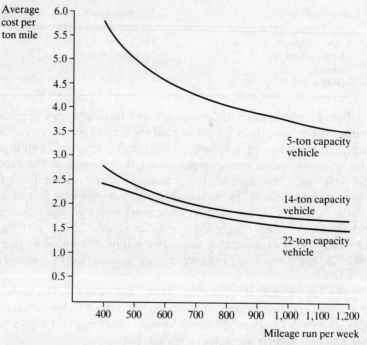

Fig. 3.1   Road haulage costs per ton mile capacity offered (1975 prices)
(*Source: Commercial Motor* tables of vehicle operating cost).

It will be seen that for these examples, cost per ton mile of capacity declines dramatically as vehicle size and utilisation increase, from a maximum of 5.71p down to 1.48p. (Allowing for typical load factors will add 50–100% to these costs.) Twenty-two-ton capacity vehicles are around the heaviest currently permitted in Britain, but where still heavier vehicles are permitted, this relationship can be expected to continue. However, the ability to benefit from the economies of large vehicles will be limited by consignment size and the ability to aggregate consignments to make up a full load, and the physical layout of the premises to be visited. Utilisation will be influenced by many factors such as the regularity of the traffic flow and the quality of the road network, but length of haul may be the most important factor. Generally, long-haul work involves a smaller proportion of time loading and unloading and running on congested and poor-quality urban or access roads than short haul. This is reflected in road haulage rates; Edwards and Bayliss (1971) found on average a 1 per cent increase in length of haul raised rates by only 0.3 per cent (compared with an elasticity with respect to consignment size of 0.6). In practice, the characteristics of road freight lead to costs being on average much higher than appears possible at first sight; for instance, in 1976–77, users paid on average 17.2p per ton mile.

Much freight haulage work takes place on behalf of a single customer, and this greatly simplifies costing; costs may simply be calculated on a vehicle-mileage basis. Where traffic for a number of consignors is combined (as in parcels traffic), a problem of joint costs arises. Assuming vehicles are loaded to capacity, costs may reasonably be allocated between consignments according to the limiting factor on the size of the load (which may be either bulk or weight). Whenever vehicles are not loaded to capacity, as is the case much of the time, marginal cost is effectively zero for the given level of output. This may arise because of imbalance of traffic flows, seasonal or random fluctuation in demand, or because frequency of service is maintained above the minimum necessary to carry the load in order to achieve an acceptable delivery time. This situation, more typical of passenger than freight operation, may nevertheless be of considerable importance in work such as parcels traffic, and if spare capacity arises in a predictable fashion, may justify price discrimination or other departures from a simple average cost–pricing approach.

In closing it should be noted that whilst the evidence suggests constant, or possibly diminishing, returns to scale with respect to size of firm in this sector, increasing returns to scale with respect to the volume of any individual consignment or traffic flow may be expected to rule, at least below some minimum efficient size. This is because increases in consignment size and/or traffic may be expected to lead to increases in vehicle size and/or load factors and/or quality of service (frequency, and hence delivery time).

3.3 Costing bus services

Much of what was said in the previous section can be carried over directly to the costing of bus and coach services. Thus the traditional approach of simply calculating an average cost per bus or seat mile for the company as a whole failed to reflect the effect of variations in vehicle size and, far more important, vehicle and crew utilisation between services. This problem came to the fore in Britain when the National Bus Company came to apply to county councils for grants for the operation of loss-making rural services, under the terms of the 1968 Transport Act. As a result, a new route-costing system, rather more sophisticated than that suggested above for freight hauliers, was introduced; it also became the basis of method recommended for use by municipal operators (CIPFA, 1974). A similar approach has been recommended in the US (Miller and Rea, 1973).

The basis of the system is again the allocation of costs by *a priori* reasoning, but this time according to three variables, and with three categories of avoidability, on the lines of the following matrix:

	Bus hours	*Bus miles*	*Peak vehicles*
Variable	Crew	Fuel, oil, tyres	
Semi-variable	Maintenance		Vehicle depreciation
Fixed			Garages, overheads

The argument for identifying separately peak vehicle requirements (that is to say, vehicles required at the systems peak) is that it is the size of this peak which determines fleet size, and therefore garage requirements, etc. Outside this period, services may be expanded without requiring the company to acquire additional vehicles. On average, some 70 per cent of costs are allocated by bus hours, 10 per cent by bus miles and 20 per cent by number of peak vehicles. Around 60 per cent of costs are variable, 30 per cent semi-variable and 10 per cent fixed.

As an example of the use of the method, consider the (grossly exaggerated) example of a company operating the following two routes:

	Urban	Rural
Peak buses	4	1
Annual bus miles	80,000	120,000
Annual bus hours	4,000	3,000

It incurs the following costs (£ p.a.):

Crews	50,000
Fuel, oil, tyres	10,000
Maintenance	20,000
Depreciation	10,000
Garage and overheads	10,000

Allocation of costs between the routes varies as follows (£ p.a.):

	Average cost	'Road haulage' method	NBC method
Cost per bus mile	0.5	0.05	0.05
Cost per bus hour	–	12.85	10.00
Cost per peak vehicle	–	–	4,000
Urban route (total)	40,000	55,400	60,000
Rural route (total)	60,000	45,600	40,000

The differences may not typically be this great, but certainly routes with higher average speeds and less of a peak problem (generally inter-urban and rural routes) will have lower costs per vehicle mile than will urban routes. In converting to costs per passenger mile, of course, load factors will be important. Further categorisation may be important, for instance into one-man-operated and two-man-operated bus hours; single-deck, double-deck and mini- or midi-bus operation, etc. In practice, the difference in total cost between single- and double-deck vehicles is probably only of the order of 10 per cent; reduction to mini-bus capacity only saves a further 15 per cent (assuming one-man operation in each case).

A number of criticisms may be made of this approach. In the first place, a number of the cost allocations may give rise to debate – for instance, are maintenance and depreciation really entirely independent of mileage run? – and use of statistical cost functions for individual cost categories may be necessary to resolve the issue. Secondly, the essential assumption behind such an allocation method is that constant returns to scale with respect to the three chosen variables characterise the industry. This has received some support from statistical studies (see below). The third and most significant criticism of the method is that it ignores the problem of indivisibility in crew hours. This is a particular problem in staffing peak extra services. Now a modest peak may be catered for cheaply by overlapping shifts, by timing meal breaks away from the peak and by overtime. Beyond this, unless it is possible to obtain part-time labour, additional shifts of men must be taken on for a minimum number of hours each. Even if it is possible to use these for split shifts (covering both morning and evening peaks, with time off in the middle of the day), it is likely to leave some spare driving time; moreover, staff have to be compensated for working such inconvenient hours, so the cost per driving hour will be raised.

This distortion may not be too severe in the case of rural and inter-urban routes (although it is likely to be allowed for in subsequent modifications of the system), but it is crucial for city operators who tend to suffer a far more severe peaking problem. It is especially important when considering adjustments to peak or off-peak frequencies, as opposed to routine monitoring of trends. Three possible ways of dealing with it have been suggested.

Bradford Bus Study approach (Travers Morgan, 1976).

The approach used here was to divide costs into crew, vehicle-related and mileage-related costs. It was argued that on average the marginal costs of additional vehicles could be measured in the following way:

Peak-only services – 1 bus plus 1 split-shift crew.

Off-peak-only services – 2 straight shifts less 1 split-shift.

All-day services – 2 straight shifts plus 1 bus.

This led to the marginal cost per bus (in addition to 3.5p per mile mileage-related costs) shown in Table 3.1. The main use of such figures is in costing adjustments to peak and off-peak service levels.

It should be noted that to use these marginal costs as a basis for calculating the profitability of peak and off-peak services separately as was done in the *Bradford Bus Study*, is rather misleading. A substantial change in the peak/off-peak ratio would be bound to alter the relative size of peak and off-peak marginal costs. A more appropriate approach is to recognise that there are substantial joint costs of peak and off-peak services (provision of vehicles used on both; cost savings from providing crew hours in straight rather than split shifts), but that one may reasonably estimate separately the avoidable costs of peak and off-peak services. If the undertaking is to behave commercially, it is necessary that these costs are covered by revenue from the

Table 3.1 Marginal costs of buses in Bradford

(£ per day) 1973 prices

	Platform shift labour costs	*Overhead costs*	*Total costs*
Two-man operation			
Peak periods	14.53	22.54	37.07
All day	27.07	22.54	49.61
Off-peak	12.54	0	12.54
One-man operation			
Peak periods	8.96	22.54	31.50
All day	16.81	22.54	39.35
Off-peak	7.85	0	7.85

Source: Parker and Blackledge (1975). N.B. Bus costs more than doubled in 1973–5.

two periods respectively, and that the joint costs are covered in some unspecified proportion from the two periods taken together. Nor does the principle of marginal cost pricing require that revenue per bus mile covers cost per bus mile for the two periods separately. Use of the same vehicles for peak and off-peak services leads to substantial spare off-peak capacity (in Bradford, the average load factor in the off-peak is below 25%). Whilst it may be reasonable on heavily loaded peak services to regard the average incremental cost of providing additional seat miles as a reasonable approximation to marginal cost, in the off-peak it clearly is not. In fact, at existing fares and service levels, off-peak marginal cost per passenger mile is typically zero. The implication of this for pricing policies is considered in Chapter 4.

Arthur Anderson approach (McClenahan and Kaye, 1975)

Several criticisms may be aimed at the *Bradford Bus Study* approach to this problem. In the first place, the relationship between peak service levels, vehicles and crews is not quite as direct as is suggested. Even in the peak period (however defined) there may be times and places where spare capacity exists, or may be created by minor rescheduling. More significantly, it is not true that a complete off-peak service can be provided on a basis of two straight shifts per vehicle once meal breaks and early morning and late evening services are allowed for, whilst the method also needs extending to cover weekend services.

The Arthur Anderson approach attempts to circumvent these difficulties by estimating a relationship between crew hours paid, off-peak bus hours and peak bus hours. This is estimated using regression analysis in the form:

$$\frac{\text{Crew hours paid}}{\text{Off-peak bus hours}} = a + b\,\frac{\text{Peak bus hours}}{\text{Off-peak bus hours}}$$

(the curious functional form presumably being designed to avoid multicollinearity). It was found that on average an additional peak bus hour required rather more than an additional crew hour paid, and an additional off-peak bus hour required less.

Complete rescheduling

The only completely reliable way of estimating the costs of adjustments in services is to undertake a complete rescheduling exercise. A major attraction of computerised bus scheduling methods is that such a rescheduling may be performed rapidly and (relatively) cheaply. Thus, for instance, the VAMPIRES programme, developed by Wren at Leeds University, works by taking a desired timetable and achieving as close a schedule as is possible within a fixed allocation of buses. By rerunning the programme with different allocations of buses, the marginal costs of particular trips may be estimated (where peaks occur in different locations at slightly different times, minor retiming of services may permit considerable cost savings without reducing the peak capacity provided). In some cases (such as London Transport) where vehicles tend to be specific to a single route, complete rescheduling may be a very much simpler process.

As mentioned above, the fundamental assumption behind all of these cost allocation methods is that bus operators experience constant returns to scale with respect to fleet size. This has been tested empirically by a number of studies, of which the most thorough is that of Lee and Steedman (1970). They used cross-section data for municipal operators to estimate separate equations for fuel cost, repair and maintenance costs, management and general costs and traffic operations cost. There was evidence of diseconomies of fleet size with respect to repair and maintenance cost, and slight but insignificant economies in the case of management and general costs. For traffic operations, costs fell with fleet size for constant factor prices, but this was offset by the fact that larger firms tended to pay higher wages. This may, of course, be explained by the fact that fleet size is almost perfectly correlated with size of city; this may also distort other relationships, since larger cities tend to have more congestion and greater peakiness of demand. Attempts were made to allow for this by direct introduction of variables such as average speed of buses in operation and residential density. Similar results have been obtained in the US by Miller (1970), who also found high route density (i.e. the mean frequency over the network) to be a source of some cost savings. By contrast, the later study by Wabe and Coles (1975), which found evidence of diseconomies of scale, ignored both factor prices and characteristics of the area in which operating, and this runs the risk that the results are biased by misspecification.

Overall, the conclusion seems to be that at best, large fleet size offers no significant cost savings (although it may permit other advantages, such as better marketing and co-ordination of services). Again, this should not be taken to mean that there are no economies of scale with respect to the size of individual traffic flows. As with freight transport, but probably more significantly, higher traffic levels on a particular route permit some combination of large vehicles, higher load factors and better (i.e. more frequent) services. Moreover, the role of indivisibilities means that spare capacity on existing services is common; quite often, the marginal cost of carrying additional passengers may be virtually zero. Nor is this merely a short-run phenomenon; it occurs because economies of scale in vehicle size make it worth operating a vehicle large enough to cope with most peaks in demand, unless particular factors such as the use of poor-quality roads or provision of faster or more frequent services make operation of a smaller vehicle desirable or necessary.

3.4 Road infrastructure costs

All the cost information quoted above includes tax paid by the operator for the use of the road system, and thus represents the kind of information used by the operator for his own decision-taking. However, from the point of view of social decision-taking it is necessary to consider what relationship these taxes bear to the true costs of road infrastructure. Now one is immediately faced with a massive problem of joint costs, since the road system is generally available to road traffic of all types. Following the example of some American literature on the subject (e.g. Meyer *et al.*, 1959), the British Ministry of Transport developed a method of allocating road track costs on the basis of 'cost responsibility'; in other words each category of costs was allocated between vehicle classes according to the degree to which each class of vehicle was believed to cause them. A study of track costs was published in 1968 (MOT, 1968). Updated estimates for 1975–76, are published in the Transport Policy Consultation Document (DOE, 1976, Vol. 2, paper 6). As an example of the approach, it is perhaps worth looking at these figures in some detail.

The current costs of road infrastructure (maintenance, lighting, cleansing, policing) are allocated between vehicles on the basis of four variables.

1. Vehicle miles. This variable is taken to explain costs such as policing and courts (although different vehicle types in fact have different degrees of accident involvement per vehicle mile – for instance, in 1977, cars and taxis were involved in 2.09 accidents per million miles, light vans in 1.94 and heavy goods vehicles in 1.44. On the other hand, 5.6 per cent of heavy goods vehicle accidents involved fatalities as opposed to just over 2 per cent in the case of cars and light vans (Foster, 1978).

2. Passenger car unit (p.c.u.) miles. Costs which are believed to vary with the capacity of the infrastructure rather than its use are allocated on the basis of p.c.u. miles. (Passenger car units define the relative contribution of different types of vehicle to traffic congestion in comparison with passenger cars; since road capacity is varied to ease congestion, this may be an appropriate approach.)

3. Gross vehicle weight (g.v.w.) miles. This encompasses costs which are believed to vary with the g.v.w. of the vehicle in question.

4. Standard axle miles. The bulk of maintenance costs (including all reconstruction work) is believed to be caused by axle loadings, in accordance with the fourth power rule. This rule, which originated in tests in the US (AASHO, 1962) has been the cause of debate for two decades, but the Consultation Document cites evidence from tests conducted – at the TRRL (Great Britain) and in South Africa – to the effect that, if anything, the fourth power rule understates the dependence of maintenance costs on axle loadings. The number of standard axles expresses the damage done by the vehicle relative to the damage caused by a single 10-ton axle. It is calculated as follows:

$$\text{Standard axles} = \frac{1}{10^4} \sum_i t_i^4$$

when t_i = average effective loading of the ith axle of the vehicle (tons). It is necessary to take account of effective loadings, since vehicles may spend a relatively small part of their working life loaded to the maximum permitted level.

Application of the formula at 1975/76 prices (to iron-out some supposedly random fluctuations, the mean of three years' data was used) gives the equation:

Maintenance cost per vehicle mile is:
0.0838p per vehicle mile
0.0212p per g.v.w. mile
4.5198p per standard axle mile
0.1291p per p.c.u. mile

As examples, the maintenance cost caused by a 32-ton, 4-axle goods vehicle with a standard axle rating of 1 and a p.c.u. value of 3 would be 5.7p per mile. For a 10-ton 2-axle bus with a standard axle rating of 0.4 and a p.c.u. value of 3, the answer would be 2.5p per mile.

It should be noted, however, that the formula is based on an allocation of total cost. If there are indivisibilities and scale economies present, it may overstate the marginal cost per vehicle mile. In any event, in terms of magnitude, the treatment of capital cost is far more significant (capital expenditure accounted for two-thirds of total expenditure in the period considered). In the 1968 document, two methods of treating capital costs were suggested. The first, the 'public enterprise' approach, attempted to assess the appropriate capital charge to levy on the road system if it were treated as a normal nationalised industry, paying depreciation and interest on the capital tied up in the form of land and past investment. The arbitrary assumptions involved in this approach, and an apparent belief that the second approach was more closely related to the concept of long-run marginal cost, led the authors of the 1976 paper to adopt the second approach, termed 'pay as you go', whereby capital outlays for each year were treated simply as a current cost. Now, if both the rate of traffic growth and the level of capital spending were expected to show long-run stability, this approach might not be too much of a distortion (although it still ignores any charge for capital already locked up in the road system, some of which, at least – the value of land – might be recouped, and also ignores interest charges on new investment). In the face of fluctuations in traffic growth and capital expenditure, it is capable of producing illogical fluctuations in the capital cost assessed per unit of output. For instance, a cutback in road investment – leading to more congestion – would result in *lower* charges, and vice versa.

Given the total to be allocated, a certain part (15%) is assessed as the avoidable cost of fitting structures to carry heavy vehicles (over 3.5 tons gross weight), costs associated with car parking are allocated to the private car, and the remaining costs are spread across vehicles according to their p.c.u. mileage. This approach is presumably based on the view that investment in roads is brought about by congestion, and that relative p.c.u. values represent the contribution of each vehicle type to congestion. In fact, if road investment is justified by cost–benefit procedures, the higher value of time savings assessed for goods vehicles and buses and coaches than for the private car, due mainly to the fact that the crews of these vehicles are always travelling in working time and also, in the latter case, to the high occupancy rates associated with the vehicles, means that goods vehicle and bus flows contribute to the case for new investment more than do private cars, but not necessarily in proportion to p.c.u. values (Table 3.2). In any case, it should be pointed out that additional traffic will lead to a greater impact on capital expenditure at some times and locations (congested or poor-quality roads) than others, and at best the resulting figures can only be a broad average. Moreover, the figures do not allow for the social and environmental costs of expansions in road capacity (except inasmuch as they are reflected in sums paid out as compensation). Nor, of course, do they include the costs of additional traffic in terms of congestion, accidents and social and environmental impact.

However, for what they are worth, the costs estimated for various types of goods vehicle for the UK in 1975/76 and 1976/77 are presented in Table 3.3. They reveal a very substantial underpayment of infrastructure

Table 3.2 Value of occupant's time per vehicle

(*1973 prices*)

Vehicle	Value
Car	81p
Light van	120p
Goods vehicle	128p
Public service vehicle	633p

Source: Dawson and Vass (1974).

Table 3.3 Goods vehicles costs and revenues for selected vehicles

	1975–76					
max. gvw (tons)	*capital and maintenance costs per vehicle (£)*	*fuel tax per vehicle (£)*	*vehicle excise duty (£)*	*total revenue per vehicle (£)*	*ratio of revenue to costs 1975/76*	*ratio of revenue to costs 1976/77*
Rigid vehicles						
2 axle						
5	137	123	104	227	1.66:1	1.8:1
12	447	304	216	520	1.16:1	1.3:1
14	614	361	270	631	1.03:1	–
16	1270	552	306	858	0.68:1	0.8:1
3 axle						
16	624	395	324	719	1.15:1	1.3:1
18	769	453	360	813	1.06:1	–
22	1593	742	450	1192	0.75:1	–
24	2189	899	504	1403	0.65:1	0.7:11
4 axle						
24	1632	873	540	1413	0.87:1	1.0:1
26	2490	1255	558	1813	0.72:1	–
28	3018	1399	576	1975	0.65:1	–
30	3546	1543	594	2137	0.60:1	0.7:11
Articulated vehicles						
3 axle						
12	382	268	270	538	1.41:1	1.5:1
16	594	372	342	714	1.20:1	1.3:1
22	1641	770	450	1220	0.74:1	–
24	2221	904	486	1390	0.63:1	0.7:1
4 axle						
24	1327	702	522	1224	0.92:1	1.0:1
30	2770	1104	612	1716	0.62:1	–
32	3779	1435	630	2065	0.55:1	0.6:1
5 axle (tri axle tractor)						
32	2491	1235	648	1883	0.76:1	0.8:1

Source: DOE (1976) plus supplementary DOE papers and Hansard (July 14th, 1976).

costs according to this rule for vehicles with heavy axle-loads. Figures given are for vehicles of average mileage; the degree of undercharging rises rapidly with respect to mileage (for instance, a 32-ton, 4-axle truck covering twice the average miles p.a. would in 1975/76 have only paid 46% of its assessed track costs). For buses and coaches, the average ratio of revenue to cost in 1975/76 was 0.8, but this was before allowing for rebate of fuel tax on stage services; if this is allowed for, the average figure drops to 0.25 (the figure for stage services will, of course, be lower).

3.5 Costing rail services

It is commonly believed to be more difficult to cost rail services than road. This is apparently due to the following causes:

(a) Rail operators are responsible for the provision of their own track, and it is track which is most subject to joint use, scale economies and indivisibilities. From the point of view of the road operator, he is faced with a fairly simple tax structure, although from the social viewpoint, the problems of costing road track have to be faced as well.

(b) The unit of capacity of railways – the train – is larger, and there is more joint use of assets between quite different traffics.

(c) Rail assets (even ignoring track and signalling) are longer lived than road.

Now, traditionally, railways have used cost allocation methods similar to those described above for road transport. For each asset, the proportion of its time or mileage (or other appropriate measure of use) devoted to each service has been calculated. Costs are divided accordingly, using the most plausible measure of output available.

For instance, crew costs are naturally allocated between services on the basis of the time spend working on each. Fuel costs depend fairly closely on the total weight of trains shifted (gross ton miles). Rolling-stock maintenance and depreciation costs are assumed to depend partly on the distance travelled, but also to have a fixed element per unit time. Terminals costs are more complicated, but are taken to depend both on the number of trains and the amount of traffic handled (freight tons or passengers). Traditionally, track costs were allocated according to the total weight of trains (gross tonne kilometres) and signalling costs according to the total number of each type of train handled. Of course, the analysis would be very much more disaggregate than this brief summary implies, both spatially and by type of asset.

Such an allocation procedure involves the usual assumptions of divisibility and constant returns to scale; it also at best reveals only long-run costs, on the basis of full adjustment of the stock of assets to the work to be done. With respect to train working costs (crew, fuel, rolling-stock and maintenance and depreciation), the assumption of constant returns to scale may be appropriate with respect to the production of train kilometres (although economies of scale may be achieved by the operation of longer trains). Indivisibilities are a problem, however, in that staff and assets may be used on a number of different services during the working day or according to season. The costs which could be avoided by withdrawing a particular service depend upon the extent to which it would be possible to save assets or shifts of men by rescheduling the jointly worked remaining services. A particular hindrance to this is the presence of peaks in demand for railway assets, and more accurate costings may be achievable by allocating costs according to peak use of assets, rather than total use, where such peaks in demand are known and predictable.

With respect to terminals costs, the relationship between cost and output is less direct. Indivisibilities are more significant; there is a minimum incremental unit of one platform, and one member of staff. Size may permit economies of scale through specialisation of staff and employment of superior equipment; on the other hand, this relationship may be clouded by the fact that commercially a higher standard of accommodation is justified the larger (and the longer distance) the flow of traffic. All this suggests that terminals costs may be much more appropriately handled by statistical techniques than by *a priori* allocation, and a number of railways, including BR, make use of regression analysis in this context.

In current BR costing methods, the twin problems of jointness of use between services and jointness over time are handled by presentation not of a single cost figure but of a matrix of costs (BRB, 1978):

	Specific	*Joint*
Expenses	a	b
Costs	c	d

Specific costs are those pertaining to staff, assets, etc. used solely on the service in question; joint costs are those shared with other services. Expenses exclude capital charges; costs include them. Thus: (a) represents the immediate avoidable cost (subject to the time-lag necessary to reduce or redeploy staff); ($a + b$) represents potential savings if other services can be adjusted or withdrawn concurrently; ($c + d$) represents the full long-run potential cost when all assets require renewal. Clearly, the joint cost element will be minimised if services are examined in groups which maximise common use of resources; within BR, movement and terminal costs (and revenue) are budgeted on a regular basis for some 700 such 'profit' centres.

It is when one turns to track and signalling costs that indivisibility, scale economies and longevity pose the greatest problems. These costs include maintenance of basic structures (embankments, tunnels, etc.) which depend mainly on geological conditions, and signal operating, which depends upon the number of signal boxes and the hours for which they are open. But the major items are maintenance and renewal of the track. This generally takes place according to prescribed standards, given the volume and speed of traffic on the route (in Britain, standards are prescribed for four categories of each). As long as track does not shift between categories, track costs vary little. For instance, a BR cross-section regression analysis has shown 87 per cent of track and signalling costs to be invariant with traffic volumes as long as installed capacity is held constant. Similar results hold for other European railways, although where track maintenance standards are lower, as in the US and many developing countries, the variable portion of track and signalling costs may be much higher (perhaps 50%).

Even in the long run, the main capacity decision with respect to track is whether to have one, two or four running tracks (although the number of passing loops is also important, and capacity may also be adjusted more closely to demand by alternating sections of one- and two-, or two- and four-track route. Three-track route with bi-directional signalling on one track is another possibility; it is particularly useful where there are major peaks in demand for one direction at a time.) With respect to signalling the type (in particular the number of aspects) and spacing of signals are important influences on capacity. In addition to these indivisibilities, economies of scale appear to be significant. Thus, for instance, in Table 3.4 Foster and Joy (1967) quote the annual costs for continuously welded main line track. Note that expansion from single to double track costs considerably less than double the original cost, whilst leading to on average around a quadrupling of practical capacity by eliminating conflict between trains in opposite directions. The move from two tracks to four tracks offers less in the way of scale economies, although a more than proportionate increase in practical capacity is again to be expected, because segregation of trains by speed permits reduced mean headways.

Given the presence of significant indivisibilities and economies of scale, any allocation of total track costs between services will be arbitrary and misleading, except where the track is specific to a single service. For this reason, such allocations are no longer undertaken by BR (Fowler, 1979). What can be meaningfully assessed is the 'avoidable' track cost of different services and sectors of the business on given assumptions about the volume of other traffic. For instance, removal of a particular service may permit elimination of sidings, passing loops or even reduction in the number of running tracks. At a more aggregate level, removal of a whole sector of the business may permit much greater cost savings (for instance, in the absence of inter-city passenger trains, no track would need to be maintained to standards suitable for speeds above, say, 75 mph). Nevertheless, even the concept of

Table 3.4 Annual cost per mile of rail track

(£, 1967 prices)

	No. of tracks		
	1	2	4
Interest	3,020	4,260	7,900
Renewal of track and structures	1,400–2,840	1,895–3,442	3,422–4,474
Signalling	2,600	4,030	8,060
Total	7,020–8,460	10,190–11,730	18,380–20,430

Source: Foster and Joy (1967).

avoidable cost is not without ambiguity, depending as it does on the state of the system as a whole. For instance, on a particular route, removal of freight services with no other change may not reduce running track requirements, whereas removal of freight services in combination with reduction of other services may. In the reverse case, expansion of inter-city passenger train services may be possible within the existing infrastructure only provided that freight traffic does not rise too rapidly, or provided secondary routes remain open and have spare capacity for freight services. In other words, calculation of avoidable cost is only meaningful within the context of an overall framework of systems planning; by itself, it is potentially misleading if regarded as an aid to decision-taking.

Difficulties also arise in connection with administration costs. Some administrative tasks are directly related to traffic volumes and could be treated in the same way as movement costs. Others are related directly to the number of terminals or amount of infrastructure maintained, and should therefore be treated in the same way as terminals costs or as track and signalling costs. There may remain a true overhead cost element which cannot sensibly be further analysed, but it seems unlikely that this would be very large.

It is not easy to give an indication of the size and composition of railway costs comparable to those given for road transport because of the diversity of railway costs according to the precise details of the services involved. However, three hypothetical but representative examples of passenger services are illustrated in Fig. 3.2.

Inter-city

At typical levels of utilisation for British inter-city services, seat miles may be produced at a direct cost of around 0.75p. Thus, at 1975 fare levels, which averaged 2.5p per passenger mile for inter-city routes, it is worth expanding services even at relatively low load factors if the traffic carried would otherwise be lost; the short-run avoidable costs of inter-city passenger services are particularly low. On the other hand, the burden of track and signalling costs may be heavy. In the absence of a contribution from other services, for an hourly service, a surplus of some £2.50 per train mile may be needed to cover in full the costs of modern double-track main line. In other words, track costs may double the cost of providing frequent inter-city passenger services unless there are other profitable or grant-aided services with which the track may be shared. Even single-track main line will require a contribution of the order of £1.75 per train mile for an hourly service, whilst leading to a poorer quality service in speed and reliability and hence increased movement costs. The situation for lower frequency services is correspondingly more difficult.

Suburban

A number of factors combine to produce considerable variability in the movement costs of suburban services; the most important of these are

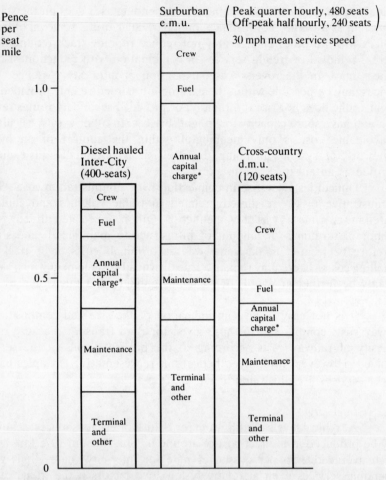

* Replacement cost annuitised at 10 per cent

Fig. 3.2 Representative direct costs of BR passenger services (1975 prices).
Note: costs vary greatly according to characteristics of individual services. These figures can *only* be regarded as broadly representative.

probably variations in route length, train length and peakiness of demand. However, for a typical service provided by electric multiple units an average direct cost of 1.15p per seat is estimated. The importance of the peak for this sort of service should be stressed; in off-peak hours, additional capacity could be provided for less than half this figure. On the other hand, in the peak, additional services will probably require extra rolling-stock and crews for only one return journey per day. In this case, the incremental cost per passenger mile will depend critically on the length of the journey (Fig. 3.3) and for short

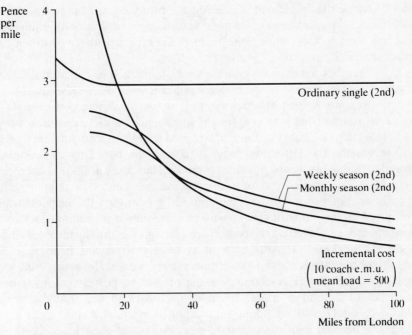

Fig. 3.3　Revenue and marginal cost on London commuter services (1975 prices).

journeys will be extremely high even if track and terminal capacity is available.

　　With closely spaced stations, terminals costs form a significant part of the above figure and track and signalling – if they are specific to the service in question – may add a further 100 per cent. With low average load factors, it is easily seen how such services are typically unprofitable.

Cross-country and rural services

　　At the opposite extreme, consider a rural service, operating every two hours over a 40-mile route. The estimated cost per seat mile is very similar to that for an inter-city service, but with a very different composition of costs. Crew and terminal costs each form around a third of the total, suggesting that there are substantial unexploited economies of scale from longer trains. If no other traffic uses the line, track and signalling costs are unlikely to be less than a further 0.75p per seat mile, giving an average total cost per seat mile of, say, 1.5p. Given that the mean load factor may well be as low as 20 per cent, it is easy to see how this type of service may be very expensive in comparison with road-based public transport.

　　The above discussion may come as a surprise to those accustomed to thinking of rail as a high-cost mode of transport. It is clear that given ideal circumstances, rail can provide passenger transport at a total cost of less than 1.5p per mile. Unfortunately, ideal circumstances – that is, a heavy regular flow of traffic the full length of the route – rarely occur in practice; spatial and time-of-day peakiness in demand lead to poor utilisation of equipment and low load factors. This is the main problem, particularly of urban and suburban public transport.

Freight train costs vary perhaps even more than passenger train costs, and only a brief résumé of the major significant variables will be given here. When assets are valued at replacement cost, the dominant cost element in trainload freight (that is to say, freight where each consignment makes up a complete train) is almost certainly the capital charge on locomotives, wagons and terminals (the latter two may, of course, be borne by the customer directly if these assets are privately owned). Thus asset utilisation is crucial. The most favourable type of traffic, therefore, comes in regular, large consignments (costs are usually minimised by operating the heaviest trains permitted by the infrastructure) of sufficient frequency for rolling-stock to be permanently employed on the traffic (even though this usually involves empty backhaul working). Length of haul is largely irrelevant if these other conditions are satisfied and no transhipment between modes is involved – for instance, much merry-go-round working of coal to power stations is over distances of around 30 miles. Irregular or low-frequency trainload traffic almost certainly involves poorer utilisation of assets and staff; even if the assets can be used jointly between different flows, additional marshalling and empty running will probably be involved, and it is unlikely that the flows will exactly balance to form an even spread of demand for the traffic. On the other hand, such traffic will be less attractive to road hauliers, too, although they have greater flexibility in the face of fluctuations in volume as a result of their lower fixed costs. On BR, where in 1976–77 83 per cent of the total freight tonnage was conveyed in trainloads, the average cost per ton mile for all freight was 2.9p.

Where consignments are too small to make up a complete train, the only way a railway can handle the traffic is by combining consignments for different origins and/or destinations. This, of course, involves trip working (from terminal to marshalling yard and vice versa) and marshalling. These processes are not only expensive in themselves; they also reduce asset utilisation and quality of service by the delay they impose. Wagonload traffic, then, will differ in costs in particular according to the amount of trip working and marshalling involved relative to the length of haul. Since this ratio usually falls rapidly as length of haul increases, the movement costs per mile of wagonload services will be strongly related to length of haul. They will also be influenced by the ability to pool similar flows; if a block of wagons for the Glasgow area may be marshalled at London and worked through to Glasgow as a single train, or major section of a train, so that marshalling is only involved at the two ends, costs will be much lower than if Glasgow traffic has to be combined with that for many other destinations, so that remarshalling one or more times *en route* is needed.

When transhipment is involved, a further element of delay is introduced, and additional resources involved (particularly road vehicles and crews), utilisation of which will also be important. Again, these costs are largely independent of the overall length of haul, so that longer distance traffic will be better able to support the costs of transhipment than will shorthaul. (It should be noted that for long-haul parcels traffic, the situation is somewhat different, in that transhipment between road vehicles at the sorting stage is normal anyway.)

The examples discussed here have stressed the significance of economies of scale in rail transport. As the traffic flow on any particular route increases, so it can be handled in longer trains, with less intermediate marshalling or changing of trains and with better utilisation of resources, especially track and signalling. Large flows also permit economies of scale in terminals and marshalling. This is why, other things being equal, one expects to find that the less densely used is a section of the rail network, the higher the average costs. (Marginal costs, however, may actually be lower on such sections.) Lightly used routes tend to have particularly high costs for passenger services where frequency is determined not so much by the need to provide adequate capacity but in order to give a commercially or socially acceptable level of service. (Frequency may also be important in wagonload freight services, too – many customers require an overnight transit – but delays of a few hours are seldom so crucial as for passenger traffic.)

3.6 The role of statistical cost analysis

At various stages in this chapter we have referred to the estimation of cost functions by means of multiple regression analysis, both in the aggregate for a cross-section of firms and for individual functions for a cross-section of components of an individual firm. The great strength of the statistical approach lies in the fact that rather than relying on *a priori* judgement as to what resources would be needed to handle certain amounts of traffic, it tests this in practice. As against this, a number of serious problems limit its usefulness (Johnston, 1960).

Obtaining appropriate cost data

Cost data is normally presented in terms of arbitrary 'accounting periods'. This causes two problems. Firstly, within the accounting period, there may have been fluctuations in output, and if the relationship between cost and output is non-linear, the exact path of these fluctuations will influence the result. Secondly, certain costs (particularly depreciation) are spread across accounting periods in a somewhat arbitrary fashion. It is necessary either to exclude these costs, or at the least to put them on a comparable base in terms of asset valuation and assumed life. A further factor for which adjustment is necessary is variations in factor prices. This is a particularly serious problem, since if the variation is large enough it may lead to the adoption of a completely different technique with a different cost function.

It may be thought that some of these problems will be mollified by studying component parts of an individual firm. The problem here is to ensure that the data do reflect the true position, and have not been derived by allocating a total between the components. If the latter is the case, all a statistical analysis will do is to find the formula by which the allocation was performed!

Ensuring comparability

One point to be stressed is that passenger miles and freight ton miles of transport comprise a multitude of diverse commodities, according to the route, length of haul and time of day and consignment size in which they are carried. It is necessary to ensure a comparable traffic mix between observations, or to introduce supplementary variables which reflect traffic characteristics. Because of the significance of varying load factors it is often better to examine output in terms of car miles rather than traffic units (passenger miles or freight ton miles). Similar problems of comparability arise with respect to inputs. For instance, the cost and capacity of a mile of railway track may differ greatly according to the type of track (e.g. continuously welded or jointed) and the type of signalling (e.g. semaphore versus power-box).

Lagged adjustment of capacity to output

Because of the long life of assets in the transport sector (particularly railway equipment) undertakings may often be operating with a capacity that is not at the optimal level for the output in question. This is particularly a problem in time series work, but also applies to cross-section analysis. In any case, indivisibilities may prevent a close tailoring of capacity to output. Thus it is usually best to distinguish separately variables reflecting the capacity of the system (miles of track, number of vehicles) and variables reflecting the output and sales (vehicle miles, passenger miles). What is then estimated is a short-run cost function; further consideration of the scope for capacity adjustment is necessary to obtain long-run costs.

Simultaneity

Suppose that we are trying to estimate the relationship between average cost and output. If average cost pricing is followed, since sales will be influenced by price, and output by sales, we have a simultaneous system, no individual equation of which can be identified without further information. Certainly, a regression of cost on output will yield biased results. It is necessary to seek for more explanatory variables, so that a simultaneous model in which the individual equations may be identified and estimated by simultaneous equation methods, may be built (Johnston, 1963). In practical work, it is often argued that external constraints and subsidies so weaken and lag the relationship between prices and costs that single equation methods are satisfactory.

As an example of the use of multiple regression techniques in analysing costs, one may examine the extensive work that has been performed using cross-section data for US railroads. For instance, Meyer *et al.* (1959) divided costs into a number of functional categories, and regressed costs on measures of output and size. There was generally a positive constant (threshold) cost, which indicated the presence of economies of scale, as well as significant coefficients on the size variables for some cost categories. These indicate economies from density of utilisation.

More recently, attempts have been made to derive explicitly separate short and long-run cost functions, by means of explicit assumptions about the underlying production function. For instance, Keeler (1974) assumes the existence of a Cobb–Douglas production function relating loaded car miles (Q) to track miles (X_1), replacement value of rolling-stock (X_2), fuel (X_3) and labour inputs (X_4). (He also distinguishes between passenger and freight traffic, which for simplicity we shall ignore.) Now total cost will be given by $C = \sum_i P_i X_i$ and output by $Q = a X_1^{b_1} X_2^{b_2} X_3^{b_3} X_4^{b_4}$. The minimum cost way of producing any particular value of $Q(\bar{Q})$ is given by minimising:

$$Z = \sum_i P_i X_i - \lambda(a X_1^{b_1} X_2^{b_2} X_3^{b_3} X_4^{b_4} - \bar{Q}) \qquad [3.1]$$

to yield a log-linear equation relating cost to output and the four input prices[1] (see notes at chapter end).

If we could observe long-run equilibrium, we could estimate this directly by multiple regression. But what we observe, unfortunately, is a set of positions on short-run cost curves. Assuming that in the short run, track miles (but not rolling-stock) is fixed, we may repeat the analysis with $X_1 = \bar{X}_1$. The result now is the short-run cost function [3.2]:

$$C = P_1 \bar{X}_1 + K' Q_1^{1/(p-b_1)} X_1^{-b_1/(p-b_1)} P_2^{b_2/(p-b_1)} P_3^{b_3/(p-b_1)} P_4^{b_4/(p-b_1)}$$
$$[3.2]$$

where

$$K' = A^{-1/(p-b_1)} \left[\left(\frac{b_2}{b_3} \right)^{b_3/(p-b_1)} \left(\frac{b_2}{b_4} \right)^{b_4/(p-b_1)} \right.$$
$$\left. + \left(\frac{b_3}{b_2} \right)^{b_2/(p-b_1)} \times \left(\frac{b_3}{b_4} \right)^{b_4/(p-b_1)} + \left(\frac{b_4}{b_2} \right)^{b_2/(p-b_1)} \left(\frac{b_4}{b_3} \right)^{b_3/(p-b_1)} \right]$$

Unfortunately, this requires non-linear estimation techniques (unless the fixed cost $P_1 \bar{X}_1$ is known, in which case log-linear regression will suffice, with $\log (C - P_1 \bar{X}_1)$ as the dependent variable), but when the parameter values are known, equation [3.1] is known also, as is p (the long-run cost elasticity).

The basic assumption underlying this approach is that smooth continuous substitution is possible between the four types of inputs examined. Now, whilst it is possible in some contexts to substitute between inputs (e.g. more track may reduce delays and requires less rolling-stock), it seems extremely doubtful whether the relationship is smooth and continuous; moreover, quality of service is unlikely to remain constant when such substitution takes place. Thus the result of Keeler's work, that overall there are no scale economies in rail transport, must be taken as reinforcing the belief that such scale economies as do occur in practice must primarily be due to indivisibilities and excess capacity. None the less, the finding that if one were free to vary output and capacity in proportion, scale economies would not exist, is interesting, and indeed surprising in suggesting that, in US circumstances at least, there are no economies of bulk buying, administration or managerial specialisation open to railroads as a result of absolute size. The results do conflict with the view that there is a major central core of administrative services which cannot be varied even in the long run with respect to changes in output and system size.

3.7 Conclusion

In this chapter, we have considered a variety of costing methods for road and rail passenger and freight operations. A number of general conclusions emerge from the discussion. In the first place, there is no single costing system which clearly emerges as being superior for all modes and all situations. Cost analysis, is very much a case of 'horses for courses', and attempts to achieve comparability between different modes by adopting equivalent costing rules (for instance, with respect to the allocation of track costs) are almost certain to produce distorted results. Comparability studies must rather start from first principles, and measure the relevant concepts in the most appropriate way for each mode. Secondly, it is not possible in general to label one mode higher cost relative to the other. Again, average figures are misleading; it all depends on the case at hand.

The most important distinction to make in cost analysis is between decisions involving marginal adjustments to traffic levels or levels of service, and decisions involving changes in the scope or quality of the set of services provided. The appropriate information in the former case is the marginal cost of the traffic in question; in the latter, it is the avoidable cost of the entire block of output under consideration. The two figures may be far apart, because of the presence of indivisibilities and scale economies. The problem may be more serious in rail transport, but also exists in road, particularly with respect to infrastructure costs.

Note

1. Minimising [3.1] yields a set of three equations of the form:

$$\frac{P_2}{P_1} = \frac{b_2}{b_1} \frac{X_1}{X_2} \tag{3.3}$$

plus the result:

$$\bar{Q} = a X_1^{b_1} X_2^{b_2} X_3^{b_3} X_4^{b_4} \tag{3.4}$$

Upon substituting the set of equations [3.2] into [3.3] and inverting, we obtain:

$$X_1 = \bar{Q}^{1/c} A^{-1/c} \left(\frac{P_2}{P_1}\frac{b_1}{b_2}\right)^{b_2/c} \left(\frac{P_2}{P_1}\frac{b_1}{b_3}\right)^{b_3/c} \left(\frac{P_4}{P_1}\frac{b_4}{b_1}\right)^{b_4/c} \qquad [3.5]$$

where $c = b_1 + b_2 + b_3 + b_4$, and similar expressions for X_2, X_3 and X_4. Substituting all these into the cost identity and simplifying gives:

$$C = K\bar{Q}^{1/c} P_1^{b_1/c} P_2^{b_2/c} P_3^{b_3/c} P_4^{b_4/c} \qquad [3.6]$$

where:

$$K = A^{-1/c}\left[\left(\frac{b_1}{b_2}\right)^{b_2/c}\left(\frac{b_1}{b_3}\right)^{b_3/c}\left(\frac{b_1}{b_4}\right)^{b_4/c} + \left(\frac{b_2}{b_1}\right)^{b_1/c}\left(\frac{b_2}{b_3}\right)^{b_3/c}\left(\frac{b_2}{b_4}\right)^{b_4/c} \right.$$

$$\left. + \left(\frac{b_3}{b_1}\right)^{b_1/c}\left(\frac{b_3}{b_2}\right)^{b_2/c}\left(\frac{b_3}{b_4}\right)^{b_4/c} + \left(\frac{b_4}{b_1}\right)^{b_1/c}\left(\frac{b_4}{b_2}\right)^{b_2/c}\left(\frac{b_4}{b_3}\right)^{b_3/c}\right]$$

Chapter 4

Management objectives and the finance of public transport

4.1 Management objectives and decision rules

If the objective of a public transport operator were purely to maximise his profits, the basic decision rules he would have to follow would appear to be fairly clear. He would raise fares whenever demand was inelastic. He would raise fares even when demand was elastic if this enabled a bigger reduction in cost (through reducing service frequencies, reducing vehicle size or shortening train length) than the loss of revenue. He would only operate trips which added more to his revenue (allowing for the fact that some of the passenger journeys on that vehicle trip might have been made, in any case, on other vehicles, whilst on the other hand extra journeys might be fed on to other services) than they added to his costs. There would be no true cross-subsidisation, although almost any method of allocating costs between routes might well show apparent cross-subsidisation.

In practice, his life would not be at all this simple. He would have to allow for the fact that, whatever short-run studies of the price-responsiveness of demand might say, over-exploitation of the customer might lead to a long-run relocation of homes and jobs or a rise in car ownership which would detract from his long-run profitability. Moreover, a simple profit-maximising objective would seem an extraordinary one to set a public transport operator with a monopoly protected by controls on entry; it is usually only advocated in circumstances where competition is permitted, and then he would have existing and potential competition to worry about.

The desirability of permitting competition is considered further in Chapter 5. For the rest of this chapter, we shall assume that the operator has an area monopoly of public transport, and that profit maximisation is ruled out as a potential objective.

However, State-regulated or State-owned monopolists may still be instructed to behave commercially. What this usually means in practice is that they should be financially self-supporting, earning a target rate of return on capital employed and possibly financing part or all of their capital requirements internally. In other words, what is involved is the imposition of a constraint; for instance, that total revenue should cover total costs (including interest at the target rate). But only where the target rate is equal to the maximum that can be achieved will this completely determine the firm's policies. Otherwise, there is an element of management discretion.

For instance, consider a very simple example in which the passenger miles carried by a bus operator (Q) is a constant-elasticity function of the fare per passenger mile (P) and the vehicle miles he operates (B) (in other words, the frequency and/or density of his services), i.e. $Q = \alpha P^{\beta} B^{\gamma}$. Assume that costs ($C$) are proportionate to B, i.e. $C = cB$. The constraint imposed by the requirement to break even is then:

$$PQ - C = 0 \qquad\qquad [4.1]$$

Or

$$\alpha P^{\beta+1} B^{\gamma} - cB = 0 \qquad\qquad [4.2]$$

By implicit differentiation the slope of this constraint is as follows:

$$\frac{\mathrm{d}P}{\mathrm{d}B} = \frac{1 - \gamma}{1 + \beta} \frac{P}{B} \qquad\qquad [4.3]$$

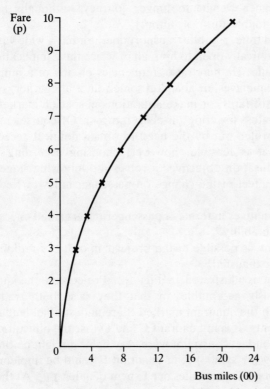

Fig. 4.1 An example of the relationship between break-even bus miles and fare.

It is reasonable to assume that the elasticity of demand with respect to mileage run (γ) lies between 0 and 1, and that the elasticity of demand with respect to fares (β) lies between 0 and -1. Therefore $dP/dB > 0$, and we have a locus of possible combinations of P and B such as is given in Fig. 4.1. In this example, we took $\alpha = 1$, $\beta = -0.4$, $\gamma = 0.7$ and $c = 50$. Here, P is measured in pence and B in million bus miles. The implications for break-even bus mileage of increasing bus fares in 1p steps from 1p to 10p are shown. Obviously, in practice, it would be dangerous to assume that the relevant elasticities could be treated as constant over such a wide range. Outside the range of current experience the schedule may become negatively sloped or it may be impossible to break even at any price. But within the range of most current operations, the choice appears to be between low service quality (frequency and route density) and low price or high service quality and high price (Webster, 1975).

How should one choose between these alternatives? It is usually implicit in discussions of nationalised industry pricing policies that, subject to the financial constraint, they are to maximise sales. However, in a multiproduct firm, this is not a clear concept. The simplest interpretation of this objective for a transport operator would be that he should maximise the passenger mileage he carries (the alternative of maximising passenger journeys fails to give higher weight to longer journeys although they are presumably a more valuable form of output).

At any point in time, a public transport operator has a wide variety of courses of action theoretically open to him, all of which have implications for traffic, costs and revenue. He may raise frequencies on any of a number of routes. He may cut frequencies, or abandon some routes altogether. He may alter the general level of fares, or make alterations in specific markets (e.g. raising season-ticket rates; lowering off-peak returns). Of course, many of these options may be ruled out by the need to obtain political acceptance. Within the subset that is feasible, however, choosing according to the passenger miles maximisation objectives involves the following stages:

1. Calculate the affect of the change on passenger miles carried, costs and revenue.
2. Rank the alternatives in terms of passenger miles gained or lost per £ change in profitability.
3. Accept as many as possible of the projects in order of ranking until the budget is exhausted.

The procedure is illustrated in Fig. 4.2. Projects in the quadrant marked A are obviously acceptable, in that they raise both traffic and profitability. Projects in the quadrant marked B are undesirable, leading to a worsening on both counts. It is in quadrant C and D that the difficult choices are to be made. If the budget constraint were very tight, it might be that only the projects marked by the symbol X in quadrant C could be implemented. These involve a ratio of passenger miles per £ spent of at least θ_1. At the same time, in quadrant D, one can find some money-making ventures (also denoted X) which lose less than θ_1 passenger miles per £ raised. These should

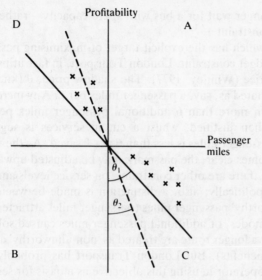

Fig. 4.2

also be implemented. In other words, one might adopt a package of measures such as raising fares but improving frequencies (or vice versa).

Suppose that the budget constraint were eased. At the margin, some additional projects in quadrant C could now be undertaken. At the same time, some of the measures which lose traffic in quadrant D could be avoided. Thus a new line, with slope θ_2, might be drawn to separate accepted from rejected options.

The significance of the angle θ is obvious. It is the marginal level of passenger miles per £ that is acceptable given the level of the budget constraint. Put another way, it is the shadow price of public funds in terms of passenger miles (an extra £ would give the operator the opportunity to attract θ additional passenger miles). If θ was known, or could be estimated in advance, the operator could then follow these two rules:

1. Reduce fares whenever the increase in passenger miles exceeds the loss of revenue plus any additional operating costs multiplied by the shadow price of public funds (and vice versa).
2. Increase bus mileage operated whenever the increase in passenger mileage resulting exceeds the additional costs less additional revenue multiplied by the shadow price of public funds (and vice versa).

It should be noted that the effects of fares changes on costs are indirect, and only occur where the service is operating at capacity. Since the extra costs of operating a large vehicle rather than a small one are too small to justify the provision of separate fleets for peak and off-peak services, off-peak bus services frequently have very low load factors. It is only during the (relatively short) peak period, and only then at specific locations, that the capacity constraint will be binding and service levels and costs require adjustment. (Even then one could regard the effect as being a decline in the quality of service – a longer wait for a bus with spare capacity – rather than an absolute capacity constraint.)

One operator which has the explicit target of maximising passenger mileage subject to a budget constraint, London Transport, in fact utilises the concept of a shadow price (Whitley, 1977). The shadow price, θ (known as the 'passmark'), is estimated as, say, 6 passenger miles per £. Any increase in services which will earn more than 6 additional passenger miles per £ of additional subsidy is then justified, whilst a cut in services is suggested whenever the loss of passenger miles is less than 6 per £ saved. As the impact of all such changes becomes clear, the passmark may be adjusted upwards or downwards. Obviously, there are other constraints on service levels and fares which are determined politically; also, a distinction is made between 'aim-worthy' and 'non-aimworthy' passenger miles (passenger miles attracted from other public transport modes, or additional passenger miles caused solely by rerouteing services over a longer route are treated as 'non-aimworthy' and are ignored in computing benefits). But London Transport has probably gone further than any other operator in using this objective as a basis for scientific decision-taking.

An alternative way of weighting journeys by journey length might be to use the actual fares paid as weights; in other words, to maximise sales revenue. However, whilst this may be appropriate where fares are set externally, in the case of an operator with substantial monopoly power, it would encourage him to exploit that power to the full in raising prices, whilst using the resulting revenue to improve service quality up to the maximum point permitted by the budget constraint. In the simple case where bus miles are homogeneous, this is equivalent to maximising the bus mileage operated (i.e. maximising the quality of service in terms of frequency and/or density). However, where bus miles differ in effects on demand and operating cost, a simple maximisation of bus mileage would lead to a greater emphasis on additional low-cost bus miles, whereas revenue maximisation would place more emphasis on bus miles which attract most revenue per £ loss. Neither of these objectives appears to be as desirable as that of maximising passenger mileage, although they may be attractive to an operator who wishes to preserve the maximum output (and the maximum job-opportunities) possible under difficult financial circumstances.

However, passenger-mileage maximisation has its shortcomings. The most important one is that it takes no account of the fact that changes in passenger miles on different services may be indicative of different changes in user benefits. For instance, suppose one is seeking to raise revenue by a marginal increase in fares, with no adjustment to services. The increased revenue from a one-unit rise in a particular fare would be:

$$Q + P \frac{\partial Q}{\partial P} = Q(1 + e)$$

where e = price elasticity of demand. The loss of passenger miles would be $\partial Q/\partial P = e(Q/P)$. The loss of consumers' surplus from a marginal rise in price would simply be Q. Thus, the ratio of the loss of passenger mileage to the additional revenue raised would be:

$$\left(e\,\frac{Q}{P}\right)\Big/Q(1+e) = \frac{e}{P(1+e)}$$

The ratio of loss of user benefit to the additional revenue raised will simply be:

$$\frac{Q}{Q(1+e)} = \frac{1}{1+e}$$

Therefore, the ratio of the loss of consumers' surplus per £ raised to the loss of passenger miles per £ raised will be:

$$\frac{1}{1+e}\Big/\frac{e}{P(1+e)} = \frac{p}{e}$$

Now if this ratio were constant for all services, then passenger miles could be used as a perfect index of consumer benefits. Unfortunately, it is not. For instance, at the same fare, demand elasticities tend to be lower in the peak than in the off-peak. Thus the loss of a peak passenger mile will be equivalent to a greater user disbenefit than the loss of an off-peak passenger mile. Giving equal weight to all passenger miles biases the decision-taker towards seeking to attract too many low-value off-peak trips and too few high-value peak trips.

This bias is easily offset, however, by adopting a weighting system for passenger miles subject to differing elasticities. For marginal adjustments to price, passenger miles would simply be weighted by the ratio of the fare to the price elasticity of demand.[1]

The pricing rule would then become: lower price as long as the (weighted) value of additional passenger miles resulting exceeds the shadow price of public funds multiplied by the loss of revenue. A problem still exists in that the same weights would not, in general, be applicable for changes in passenger miles due to service level changes; unless rather stringent conditions hold,[2] a separate set of weights must be derived by considering the marginal benefits generated per extra passenger mile from each case. This detracts from the simplicity of the approach.

This approach also ignores external costs and benefits. As was shown in Chapter 1, the external benefit generated by attracting additional trips to public transport depends both on the probability that the trip would otherwise have been made by private car, and on the extent that the marginal social cost of private car use exceeds its price. The latter, and perhaps also the former, will be higher in the peak than in the off-peak. For marginal changes in congestion, we may use the approach to external benefits outlined in Chapter 1 (i.e. the benefit of an increase in bus traffic should be increased by the congestion savings, and valued in £s per passenger mile). Thus, a new set of weights incorporating external benefits could be derived. As always, the problem is one of obtaining adequate information to carry this out.

Thirdly, the distributive consequences of alternative policies may need consideration. Generally, the poorer a user is, the more he is likely to prefer a low-price, low-quality service to the reverse. Furthermore, different services, trip lengths and times of day may be associated with a different mix of users in terms of income groups. A simple passenger-mileage maximisation policy would ignore such issues; again, they may be taken into account by weighting systems, in which social benefits are given differing weights according to their incidence.

The more weighting systems are introduced, the more one detracts from the principal advantage claimed for the passenger-miles maximisation criterion, its simplicity. It may well be thought that there are considerable advantages in using a more orthodox measure of benefits (namely revenue plus consumer surplus plus external benefits) in policy decisions, particularly those of a strategic nature. Unfortunately, conventional methods of user benefit measurement are not always well understood by operators, politicians and the public at large; nor are they readily monitored to make sure that decisions taken are having the desired effect. As a result, such measures are often dismissed as 'fairy gold' by operators who take much more readily to the objective of getting 'bottoms on seats'. Perhaps the answer is to use simple passenger-mileage measurements for short-run monitoring and minor service adjustments (with a very crude weighting system giving a higher weight to certain categories of passenger miles – for instance those during the peak – than to others), whilst using a more sophisticated multiple-criterion framework for longer-term strategic decision-taking.

Suppose that, instead of passenger-mileage maximisation, we switch to maximisation of the sum of producers and consumers' surplus (in other words the total amount that consumers are willing to pay for the services they consume, measured by the area under the demand curve less the cost of providing them). The above analysis may be repeated, but substituting changes in the sum of the two surpluses for changes in passenger miles in all the derived rules (Nash, 1978). Assuming there is a budget constraint, there will again be a shadow price of public funds, and changes in fares and service levels will be judged according to whether the extra surpluses generated exceed the extra subsidy required multiplied by these shadow prices. Again, external benefits may be added to the surplus if they can be valued in money terms.

4.2 Numerical examples

For illustrative purposes, a specific numerical example is introduced. A good deal of effort has been put into attempting to estimate the elasticity of passenger miles (Q) with respect to price (P) and bus miles run (B) in recent years. Plausible values would seem to be -0.5 and 0.7 in the off-peak period and -0.25 and 0.3 in the peak respectively (Smith and McIntosh, 1973; Fairhurst and Morris, 1975). However, it would be inappropriate to assume a constant elasticity demand function for our present purposes. This is because, with these elasticities, a rise in price would always produce an increase in revenue, whilst (with constant returns to scale) a reduction in bus mileage would always cause a smaller proportionate reduction in revenue than in costs. If this is really the case, then the problems of bus operators may not be as great as is commonly thought! But it seems more realistic to assume that beyond a certain rise in price, demand becomes elastic, and similarly for a certain reduction in bus mileage. A functional form which reflects these assumptions is the semilog form:

$$\log Q = a - bP - c\,\frac{1}{B} \qquad [4.4]$$

This yields elasticities of:

$$e_P = P\,\frac{\partial \log Q}{\partial P} = -bP \qquad [4.5]$$

$$e_B = B\,\frac{\partial \log Q}{\partial B} = \frac{C}{B} \qquad [4.6]$$

Note that each elasticity is assumed independent of the value of the other variable. This is convenient, but may be unrealistic in practice.

One set of values of the parameters which gives the above-mentioned elasticities at $P = 5$ (in pence per mile) and $B = 1$ (in 100 miles per day) are as follows (writing subscripts P and O for peak and off-peak respectively):

$$\log Q_P = 4 - 0.05P_P - 0.3/B_P \qquad [4.7]$$
$$\log Q_O = 4 - 0.1P_O - 0.7/B_O \qquad [4.8]$$

These equations are used subsequently in numerical illustrations. Cross-price effects between peak and off-peak are ignored.

The cost function used will assume a constant utilisation of buses used on peak-only and day-long services and constant returns to scale. It is assumed that overcrowding results in deterioration of service quality rather than in the provision of extra buses. Costs will therefore depend solely on bus miles operated in the peak and in the off-peak. Plausible parameters would seem to be (in £s per 100 miles):

$$C = 80B_P + 20B_O \qquad [4.9]$$

As a second example, results are reported for the set of equations:

$$\log Q_P = 4 - 0.04P_P - 0.3/B_P \qquad [4.10]$$
$$\log Q_O = 4 - 0.12P_O - 0.5/B_O \qquad [4.11]$$
$$C = 60B_P + 40B_O \qquad [4.12]$$

This example might be interpreted as comprising two routes, one of which (route P) is most heavily used for the journey to work, and the other (route O) having a higher proportion of leisure travel. Of course, differences in costs and demand elasticities between routes may occur for many reasons other than journey purpose, including differences in service speed, population density, income and car ownership levels. A full optimisation on a route by route basis would need to take these into account.

The implications of following each of the suggested objectives in this numerical example were computed using an iterative non-linear optimisation programme, and are set out in Tables 4.1 and 4.2. Net social benefit is measured as:

$$\text{NSB} = \int_0^{Q_P^1} f_P^{-1}(B_P, Q_P) \, dQ_P + \int_0^{Q_0^1} f_O^{-1}(B_O, Q_O) \, dQ_O - C$$

[4.13]

where $f_P^{-1} f_O^{-1}$ are the inverses of the demand functions specified above.

Whilst the results may depend on the rather arbitrary assumption on functional form, nevertheless some interesting suggestions have arisen from these examples. Firstly, revenue and bus-mileage maximisation subject to a budget constraint lead to an expansion of bus mileage far beyond that justified in terms of NSBs, (bus-mileage maximisation expands off-peak mileage relative to peak compared with revenue maximisation, which places greater weight on the extra revenue brought in by expansion of peak bus mileage). This is important since the natural inclination in a declining industry may be to try to preserve the levels of output and employment at the expense of high fares; moreover, it appears that the Traffic Commissioners have tended to influence operators in this direction (Hibbs, 1975).

Unconstrained social welfare maximisation involves zero fares (but it should be remembered that this is ignoring capacity constraints and the externalities, in the form of service deterioration imposed by one passenger on another. In practice, positive fares would undoubtedly be justified at any rate in the peak.) By comparison, constrained social welfare maximisation implies a higher peak than off-peak fare, and some reduction in both bus-mileage figures and in NSBs. Constrained passenger-mileage maximisation implies a lower off-peak fare and higher off-peak service level than social welfare maximisation (the latter places a higher weight on extra passenger miles when demand is inelastic), but the result is much closer to that of social welfare maximisation than for any other alternative considered.

It is often suggested that cross-subsidisation should not occur between individual routes (e.g. Gwilliam and Mackie, 1975, p. 372) or between times of day (Travers Morgan, 1976). Tables 4.3 and 4.4 calculate financial results separately for O and P for the two examples. (In this calculation, it is assumed that the cost functions given above hold for all possible values of B_O and B_P; in practice, the presence of joint costs makes it unlikely that the form given is appropriate for more than marginal adjustments.) It is seen that cross-subsidisation between routes and times of day may occur with any of these alternative objectives.

Table 4.1 Example 1 – results

Objective	Constraint	B_O	B_P	P_O	P_P	Passenger miles	Revenue	Cost	Profit	Net social benefit
Social welfare	None	4.01	1.87	0	0	91	0	230	−230	1,159
Social welfare	Break even	3.62	1.70	1.85	3.65	75	208	208	0	1,137
Profit	None	2.30	1.07	10	20	30	454	132	322	771
Passenger mileage	Break even	4.64	1.54	0	6.79	79	216	216	0	1,111
Revenue	Break even	9.91	4.56	10	20	38	563	563	0	563
Bus mileage	Break even	20.61	1.10	10	20	34	500	500	0	494

Table 4.2 Example 2 – results

Objective	Constraint	B_O	B_P	P_O	P_P	Passenger miles	Revenue	Cost	Profit	Net social benefit
Social welfare	None	3.13	2.46	0	0	94	0	273	−273	1,389
Social welfare	Break even	2.54	2.30	1.64	4.62	77	240	240	–	1,360
Profit	None	1.17	1.62	8.40	25.00	30	526	144	382	932
Passenger mileage	Break even	3.15	2.24	0	7.60	82	260	260	–	1,341
Revenue	Break even	6.12	6.40	8.40	25.00	38	629	629	–	761
Bus mileage	Break even	2.90	10.98	8.40	25.00	37	613	613	–	825

Table 4.3 Example 1 – financial out-turn

Objective	Constraint	Off-peak revenue	Off-peak cost	Surplus	Peak revenue	Peak cost	Surplus
Social welfare	None	0	80	-80	0	150	-150
Social welfare	Break even	69	72	-3	139	136	+3
Profit	None	149	46	+143	304	86	+218
Passenger mileage	Break even	0	93	-93	216	123	+93
Revenue	Break even	191	198	-7	312	365	+7
Bus mileage	Break even	194	412	-218	306	88	+218

Table 4.4 Example 2 – financial out-turn

Objective	Constraint	Off-peak revenue	Off-peak cost	Surplus	Peak revenue	Peak cost	Surplus
Social welfare	None	0	125	-125	0	148	-148
Social welfare	Break even	60	102	-42	180	138	+42
Profit	None	109	47	+62	417	97	+320
Passenger mileage	Break even	0	126	-126	260	134	+126
Revenue	Break even	152	245	-93	477	384	+93
Bus mileage	Break even	160	439	-279	453	174	+279

4.3 Alternative methods of administering grant aid

The above discussion has concentrated on the problems of an operator faced with a general set of objectives and an overall budget constraint. The attraction of this approach is that it gives the operator maximum freedom to plan and market his services without direct political involvement. It is to be expected that the operator will normally be closer to the market than the grant-aiding authority, and will be in the best position to estimate the effects on costs, revenues and benefits (however measured) of changes in services and fares.

On the other hand, where grant aid is involved, it may be felt that none of the available simple objective functions adequately reflects the motives of the political authority in giving subsidies to public transport. In this respect, it is the officers of the grant-aiding authority (and, ultimately, the politicians themselves) who are closest to the 'political' market. This view leads to a rather different relationship, with the grant-aiding body stipulating services to be provided, and (perhaps) also fares to be charged, and the operator simply receiving compensation for any losses involved in fulfilling the contract (Beesley, 1971). Such a transfer of decisions to the political arena may be seen as more democratic, although the experience of most countries is that it can lead to inconsistency and an unwillingness to face up to the need for change.

Needless to say, the pictures drawn here are of the two extreme ends of a spectrum of alternatives; in practice, most arrangements will fall between the two. For instance, where the former policy – general objectives and global grant aid – is followed, the grant-aiding authority may still retain control of certain variables – the route system to be operated or the fares to be charged (this is the case with London Transport). Under the latter policy, the grant-aiding authority is likely to seek the advice of the operating authority on the consequences of alternative courses of action, and may leave it the power to make some decisions – for instance, minor revisions of services – independently. Moreover, the exact division of powers is not necessarily obvious from the institutional arrangements; the degree to which informal exchanges occur and to which statutory powers are used is also important. But the distinctions remain useful in analysing the situation of particular operators.

If one wishes to move towards making grant aid more specific, there are various ways in which this may be done. The most obvious, perhaps, is to give grants for individual services. Alternatively, compensation may be provided for specific types of obligations, but on a network basis. Or, thirdly, support may be given for specific types of traffic.

The first of these approaches, specifying grant aid for individual services, was the approach adapted to support for rail services in Britain in the period 1968–74. The major problem is that there is so much joint use of staff and assets, and so many passenger journeys involving more than one service, that any allocation of costs and revenues between individual services is bound to be somewhat arbitrary. One can, in principle, work out the avoidable cost of any particular service, but this will depend on what assumptions are made about changes to the other services with which it shares costs and revenue. The minimum level for sensible allocation of grant aid is likely then to be the cost centre, as discussed in Chapter 3. Even then, the sum of the avoidable costs of individual cost centres will not add up to the total cost of the system as a whole, and there may be a need for additional non-specific support (or support specific to certain assets, such as railway infrastructure, rather than to groups of services).

Grant aid on an avoidable cost basis contributes nothing directly to fares and service level decisions (it can only be calculated after they are taken), but at least it does not distort them. Grant aid based on the allocation of total cost according to some 'reasonable' formula may actually distort decisions, since a decision to alter the level of a particular service will affect not just costs and revenues but also the way in which costs are allocated between services, and therefore the amount of grant aid given to related services. For instance, in Britain it was the practice to allocate track maintenance costs according to gross tonne kilometres and signalling costs according to train kilometres. A decision to increase commercial service levels would lead to a reallocation of these costs away from grant-aided services, and thus to a reduction in the amount of grant aid received. Such problems also exist where bus services are interdependent, although they are usually less severe.

The approach to support permitted by EEC regulations and adopted towards most Western European rail systems is that of global support for specific obligations – for instance, with respect to fares, service levels, route structure or obligations such as pensions or social security payments which other modes of transport do not have to bear. Presumably the philosophy behind this approach is that railways should be fundamentally profit-maximising organisations, but that they should be subjected to, and compensated for, constraints where this conflicts with social welfare. In practice, most railways are so far from profitability, and the constraints on their commercial freedom so severe, that the whole approach appears to be somewhat removed from reality.

The third possible method of giving subsidies mentioned above is to link them to sales of specific types of service. This has recently been suggested by the Chairman of the BRB as a possible means of support to BR (Parker, 1978), where it is given the label of 'social fares'. The principle is that the operator would receive a fixed sum of money per traffic unit carried of a particular type. Traffic yielding high social benefits would receive a relatively high social fare; traffic yielding no social benefits a social fare of zero.

The attraction of this approach is that it gives extremely clear objectives for management in the field; they simply have to maximise profits, including the social fare. Thus they will raise fares as long as the additional revenue from customers is greater than the loss of revenue in social fares from lost traffic. Additional services will be judged on the revenue plus social fares from the traffic they attract, relative to the additional costs. Moreover, if the social fare is appropriately set, the result is equivalent to one of passenger mileage maximisation. (The proof of this is given in the Appendix.) In other words, even if the operator were set the objective of maximising passenger miles subject to a budget constraint, he could interpret this in terms of a social fare just as easily as in terms of a 'passmark' in passenger miles per £. As with weighted passenger-miles maximisation, the problem arises that different social fares may be required according to *how* the traffic is affected (price reductions or service improvement) as well as traffic type.

A second possible problem arises from misinterpretation of what the 'social fares' mean. It must be stressed that a 'social fare' is determined as a way of influencing decision-taking; it does not represent the amount of subsidy going to a specific group. Thus a positive social fare for a sector is quite consistent with operating that sector at a profit (although not with *maximum* profits). This might easily be misunderstood in a way not likely with the passenger-mileage maximisation approach.

Finally, as with simple passenger-mileage maximisation, the approach is of doubtful value for non-marginal adjustments, such as service closures (unless a replacement service of broadly similar quality is available). The social fare can only represent the marginal benefit from additional passenger miles. Major changes will almost certainly change that marginal value.

4.4   The appropriate level of subsidy

In the above discussion we have considered subsidy policy without mentioning what is usually thought to be the crux of the matter – namely whether there is a case for subsidy at all, and if so, how large should be the subsidy. Now it should be clear from the above discussion that we see the fundamental case for subsidisation of public transport as lying in the fact that fares matched to marginal cost are unlikely to bring in sufficient revenue to cover total cost. This much is obvious for rail transport but also applies to.bus transport, inasmuch as an increase in traffic permits either a more frequent and better service *or* use of a larger vehicle. In the first case there are external scale economies (Mohring, 1972) and in the second, internal. Furthermore, joint use of vehicles between peak and off-peak means that in the off-peak, load factors are so low that marginal cost is usually zero. Subsidies for second-best purposes, to direct traffic from private transport, or for social service reasons, to provide a basic level of mobility for all, need to be regarded as additional cases for support – not as the sole reasons for departing from a break-even situation.

On the other hand, raising revenue by taxes and rates has administrative costs and may have distorting influences elsewhere in the economy. For this reason alone, the appropriate shadow price of public revenue in terms of social benefit is likely to exceed one. Furthermore, political considerations often impose an absolute budget constraint on the public sector as a whole, so that the true cost of an increased subsidy to public transport may be the giving up of other public sector expenditure. In each case, the principle is clear. The shadow price attached to public funds devoted to public transport should be equal to that in other sectors. What is not clear is how social benefits should be measured to derive these shadow prices, particularly in sectors such as housing, education and health, where social benefit measurement is even more difficult than in public transport. Ultimately, of course, the decision will be made politically. But an essential input into it will be studies of the consequences of alternative levels of subsidy, and alternative constraints, on public transport operators.

It is here, too, that studies of the incidence of subsidies by income group become relevant, not as an absolute free-standing consideration, but in order to judge the distributive consequences of alternative levels of public transport support, in comparison with spending elsewhere. For instance, Table 2.3 above illustrates the pattern of expenditure on private and public transport in Great Britain in 1973. It is clear that if the sole purpose of the expenditure were to aid the poorest members of society, governments would not spend money on any form of transport, public or private. (Housing subsidies or social security benefits would be a better choice.) On the other hand, if choosing between transport policies, it would appear that raising revenue from motor taxes and spending it on bus subsidies would be a progressive policy in terms of redistribution. Obviously, more detailed information is required on the specific changes in mind (for instance, whilst on average, expenditure on rail fares rises with income, this is largely due to the influence of rail commuters: passenger mileage on inter-city leisure journeys is fairly evenly spread across all groups but the very poorest). Nor are we arguing that distributive consequences should be the *only* factor in such decision-taking; only that they need to be borne in mind (Dalvi and Nash, 1977).

This approach does not, unfortunately, lead to a neat formula for deciding the level of spending on public transport. It does, however, provide a realistic framework within which information on the consequences of alternative decisions may be improved.

4.5 Subsidies and internal efficiency

So far we have said nothing about the effect the method of administering subsidies has on the internal efficiency of the firm; i.e. the amount of resources used to produce a given level of output. Yet this aspect could easily be more significant than the effect on resource allocation. Indeed, some authors argue that any subsidy system at all will seriously damage the incentive to efficient operation (Pryke, 1977), by leading the operator to assume that whatever financial difficulties he gets into, he will always be baled out.

The generally agreed conditions that are necessary for a subsidy to be given with minimum damage to incentives for efficiency are that the amount of the subsidy should be stipulated in advance, that the objectives with respect to which the subsidy is to be used should be stated in a clear and easily monitored form and that the budget constraint should be binding. In general, these conditions could be met by any of the specific objectives considered in this chapter. There is a danger that when the operator is merely recompensed for obligations laid upon him, if he performs better than anticipated, the budget constraint ceases to be binding, and he is left with room for discretionary spending with no clear guidance as to how to allocate it. For this reason a system embodying a specific maximand may be preferred.

An important factor leading to internal efficiency in the presence of a budget constraint is that a failure to produce with maximum efficiency will almost inevitably lead to lower output and sales, and to less employment. Just as in the private sector, this is likely to be contrary to the private interests of workforce and management alike. Where deficit finance for a set of obligations is given in retrospect, no such penalty applies.

However, the arguments are not entirely on the side of *ex ante* subsidies (Beesley, 1974). If forecasts do not hold good, sticking rigidly to *ex ante* cash limits may lead to cuts in services or increases in charges which it would be preferable to avoid by diverting resources from elsewhere. At the very least, it will be necessary to have a system of *ex post* adjustments, agreed in advance, in the event of unexpected changes in key exogenous variables, such as the rate of inflation or the level of gross national product.

Finally, it may be added that whenever a public transport operator has some degree of monopoly power, the absence of subsidy does not imply internal efficiency. It is possible that the operator is using monopoly profits to pay for inefficiency. In other words, the absence of subsidies does not make it any less important to set clear objectives and financial targets.

4.6 Conclusion

In this chapter, we have considered a number of alternative regimes, in terms of combinations of management objectives and methods of finance. At one extreme, the operator may be given a simple objective such as passenger mileage or social surplus maximisation subject to a budget constraint. At the other extreme, he may be simply told to operate a given set of services at a given set of fares and compensated for any losses involved. Our own preference, on grounds both of internal efficiency and responsiveness to the market, is for the former approach. However, it must be recognised that any practical approach will fall somewhere between the two, with simple criteria being used most for short-run and relatively minor decisions, and with major strategic decisions being judged more widely, with a greater political input into the decision-taking process.

Notes

1. This is equivalent to following the objective function:

$$Z = -\sum_i \frac{P_i(Q_i, B_i)}{1 + e_i} Q_i - \lambda\left[\sum_i P_i Q_i - \sum_i C_i(B_i) - G\right] \quad [4.14]$$

where G is the permitted level of grant aid

so that

$$\frac{\partial Z}{\partial Q_i} = \frac{Q_i \frac{\partial P_i}{\partial Q_i} + P_i}{1 + e_i} - \lambda \frac{\partial (P_i Q_i)}{\partial Q_i} = 0 \qquad [4.15]$$

Since the first term may be written:

$$\frac{\left(1 + \frac{1}{e_i}\right) P_i}{1 + e_i}$$

this simplifies to:

$$\frac{\partial Z}{\partial Q_i} = \frac{P_i}{e_i} - \lambda \frac{\partial (P_i Q_i)}{\partial Q_i} = 0 \qquad [4.16]$$

2. Broadly, these are that all price and quality variables may be combined to give a 'generalised cost' the demand elasticity of which is constant. In this case, weights for all purposes will be derived as generalised cost divided by its elasticity, which is equal to P/e. See Glaister and Collings (1978).

Appendix

Proof that passenger miles maximisation subject to a budget constraint is equivalent to profit maximisation subject to payment of an appropriate social fare

Passenger miles maximisation subject to a budget constraint may be represented algebraically as the task of maximising:

$$Z = Q(P, B) - \lambda[C(B) - P \cdot Q(P, B) - G] \qquad [4.17]$$

where G is the level of grant permitted to the undertaking. First-order conditions for a maximum are:

$$\frac{\partial Z}{\partial P} = \frac{\partial Q}{\partial P} + \lambda \frac{\partial [P \cdot Q(P, B)]}{\partial P} = 0 \qquad [4.18]$$

$$\frac{\partial Z}{\partial B} = \frac{\partial Q}{\partial B} + \lambda \left[\frac{\partial [P \cdot Q(P, B)]}{\partial B} - \frac{\partial C}{\partial B} \right] = 0 \qquad [4.19]$$

The Lagrangian multiplier, λ, may be interpreted as the shadow price of public funds in terms of passenger miles (in other words, an extra £1 would permit the organisation to attract an additional λ passenger miles).

Now consider profit maximisation subject to payment of a social fare. For instance, consider the case of a single type of bus service, with a social fare of s. The maximand is now:

$$z = (P + s)Q(P, B) - c(B) \qquad [4.20]$$

First-order conditions are:

$$\frac{\partial z}{\partial P} = (P + s)\frac{\partial Q}{\partial P} + Q(P, B) = 0 \qquad [4.21]$$

$$\frac{\partial z}{\partial B} = (P + s)\frac{\partial Q}{\partial B} - \frac{\partial C}{\partial B} = 0 \qquad [4.22]$$

Rearranging these gives:

$$s\frac{\partial Q}{\partial P} + \frac{\partial [P \cdot Q(P, B)]}{\partial P} = 0 \qquad [4.23]$$

$$s\frac{\partial Q}{\partial B} + \frac{\partial [P \cdot Q(P, B)]}{\partial B} - \frac{\partial C}{\partial B} = 0 \qquad [4.24]$$

If s is set equal to $1/\lambda$, these conditions are the same as those derived by maximising passenger miles with a shadow price of public funds of λ. To see this, multiply through by λ. In each case, the first term then represents the change in passenger miles, and the rest of the equation the change in profitability multiplied by λ.

Chapter 5

Competition, regulation and integration in public transport

5.1 Introduction

There are few countries in which government regulation does not play an important role in the transport market. Generally, operators of public passenger transport services are subject both to controls on entry and on prices and service levels. In the freight market, arrangements are more diverse. Entry is usually licensed, but the licence may be available to anyone who can show that he has the facilities and resources to operate the services safely, or it may (as for long-distance freight in France and in West Germany) be subject to a limit on the road haulage capacity permitted. It may limit the operator to specific routes or areas (as for inter-state traffic in the US). Licensed operators may be required to operate to a fixed published tariff (as may railways) or they may be subject to upper and/or lower limits on prices. Such a 'forked' tariff is again found in West Germany and was at one time official EEC policy (Bayliss, 1979). The aim of this chapter is to examine the reasons given for such intervention in the transport market and to assess their validity.

5.2 The need for regulation in passenger transport

There are two main reasons given for regulating the transport market: ensuring safety, and the prevention of 'wasteful' competition. Now it may be thought that the safety issue is adequately dealt with by a system of 'quality' licensing, whereby anyone will be given a licence to operate provided that his drivers and vehicles are deemed satisfactory. This certainly deals with one important aspect of the issue, provided that the balance of inspection levels and penalties is a sufficient deterrent. However, there is a further point. If direct competition is permitted between vehicles on the same route and at the same time, a dangerous race between vehicles from stop to stop may ensue. There is ample evidence that such happenings were not uncommon in London, for instance, in the cut-throat competition of the 1920s (Dyos and Aldcroft, 1969). Even in rail transport, there have been celebrated inter-company 'races', such as those on the London–Scotland route in 1895. Safe operation may require prevention of direct competition between different passenger transport operators on the same route, if there is any likelihood that such races may result.

However, this section is mainly concerned with the issue of 'wasteful' competition. It needs to be explained immediately why competition should be considered 'wasteful' in this sector, when economists so often applaud competition elsewhere in the economy. The simple answer lies in the economies of scale identified in Chapter 3 with respect to vehicle (or train) size. Competition may lead to the bidding down of average loads and hence raising of unit costs. Even if competition is strong enough to eliminate any excess profits, the resulting equilibrium will be a monopolistic competition one of excess capacity and unnecessarily high unit costs.

Two points may be made against this view, however. The first is a standard criticism of the theory of monopolistic competition; that it assumes excessive short-sightedness on the part of existing producers. Surely, it may be argued, they will realise that by operating at minimum average cost and not seeking to make more than a normal rate of profit, they can remove the incentive for new entry and retain a higher market share for themselves. New entry, then, will only be possible if the entrant has something better to offer in terms of product quality or cost, and then it is surely desirable. However, elimination of existing excess capacity may be more difficult unless some operators have the financial resources to sustain a price war.

Secondly, even if new entry does occur, reducing load factors, there is some compensation in terms of an increase in services operated, and hence in scope and quality of the transport system. However, such an increase may not be as beneficial as if planned to offer the greatest improvement; it may simply duplicate an existing service with adequate capacity rather than operating at a less popular time or over a less well-used route. For instance, if an existing service has an average load of 50 passengers, a new operator may feel there is more to be gained by aiming to take half of this traffic by duplicating the service (in the knowledge that if he succeeds, fares will have to be raised or services cut by the other operator in any case) than to introduce a new service where or when traffic is more sparse. Lack of planning may also lead to an undesirably poor standard of connections between services. For instance, suppose that the fare from Bradford to Leeds is 30p and from Leeds to London is £5. A single operator of two connecting services will pay close attention to the needs of through passengers, since their loss represents a loss of £5.30. An independent operator from Bradford to Leeds, on the other hand, would regard these passengers as no more important than local passengers, since all pay him 30p. Unless the Leeds–London operator makes a side payment to the local operator to improve connections, journeys involving interchange may be hampered. The situation would be even worse if the Leeds–Bradford operator also operated a Bradford–London direct service. He would have a strong incentive to prevent connections into and out of the Leeds–London service, for fear of passengers diverting from his own long distance service. Common control of services, or a regulatory body to co-ordinate timetables, would seem to have considerable justification in such cases.

What we are really saying is that there are positive or negative externalities of production between services. Provision of one service may raise or lower the value of another. Moreover, since the value of a particular service to its passengers differs from that to its operator (because of consumers' surplus), even a system of side payments between operators would not necessarily lead to a socially optimal set of services.

A further objection to allowing the competitive process to determine the service levels to be provided is the absence of any obvious stable equilibrium. Consider Fig. 4.1 above. For a plausible combination of demand and cost characteristics, this shows the alternative combinations of fare and bus mileage that can be provided in a given area. Any point on this curve, then, is a potential competitive equilibrium. For instance, suppose the existing situation is one of high fares and high frequencies. A new operator charging lower fares will attract some traffic from existing services (not all, since he cannot profitably match the existing services in frequency). The original operators will then be obliged to make a more than equivalent cut in their own bus mileage (since average fare is now lower, a lower total bus mileage can be supported in the area); they may cut their fares as well. The outcome will be a new equilibrium with lower fares and lower frequencies, unless a price war ensues, culminating in the departure of one or more operators from the market, or unless competition leads to greater productive efficiency, so that more bus miles may be supported at any given fare. Even if a price war does emerge, it is likely to be the operator with the greatest financial strength, rather than the one with the lowest costs, that wins. Financial strength may result from having profitable operations elsewhere or in a completely different field from road transport.

However, there is nothing stable about this new equilibrium. Further cuts in fares and service levels may ensue. Alternatively, one operator may again raise fares and frequencies, to be followed or not by the other operators, as the case may be. It is impossible to determine on *a priori* grounds whereabouts on the schedule of Fig. 4.1 the market will ultimately settle. A regulatory body, on the other hand, should be in a position to take a positive view of the combination of fares and service levels that will serve the community best, whether its decision is based on cost–benefit studies or on political judgement. It should also prevent the instability of fares and service levels that might be expected to ensue under competitive circumstances, and since transport demand is heavily conditioned by long-term location decisions, and much hardship may be caused by rapid fluctuations in price and service levels, a degree of stability is highly desirable.

Where rail also operates in the area, a further choice between competition and integration has to be made. As was shown above, rail transport enjoys considerable economies of scale with respect to the size of the flow of traffic on a particular route. If it were feasible to charge marginal cost on both rail and bus transport, this would not prevent competition between modes from establishing a desirable modal split. However, heavy subsidisation would be necessary, and planning studies to decide, on the basis of total costs and benefits, whether both should exist. If, on the other hand, a second-best pricing policy were being followed, as suggested in Chapter 4, there could be a good case for protecting the railway from bus competition on routes where it is considered a rail service is justified. At the margin, diversion of traffic from rail to bus would only be justified if the excess of price over marginal cost on the bus exceeded that on the train service. On the other hand, a comparison of total costs and benefits might lead to the conclusion that, on more lightly loaded routes, all traffic should be concentrated on buses, and the rail service discontinued.

At the same time, the flow of traffic on a rail route may be increased in some cases by the provision of road feeder services. In the peak days of railway construction, many routes were provided which could not conceivably have been profitable examined in isolation, just for this reason of expanding traffic – and profits – on the busier lines. (Another major motive behind expansion of the railway network was to forestall attempts by competing companies to gain a foothold in the area, and thus deplete existing traffic flows.) However, maintenance of rail feeder services over lightly trafficked routes is expensive, and it is likely that the bus has a substantial role to play here. Not only are there routes on which feeder services are better provided by modes other than rail, because of the small size of the flow, or because the geography of the area makes a rail service very indirect, but also there may be cases where an individual trip on a predominantly rail service is best provided by road. This may be because demand at that particular time is low, because of track occupation for engineering work, or because the provision of a path for a particular passenger train at that time involves either a large increase in infrastructure capacity or a high opportunity cost in terms of its impact on other services. Restricting an operator to a particular mode discourages him from seeking opportunities for the efficient integration of modes; he is not encouraged to ask what is the most appropriate technology for the particular task at hand.

So far, in this chapter, the argument has been almost entirely opposed to permitting competition in public passenger transport; in particular, it has been shown that those who believe that competition will ensure the establishment of an optimal level of fares and service levels are mistaken; only planning and regulation can do that. However, the advocates of competition do have some much stronger arguments. In particular, competition may lead to increased efficiency in production, to greater innovation and variety in the types of service provided and to more thorough and effective marketing. Some competition on these grounds is not necessarily incompatible with regulation, provided that the regulating authority takes the interests of all sectors of the community into account, and does not see his role as purely one of protecting the established operator. Routes may be auctioned, for instance, and licences given to the operator who makes the most attractive bid in terms of fares, service quality and required subsidy. (To a limited extent, competition of this type already exists in Great Britain in tendering for subsidised routes outside the main conurbations.) In considering proposals to start new services, the effect on existing services must be taken into account, but an adverse impact should not rule out the new service if it also offers advantages to some passengers. At the same time, the need for an element of stability has been referred to above. The interests of those working in the industry should also be considered (and the existence of strong trade unions will ensure that they cannot in practice be ignored). The belief that a regulatory body will fall too much under the influence of established operators, and offer too much protection, may lead some analysis to prefer a free market even if they accept the above arguments against it.

In conclusion then, a good *a priori* case exists for the regulation of the public passenger transport system to achieve a planned and co-ordinated system of services and fares. At the same time, competition does have very real advantages, and to the extent that these may be exploited without excessive damage to the integration of services, they should be. In particular, licensing authorities must be willing to license new services where the balance of advantage lies with them, and to transfer licences from one operator to another where the efficiency with which the service is provided is likely to be improved.

5.3 Institutional arrangements

In the face of these problems, a wide variety of institutional arrangements has emerged. Most involve preventing direct competition between different operators on the same route. There are two broad approaches to this: creation of an area monopoly and regulation of individual operators by a third party.

Area monopoly

Area monopolies have been created in many cities by placing ownership of urban railways (metros, etc.) buses and trams in a single body, usually controlled by the local authority. Externalities between services are thus internalised by means of common ownership. Creation of a similar situation in rural areas involves the problem that rail services in rural areas are usually an integral part of the national rail network with through services and joint use of assets rather than self-contained local lines (although the position in Switzerland, where many local lines in rural areas are effectively owned by the Canton whilst being legally required to integrate their services with those of Swiss Federal Railways should be noted). One solution is the creation of a single national transport company (such as CIE in Ireland). In most other countries, the railway is a major bus operator, and this has helped encourage transfer of local stopping services to buses in some cases (e.g. Sweden), even though political·opposition to rail closures remains strong. However, in a country with a large and complicated transport network, services will have to be divided into divisions for control, and integration of bus and rail services even within a single organisation may remain a problem.

An alternative to outright ownership is for a single body (the Verkehrsverbund in West German cities; the PTE in Britain) to be responsible for setting fares and service levels throughout the area, whilst subcontracting actual operations. Whilst in Britain the body in question is a major bus operator (and in one case, Tyne and Wear, operates a new rapid transit network), in the West German example it does not actually operate any services. This leaves it free to contract with municipal and private operators as seems most advantageous. This is a benefit to the extent that private operators in rural areas may be able to hold down costs by means of part-time labour, shared facilities with other businesses, etc. in ways not usually open to a large municipal undertaking.

However, contracting for rail services presents a problem in that even local services tend to operate over much longer distances than bus services, crossing local authority boundaries and linking in with the national network. Conflicting decisions by neighbouring authorities may therefore create anomolies in terms of services terminating short of the most sensible destinations, fares which differ greatly between neighbouring stations and thus distort traffic flows and a failure to link in well with the national network. Moreover, sharing the costs of such cross-boundary services is always controversial as a large part of the costs is joint. Thus, in most countries, whilst subsidy of local bus services is the responsibility of countries or the equivalent local authority, rail services are subsidised and controlled nationally. Even when all the parties concerned are subject to some form of public ownership, problems of integration remain.

Regulation

In most developed countries, and an increasing proportion of developing countries, bus operators have to apply to a licensing authority for permission to operate on a particular route; usually fares and service levels are also controlled. Sometimes the licensing authority is appointed nationally (as in Britain); sometimes (e.g. Denmark) it is effectively the local authority. In Switzerland, the Post Office – as a major operator and user – co-ordinates services.

The licensing authority can thus prevent direct competition, and abstraction of revenue from one operator by another. Usually there is a blanket ban on competition with the railway, which both protects the railway and encourages bus operators to act as feeders, since this is the only way they can share in longer distance traffic. The authority has only limited powers to secure provision of services (by means of cross-subsidisation as a condition for the granting of profitable routes) unless it is also responsible for payment of subsidies.

In Britain, the licensing authority has always afforded less protection to the railway than elsewhere in Europe; whilst it had to take abstraction of railway revenue into account in its decisions, competing services have frequently been allowed, and Britain is the only Western European country to have a national network of express coach services (operated largely by a nationalised operator, but one which is totally separate from and in competition with the railway). At the time of writing, new legislation is about to come into force which will free entry into the coach market for services with more than 50 km between stops, and shift the burden of proof in other licensing disputes on to the objectors to any new service to show that it is not in the public interest[1]. This raises the possibility of reintroducing competition on individual routes, and a consortium of private companies has already announced plans to operate a network of coach services on key trunk routes in direct competition with BR and the National Bus Company and at lower prices.

5.4 Competition in the freight market

By comparison with the passenger market, the discussion of the costs of freight operation in Chapter 3 may seem to indicate that there will be little wrong with a competitive solution to the structure of the road freight industry. In the road haulage sector, there appeared no real evidence of economies of firm size and in fact in most countries a large number of firms of widely differing sizes co-exist. Only where firms offer regular services carrying goods for a number of different customers (basically, the parcels end of the business) is there a major risk of competition leading to waste by duplication of services with low load factors. For other traffic, there seems no objection to allowing consignors to choose between competing road hauliers, with often the further alternative of using their own vehicles to fall back on. Competition can be expected to lead to minimisation of the average cost of producing the desired standard of service; prices will be based on average cost, which in the presence of constant returns to scale also reflects marginal cost. It is true that competition could lead to cutting costs at the expense of safety. But this can be prevented by government control of safety standards (construction and use regulations, vehicle testing, drivers' hours) without other interference in the market.

Fears of wasteful competition in the freight market usually centre on the issues of instability and of whether the industry provides a reasonable livelihood for operators and workforce. Since in most countries it is an industry of thousands of small firms, which can be entered by the purchase (on hire-purchase) of a single vehicle, the classical barriers to entry are relatively low. As a result, it may attract an excessive supply of would-be entrepreneurs, leading to over-vigorous competition, wastefully low utilisation of vehicles, a high risk of bankruptcy for owners and excessive hours of work and unsatisfactory conditions for drivers. The latter problem may be aggravated by the high proportion of owner-drivers, and the difficulties of union organisation in such a fragmented industry.

Two further factors may make competition in the public sector of the road haulage industry more acute than in other industries in the face of industrial fluctuations. Firstly, firms which operate own-account fleets will consider the avoidable costs of laying these up or disposing of them during a recession as against public haulier rates, and will be inclined to place the brunt of fluctuations in demand on the shoulders of the latter. Secondly, whilst the larger public haulier may be able to vary his labour force (subject to industrial relations problems, redundancy payments requirements and the risk of difficuties in attracting trained staff when the upturn comes), the owner-driver has no such option. His costs are almost entirely inescapable, unless he decides to leave the industry altogether. He may, then, accept work at rates which are in the long run grossly uneconomic, simply to pay his hire-purchase and other fixed outgoings. Such competition may pose difficulties for rail operators, too, who may find themselves undercut for short-term work by road hauliers, whilst almost all rail costs are inescapable in the short run.

If this picture of the industry is correct, there are a number of issues for public concern arising from it. Safety, again, may require regulation (for instance of drivers' hours, training and maintenance standards). A high level of bankruptcies may in itself be disturbing to customers, although they generally have the choice between seeking to obtain the lowest price, or employing an operator more certain to give a reliable long-run service (particularly where a nationalised operator is available). But the biggest issue arising from this is the degree to which regulation is desirable to protect the interests of those in the industry concerned against excessive competition.

This issue has been examined in Great Britain on a number of occasions. Walters and McCleod (1956) examined evidence from the inter-war period when controls on entry was first introduced and concluded that the rate of banruptcy was lower than for most trades where small-scale operation was the norm (it may be, of course, that all such trades have easy entry conditions leading to low profits and instability). Regarding the more recent situation, the Foster Committee (1978) did find profits in road haulage in the mid-1970s to be extremely low (on average, after allowing for replacement cost depreciation, zero) although very variable, and in general higher in the more specialised sectors of the industry. However, this was at a time of recession and low profits throughout industry. The Committee took the view that if it could not be established that these low profits were damaging customers, there was no case for government intervention.

A further issue which arises with respect to public freight transport more than passenger is the question of whether regulation is an appropriate way of reducing the environmental impact of the transport industries. (Ch. 6)

Consideration of modes of transport which experience economies of scale at some or all output levels (rail, pipeline, shipping or inland waterways) brings in two main problems. Economies of scale in rail transport mean that there will normally be a single monopoly rail operator. This need not cause problems as long as there is effective competition from other modes, but there may exist some traffic for which the rail operator has considerable monopoly power. Secondly, because of economies of scale, endeavouring to cover total cost will lead to a divergence between price and marginal cost (Friedlander,

1969). This problem is most marked in the case of infrastructure costs, but also applies to movements and terminals costs, particularly where certain services regularly have spare capacity, retention of which is required to maintain quality of service or to deal with peaks. (A somewhat similar problem is posed by the long time-scale of cost avoidability; traffic may be worth retaining for a substantial period of time, even though in the long run it cannot pay for the complete renewal of all the assets involved.)

There appear to be three main solutions to this problem.

(a) The rail operator may base prices on marginal costs, with the resulting deficit being reimbursed by the government.

(b) The rail operator may base prices on average (allocated) cost; to prevent misallocation of traffic between modes, some form of protection from road competition will then be necessary.

(c) The rail operator may seek to discriminate between traffic flows according to the maximum the consignor is willing to pay, in order to cover the difference between marginal and average cost.

A simple example may help. Suppose the road transport rates for each of n flows on a particular route are given by R_i ($i = 1, 2 \ldots n$). The rail operator's costs are determined by the volumes of all commodities carried (x_i):

$$C = C(x_1, x_2 \cdots x_n) \tag{5.1}$$

For simplicity, indivisibilities will be ignored, so that rail may be considered to offer decreasing cost at all output levels. Under the first policy, $\partial C / \partial x_i = p_i$, where p_i is the rail price (for all i). Ignoring quality differences, rail will carry all traffic for which marginal cost is less than by road ($p_i < R_i$) at the optimal output mix. Under policy (b), some form of allocation of joint costs is involved which, in the presence of scale economies, is bound to be more or less arbitrary. The result is to raise some prices above marginal cost, and – in the absence of protection – to lose traffic to a mode with higher marginal costs (other prices may be set too low, with the reverse effect).

In the case of policy (c), assuming that no other modes of transport are available and that the amount of the commodities to be transported is fixed regardless of transport costs, the railway will charge prices marginally below road haulage rates. Its revenue will thus approach

$$\sum_i R_i x_i$$

Some of the advantages and disadvantages of the various approaches may now be considered. In the first case (a), the government needs to be able to estimate the volumes and corresponding marginal costs conforming to the optimal allocation of traffic in order to determine the appropriate subsidy (if it is unable to do this, and simply resorts to deficit finance, then it will be exerting no financial discipline on the efficiency of the operator – see Ch. 3). It must watch the overall cost saving being achieved by the presence of the railway, in order to take long-run planning and investment decisions on a cost–benefit basis. The presence of the deficit means that funds must be raised by taxation or diverted from other forms of expenditure, and the opportunity cost of each of these must be borne in mind.

Approach (b) eliminates the need for external finance, but involves the government not just in a planning function but in a day-to-day administrative function in the allocation of freight traffic. Either each case will have to be considered on its merits to determine the cheapest overall method of transport (taking quality of service as well as money outlay into account), or (more usually) rules of thumb concerning the consignment sizes, commodities and lengths of haul that may be undertaken by road transport will have to be laid down. Given the diversity of the freight market, any such set of rules is bound to misallocate traffic in a certain proportion of cases. Long-term planning and investment decisions will again need to be taken in a cost–benefit, rather than a financial, framework.

By contrast, approach (c) largely eliminates the regulatory role of the government. This is because not only is the allocation of freight determined in the market, but also effective discrimination means that long-run planning and investment decisions may be taken on grounds purely of profitability. For instance, in the above example, it will be worth maintaining the railway in question in the long run only if

$$\sum_i R_i x_i > C(x_i \cdots x_n) \qquad [5.2]$$

i.e. revenue is greater than total cost. Otherwise, it will be cheaper to substitute road haulage overall even though its marginal cost is higher than for rail. A corresponding rule may be stated with respect to the costs avoidable with respect to each time horizon.

The clarity of objectives and the absence of administrative complications are great attractions of the latter approach. At the same time, a number of drawbacks must be noted.

1. A desirable outcome is only possible if the railway operator is able to discriminate efficiently and thoroughly. This is throwing a heavy burden on the skill of its marketing and sales officers; it also assumes that customers will not possess the monopoly power to retaliate singly or collectively. Given that a few other organisations (coal, oil and electricity producers, for instance) may supply a large proportion of the traffic, this is a doubtful assumption.

2. Discrimination will be rendered much more difficult if the railway is required to publish and adhere to a fixed set of rates. Traditionally, such published rates have been a legal requirement in most countries, as a protection against the railway's monopoly power. In such a situation, railways could only discriminate according to factors such as the commodity class in question, rather than with respect to the circumstances of the individual firm. Usually such discrimination was linked to the value of the commodity. (When railways have a monopoly, this approach may have some logic, since the only factor affecting the amount of traffic by rail is the amount of the commodity sold in the final market, and on average rail freight rates could be expected to

affect this less, the smaller the proportion of the final price accounted for by the freight rate. Its perpetuation in a competitive situation, where the value of the product has nothing to do with the rates charged by the competitor, may lose a great deal of valuable traffic to road.) However, if fixed rates are not required, and prices set by individual negotiation, there is still a risk that in certain areas the railway may be able to exploit monopoly power to make an excessive surplus, which may be used to cross-subsidise other traffic or to permit inefficiency (Heaver and Nelson, 1977).

3. The assumption was made at the beginning of this section that road haulage rates reflect average, and marginal cost. This may be appropriate as regards the private costs of the road transport operator. It is unlikely to be so as regards the social costs. Even if taxes can be made to cover on average the marginal costs of road traffic in terms of infrastructure costs, congestion, accidents and environmental costs (which, in the absence of any consensus on how to value the latter two, will always be a contentious issue) these vary so much from place to place and from time to time that much misallocation of traffic may still occur. Thus a case may remain for regulation and direction of traffic, at any rate where divergence between taxes and external costs appear greatest. Alternatively, subsidies to certain types of traffic to change mode may be worth while.

The situation which has emerged in Great Britain is largely that of (c) above, supplemented (since 1974) by grants towards the construction of privately owned rail sidings or terminals where the use of these affords environmental advantages. In a great many countries, however, including much of Western Europe, controls are more strict. Railways may be obliged to publish fixed rates and to carry any goods offered without discrimination (this is the case in the United States, West Germany and Italy) whilst in some cases (e.g. France and West Germany) receiving more protection from road haulage on long-haul traffic (policy (b) above). This divergence of policy *may* make sense, inasmuch as these countries have much longer average lengths of haul, so that the amount of competitive traffic between road and rail in the difficult area of wagonload services is much greater than is the case in Great Britain.

5.5 Competition in the taxi trade

In Britain, taxis currently account for less than 2 per cent of consumers' expenditure on passenger transport (compared with 6% rail and $8\frac{1}{2}$% bus) and considerably less than one-half of 1 per cent of the passenger mileage travelled (compared with 7% for rail and 11% for bus) (DTp, 1979). Yet there are two reasons why we should not dismiss it as an unimportant sector, in the context of this chapter. Firstly, the taxi and private hire market appears to be achieving the fastest growth rate of any sector of the public passenger transport, generally without the benefit of subsidies (Table 5.1). Secondly, it has been argued that existing institutional arrangements in Great Britain are seriously reducing the contribution that taxis and other small

Table 5.1 Public transport vehicles with licences current (000's)

Year	All	4 seats or less	5–8 seats (incl.)
1966	93.8	11.4	3.9
1967	94.2	11.5	3.9
1968	99.4	14.3	5.4
1969	101.6	16.0	6.5
1970	103.0	18.0	7.2
1971	106.3	20.2	7.9
1972	104.7	20.5	7.5
1973	106.5	21.4	7.3
1974	106.8	21.6	6.6
1975	111.8	25.6	6.6
1976	113.1	26.4	7.3
1977	111.6	27.9	8.1
1978	110.3	28.4	8.3

Source: DTp (1979).

unscheduled vehicle operations could make to the quality of public transport (Beesley, 1973). In support of this view, the growth of 'jitney'-type operations in countries where regulation is less stringent or not enforced is often cited, although most of the cases in point are in developing countries with low labour costs and a labour surplus.

An analysis of the effects of deregulating the taxi industry would follow very similar lines to that of section 3.1 above, but in place of bus miles we must substitute number of taxis available for hire as an index both of output and service quality. As this increases, the greater availability of taxis is likely to increase demand, but less than proportionately. In other words, as the number of taxis increases, utilisation falls (and unit costs rise). There would be little fear of long-run excess profits being made because of the structure of the industry (for instance, in London in 1968, out of 7,571 cabs, 3,636 were in individual ownership and only 616 in fleets of over 150. Cmnd 4483, 1970). If we define normal profits as the level at which neither net entry to nor net departure from the industry occurs (this may well be below the level of normal profits for the economy as a whole, because of the relative ease of entry into the taxi trade), we can construct a curve showing alternative combinations of mean fare and number of taxis. It will be downward-sloping, similar to Fig. 4.1. Again, as was argued for the bus industry in section 5.2 it is not all clear what will determine where, on this schedule of alternative equilibria, the industry will come to rest. There is thus no reason to suppose that what does occur in an unregulated industry necessarily provides the best possible trade-off between quality and price. An *a priori* case for regulation to achieve a certain position on the schedule is provided. On the other hand, it has been argued that the likelihood of a licensing authority choosing wisely, and the risk of it falling prey to interested parties, makes this solution unworkable as well (Beesley, 1973).

In practice, in most of the world's major cities, taxi fares are controlled (Cmnd 4483, 1970). This, alone, should also be sufficient to control numbers of taxis, although it is doubtful whether regulatory bodies always take this into account in their decisions; the principal motive behind control of fares appears to be one of protecting members of the public who use taxis rarely or who are strangers to the area from having their ignorance of normal fares exploited by unscrupulous taxi-drivers. Yet in some cities (including most UK cities outside London) entry is restricted to a specific number of licences as well as fares being controlled.

Now there are three possible outcomes of this situation. Firstly, the combination of price and number of licences may be set so that, on average, taxis make normal profits (i.e. they are located on the schedule of alternative equilibria referred to above). Secondly, the combination may be such that normal profits cannot be earned. In this case, the quantity restriction will not be binding; not all the licences will be taken up. Thirdly, the combination may permit super-normal profits, sheltered from new entry by the quantity restriction. In this case, a windfall gain will accrue to licence-holders. This may be thought desirable if it is felt that otherwise taxi-drivers would be underpaid, as a result of the easy entry conditions. Unfortunately, if licences are transferable, however, this sum will be capitalised in the market price of a licence (this happens in many UK cities) and new entrants to the industry will not benefit.

Another advantage sometimes claimed for quantity restrictions on entry is to stabilise the supply of taxis over time. Obviously, this could only work in one direction – preventing fluctuations upwards – and it is far from clear that, given the ease of entry and exit, such stabilisation is desirable when demand fluctuates. In any case, stabilising both numbers of licences and fares when demand fluctuates will have the inevitable result of forcing firms into excess or subnormal profits (and in the latter case, the attempted stabilisation is unlikely to succeed). In other words, given that there is a case for controlling prices, it seems that quantity licensing has little useful to add, and a number of possible disadvantages.

Although in London quantity licensing does not apply, there are other restrictions on entry. Taxis have to be to an approved design, for instance, and drivers have to have a thorough knowledge of the geography of the city. These conditions may add more than 10 per cent to costs. It has been argued that these regulations prevent the customer from choosing the combination of price and quality of service he wants. On the other hand, he has no way of knowing in advance what quality of service any individual taxi will give. Because of the large number of small firms in the industry, brand-name advertising is of limited use (although, of course, service competititon may cause the structure of the industry to change, favouring the large, readily identifiable firm). A possible solution would be a two-tier system, whereby taxis which had passed the quality examinations would be given a clearly identifiable plate and permitted to charge a higher fare (Beesley, 1973). However, this would still leave passengers desiring the higher quality service worse off, because of the reduced availability of such taxis; whether this would be compensated for by benefits to other users is a difficult judgement to make.

5.6 The effects on conventional public transport of competition from small vehicles

The above discussion of the taxi industry has concentrated on the effects on consumers and producers within the industry of alternative policies. But there are at least two important external considerations to take into account. Firstly an increase in the number of taxis may increase traffic congestion. The extent of this will depend on the additional dead mileage generated, and on the extent to which extra taxi trips are diverted from public or private transport. There is also, of course, a case for environmental and safety controls, from the point of view of the rest of society.

But the principal question to be addressed in this section is, to what extent taxi operations worsen the fares and/or service levels that can be offered by other public transport modes within a given budget constraint. Little evidence seems to be available on this, although the high-price, high-flexibility nature of taxi services would appear to compete more directly with private than with other public transport. Moreover, in many contexts, the taxi is complementary to other public transport. For instance it may act as a feeder, particularly for long journeys with heavy luggage. By providing for the occasional urgent journey, or awkward journey in terms of time of day or route, it may strengthen the overall package of public transport services available when a household is considering its level of car ownership.

Yet there are clearly circumstances in which taxis will take traffic from other public transport modes. This may be particularly the case where public transport fares are high relative to taxi fares, and where taxi-sharing is permitted or encouraged.

But the greater threat to public transport patronage comes not from the orthodox taxi, but from car or van-sharing. In the 1972/73 British National Travel Survey (DOE, 1975), 27 per cent of the passenger mileage reported by members of non-car-owning households took place as car or van passengers (this is twice the figure reported for rail). It is likely that many of these trips would not have taken place at all in the absence of the offer of a lift; even so, it is clear that lift-giving both provides an important source of mobility for non-car-owning households and a serious loss of patronage for public transport operators. These factors are probably more significant in countries such as the United States, where legal constraints on advertising and charging fares have not constrained the growth of car-sharing as they have in Western Europe.

Recently, there has been growing interest in organised car-sharing (putting strangers who make identical journeys in touch with each other by computer or manual matching systems); and the law in Britain has been changed to permit payment of costs by the passenger and (now) advertising. The incentive for this comes partly through a wish to provide increased mobility (particularly where public transport services are poor) and partly through a belief that in this way the number of cars on the road may be reduced, thus reducing congestion, energy consumption and pollution. British experience to date (Bonsall, 1981) suggests that a very small proportion of the workforce (under $2\frac{1}{2}\%$) would be willing to take part in such a scheme for the journey to and from work, but that most of this would be at the expense of public transport use.

To what extent is there a case for protecting public transport from competition from small vehicles? If public transport fares closely matched marginal social costs, including the effects of changing service levels, and if car-sharing led to no significant increase in the mileage run by private vehicles, the answer would be, fairly unequivocally, none. The difficulty arises from the fact that, even when an optimal fares structure has been selected, public transport fares very often will have little to do with marginal cost (see following chapters). But this leads to no simple answer. In some cases (particularly in the urban peak) public transport fares will be below marginal social cost, and diversion of some trips to car-sharing will be of benefit to public transport users as a whole. In other cases, in the off-peak and on lightly loaded routes, car-sharing may harm remaining public transport users. In any event, it is perhaps unlikely that restrictions on the amount of car-sharing can be enforced. A more open permitting of taking of fares would, however, make continued control of the taxi industry as advocated above more difficult, since it would be difficult in some circumstances to distinguish between casual lift-givers and professional taxis.

5.7 Conclusion

The approach we have taken in this chapter is to accept that there are valid arguments for regulation of the transport market, but to argue that these can be reconciled with a fair degree of competition. Firstly, there is a strong case for regulation of safety by some form of quality licensing (the details of this have not been considered here, but a comprehensive review is available in the above-mentioned Foster report) (Foster, 1978). Secondly, there is a case for a body to regulate fares, routes and service levels in public passenger transport, to promote co-ordination of services and to assess whether proposals from one operator offer advantages which offset any disadvantages in terms of effects on competing services. However, this is an extremely difficult task and certainly does not amount to a case for blanket protection of existing operators. It is probably best undertaken by the local authority, and co-ordinated with subsidisation of unprofitable but socially desirable services. Thirdly, there is a problem in the freight transport field, in terms of excessive competition, external costs in the road sector and of monopoly and economies of scale in rail. On the whole, the problem is best solved by allowing the rail operator freedom to recoup his costs by price discrimination according to what the traffic will bear, whilst using taxes to ensure that the competitive price established in road haulage is at an appropriate level. It must be admitted, however, that these solutions are by no means perfect. Decision-taking in this area is a difficult task of trading-off the expense and inefficiencies caused by regulation against the inefficiencies of an unregulated market.

Note
1. Since this was written, the 1980 Transport Act has come into force. There is little evidence of attempted new entry on stage services; a few firms have applied to run frequent services on busy sections of route (but usually excluding evenings and Sundays) at cheaper fares than National Bus Company but have been refused licences. On express services, the position is very different. British Coachways, the private consortium, came in on key trunk routes with much reduced fares, which National Bus Company matched. The resulting rapid growth in coach traffic, partly at the expense of rail, caused BR to cut their cheapest reduced fares on these routes, whilst the recession in business travel brought domestic air services into the price war, the final outcome of which is still very uncertain.

Chapter 6

Public transport, land use and the environment

6.1 Introduction

The predominant approach of the earlier chapters of this text has been to take evidence on operating costs and demand elasticities and to attempt to optimise public transport at a particular moment in time with respect to a given set of objectives. Moreover, such evidence on demand elasticities as is available is predominantly short-run. The question may very reasonably be asked whether this is an adequate approach. Short-run considerations may suggest free public transport for small towns, but surely this would encourage low-density sprawl, with long average trip lengths, which would inflate public transport costs over time? A policy of exploiting low elasticities of demand on a commuter service to the city centre, by providing low-quality services at high prices, may set up forces to decentralise jobs, perhaps leading to diversion of trips to private transport and increasing the social and environmental costs of the transport system as a whole. Cross-subsidisation between routes and areas and a commitment to 'accessibility for all', may remove all incentive to locate in places where public transport services are most cheaply provided, and again inflate costs over time. The importance of such long-run effects, and the ways in which they may be incorporated in decision-taking, are the subject of this chapter.

6.2 Public transport policy and the environment

In Chapter 1 we referred to the environmental advantages of public over private transport, and to the difficulties of reflecting these in pricing policy. Firstly, there is the difficulty involved in valuing environmental costs. Secondly, is the difficulty of reflecting the costs in prices charged, given that prices would have to vary both in time and space to do this adequately. The costs of congestion and pollution vary according to where and when they are produced. (The same is not true of resource depletion, so that whatever degree of conservation is desired is most likely to be achieved at minimum cost by a straightforward increase in price. See Baumol and Oates, 1971). There is more possibility of reflecting such variations in public transport pricing policy than in private, so there may be some case for second-best pricing policies. (These could be introduced into the systems of objectives outlined in Ch. 4 by attaching suitable weights to passenger miles or freight ton miles diverted from private transport.)

There are four main ways in which diversion of traffic from private to public transport may benefit the environment.

1. *By reducing noise and emissions at source.* Table 6.1 gives some representative figures for private and public transport. It is clear that the main ways in which emissions are reduced by public transport are firstly by concentrating a larger amount of traffic in a single vehicle or train and, secondly, by the greater prospect (in the existing state of battery technology, at least) of electrification. This is also true of the contribution of public transport to conservation of fossil fuels (see Table 1.1).

2. *By better segregation from the population.* In general, it appears that railway lines are better segregated from the population than main roads, and the former may more readily be placed underground in particularly

Table 6.1 Some comparisons of external costs of public and private transport

(all figures are given per vehicle or per train mile)

	Private car	Heavy goods vehicle	Bus	Diesel train	Electric train
Typical load (UK) passengers or tonnes	1.4	4.6 tons	16	95 passengers or 300 tonnes	
*Accidents**					
Deaths ($\times 10^{-6}$)	0.0379	0.0759	0.134	0.261	
Serious injuries ($\times 10^{-6}$)	0.574	0.538	1.43	0.485	
Noise					
Peak noise dB(A)	87†	92†	92†	83–93‡	
Air pollution					
Carbon monoxide	55,560	6,610	9,810	80,290	0§
Hydrocarbons	2,820	1,350	2,000	16,140	0§
Aldehydes	90	200	300	2,420	0§
Oxides of nitrogen	1,940	3,980	5,910	48,415	0§
Oxides of sulphur	220	2,630	3,910	3,430	0§
Lead	75	0	0	0	0§

* Road casualties are allocated between vehicles in proportion to their involvement in accidents of the appropriate type. This probably understates the reduction in casualties resulting from a reduction in heavy vehicles on the road.
† Maximum legally permitted in use.
‡ At 25 m; depends on type of stock and speed.
§ This ignores emissions at power stations. These are usually much less troublesome, being dispersed at high level and away from main centres of population.
Source: BRB (1976).

vulnerable areas. Whilst it may arise largely from historical accident, this does appear to be significant (for instance, in a survey conducted in Britain in 1972, 89% of residents heard and 23% were bothered by road traffic noise, whereas 35% heard and only 2% were bothered by rail, SCPR, 1978). Thus a given amount of emission may produce less annoyance than for road. The same advantage does not accrue to road-based public transport, except by the greater control of routeing that one has compared with private transport.

3. *Reduced environmental cost of construction of new infra-structure.* Table 6.2 gives some comparable figures for capacities and land-take. (The reduction in land-take is particularly important in existing urban areas, where destruction of property may be substantially reduced, or avoided altogether, if existing infrastructure can be used for public transport, whereas new infrastructure would be required for private.)

Table 6.2 Capacity and land-take of alternative urban transport systems

	Width of way (ft)	Peak vehicles/ trains per hour each way	Assumed peak vehicle/train occupancy	Peak passenger flow per hour	Peak passenger flow per foot of way
2-track rail	37	37	400	14,800	400
			800	29,600	800
3-track rail	50	52	400	20,800	416
			800	41,600	832
2-lane highway: car	62	1,000	1.4	1,400	22.6
			4	4,000	64.5
2-lane highway: bus		480	40	19,200	309
			80	38,400	619
4-lane highway: car	86	3,200	1.4	4,480	52.1
			4	12,800	149
4-lane highway: bus		960	40	38,400	447
			80	76,800	893
6-lane highway: car	110	4,995	1.4	6,993	63.6
			4	19,980	182
6-lane highway: bus		1,440	40	57,600	524
			80	115,200	1,047

Source: Derived from data in Kain, Meyer and Wohl (1965). Relates to American cities with modern equipment. All widths substantially revised if in cutting (as assumed there).

4. *Reduction in frequency and length of trips.* Households dependent on public transport tend to travel less far and less often by motorised means than those dependent on private transport. In part, this is due to suppression of optional trips, but much more significant is the substitution of walk for motorised trips. (Table 6.3). The latter is encouraged by the tendency to higher densities that goes with dependence on public transport.

Table 6.3 Mean number of trips per respondent for shopping, social and leisure purposes by mode, level of access to car and area

	Car ownership*	Walk	Car	Public transport	Total
Rural	Yes	3.2	2.9	0.3	6.5
	No	3.9	0.3	0.5	4.6
Small town	Yes	2.0	4.6	0.3	6.8
	No	4.6	0.4	1.1	6.3
New town	Yes	2.5	4.7	0.3	7.6
	No	5.5	0.4	1.3	7.4
Other suburb	Yes	2.3	5.4	0.2	7.8
	No	4.4	0.5	1.4	6.2
Inner suburb	Yes	3.4	2.9	0.4	6.8
	No	5.1	0.2	2.2	7.3

* The two levels of car ownership shown are:
  Yes: licence holder in car-owning household.
  No: non-licence holder in no-car-owning household.
Source: Hillman (1973), Table 3.10. Based on a sample survey of residents of five British communities.

There is a wide variety of policies which may be used to achieve these ends. Some of them involve the public transport operator directly – fares reductions and service improvements – whilst in other cases his involvement is solely in terms of adjusting to new circumstances. For instance, additional parking charges, tolls or supplementary licences for entering the urban area during the morning peak or physical measures of traffic restraint may be more successful than action by the public transport operator himself in diverting peak traffic to his services. The resulting traffic increase will not merely have implications for peak service levels but also, since the financial position of the undertaking is likely to be worsened, for the combination of subsidies, fares and service levels in general. Where the change is brought about by bus priorities or improvement of public transport infrastructure, there may be compensating reductions in operating costs to be taken into account.

The above measures all concentrate on the direct problem of peak hour mode split. They may have effects on other factors such as car ownership and location, but these are indirect and may work against the primary effect. For instance, restraint from using car for journeys to the city centre may promote decentralisation of work-places to locations to which the car may be used. Or the car may be left at home for use in off-peak periods, thus worsening the ratio of peak to off-peak public transport use.

By contrast, effects (3) and (4) above rely on something more than a simple change of mode for peak trips. They require pressure on location and car-ownership decisions. This may be achieved indirectly, by improving public transport, but is likely to be most effective when enforced through planning controls on new development.

Seen in this light, long-run public transport planning needs to be integrated with general strategic planning for the area in question. Alternative plans, incorporating different developments in terms of land use, mode split and transport infrastructure need to be compared in terms of costs, transport benefits and environmental quality. The difficulty of achieving this is the subject of the next section.

6.3 Modelling transport/land use interactions

It may be thought that the obvious way of producing such a range of plans is by undertaking a conventional land-use/transportation study such as has been mounted in most major cities in the last couple of decades. Such a study would consider the long-run effects of alternative policies towards public transport provision, and provide a set of strategic policies within which both investment and pricing decisions would be taken. For instance, a lower limit could be set on fares, to prevent undue sprawl; an upper limit on peak fares to the city centre to avoid excessive job decentralisation and so forth.

Unfortunately, however, the conventional land-use/transportation study either ignores or assumes away most of the feedbacks between transport provision and land use with which we are currently concerned. Firstly, it regards the location of jobs and households as fixed, so that the only way in which transport provision can influence the mean length of the journey to work is by reordering the links between the two (known as the distribution stage of the model). Secondly, car ownership is usually forecast exogenously without reference to the public or private transport facilities available, and car ownership is naturally taken as a major influence on modal choice. Thirdly, the total trips made per household is also treated as being uninfluenced by the quality of transport provision, so the models cannot investigate the significance of generation and suppression of trips in response to changes in the price and quality of public transport. (Further discussion of land-use transport models is outside the scope of this text; for a simple critique see Plowden, 1971. A more technical review is contained in Jones, 1977. For a somewhat simplistic attempt to apply a fairly conventional transportation model, but in which the numbers of trips originating and terminating in particular zones is allowed to vary, to estimating the effects of free public transport see Batty, Hall and Starkie, 1973.)

Attempts are being made to model all the above interactions as part of a full-scale land-use/transportation model. For instance, a model has been developed for Leeds in which the location of new industrial and commercial development is influenced by accessibility to labour supply and customers, whilst household location is influenced by job accessibility and the attractiveness of the area to the social class in question (Mackett, 1977). But unless and until such models become common practice, most decisions of the type dealt with in this chapter will have to be made on a more piecemeal and intuitive assessment of the long-run effects of the decision in question.

6.4 Transport cost/house price trade-off models

Public transport is most heavily used for the journey to work when jobs are concentrated together, for instance in a city centre. The most usual model used for analysing household location in this type of situation is one based on the trade-off between transport costs and house prices or rents (Evans, 1973). It is assumed that a certain number of households are to be located in the area surrounding the city centre. Close to the city centre, transport costs (including travel time) for the journey to work will be low. Correspondingly, people will be willing to pay a premium to locate there rather than farther out. On the other hand, at the fringe of the urban area, where transport costs are high, the price of land will be determined by its alternative use (e.g. agriculture). If all houses and households were identical, competition between them would ensure that house prices rose with proximity to the centre in such a way that the sum of the annual rental value of the house and transport costs for the journey to work was equal in all locations. (Fig. 6.1).

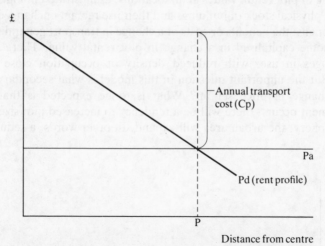

Fig. 6.1 Relationship of rents to transport costs.

Let us ignore for a moment the value of the house itself and consider just the location rent per annum of the land (per equal-sized plot). At the periphery, this is given by P_a (the rental value of agricultural land). If the distance from the periphery to the centre is p kilometres, the rent at distance d (assuming 500 work trips to the centre per household p.a.) will be:

$$P_d = P_a + 500(C_p - C_d) \qquad [6.1]$$

where C_p = generalised cost of a work trip from p to the centre;
C_d = generalised cost of a work trip from d to the centre.

If the generalised cost were proportionate to distance, equation [6.1] could be written:

$$P_d = P_a + 500c(p - d) \qquad [6.2]$$

where c = generalised cost of a work trip per kilometre

In practice, generalised cost usually rises less than proportionately with distance, both because longer journeys usually achieve a higher average speed and because public transport fares usually taper with distance. Thus it is more accurate to write:

$$C_d = C_0 + C_1 d \qquad [6.3]$$

So that equation [6.1] becomes:

$$P_d = P_a + 500C_1(p - d) \qquad [6.4]$$

Now suppose that a decision either to raise speeds or lower fares results in a lowering of C_1. The immediate effect is clearly an equiproportionate lowering of plot rental values at all locations, as illustrated in Fig. 6.2. As long as the physical stock of buildings and their use remain unchanged, this is all that happens; the benefits or costs of a change in transport generalised cost simply become capitalised in a change in plot rental value. There may be some changes in use, with reduced density of occupation close in, for instance. But the important question in this model is what secondary effects will this change in price set up? What is to be expected is that, when redevelopment occurs, there will be a tendency to increased plot size, whilst at the periphery, the urban area will expand. In other words, a reduction in

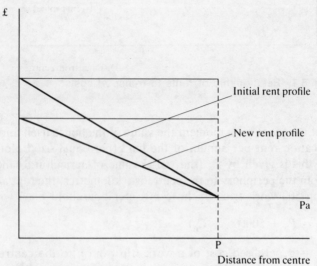

Fig. 6.2   Effect of a fall in transport costs.

the distance-related element of transport cost will produce a tendency towards lower densities and longer journeys to work.

In practice, of course, this simple model ignores differences in the housing stock inherited from the past at different locations, and differences in the structure, income and tastes of the households occupying them.

The characteristics of houses at different locations are heavily influenced by their date of construction. There is an obvious tendency for houses occupying larger plots of land to locate on the outskirts, where land is cheaper (although these may be subsequently swallowed up by further development). Peripheral locations may also be environmentally more attractive. Households, too, vary. Richer households and households with young children may be more concerned with plot size and the environment than others. Households with more than one city centre worker will have an obvious incentive to live closer in, and so forth. Thus the individual household is unlikely to be indifferent between alternative locations at existing prices. None the less, in aggregate, and after allowing for differences in the quality of housing, there seems good evidence that such a relationship between transport costs and house prices does exist (Evans, 1973). However, these differences in houses and household characteristics produce further effects of a change in the distance-related generalised cost of travel. For instance, some households may prefer, for environmental reasons, to live beyond the periphery of the built-up area in the surrounding countryside. A reduction in C_1 will encourage this. Also, differences in a household's value of time may mean that the composition of generalised cost is important. Cities with very slow, uncomfortable but cheap transport may be characterised by richer families living towards the centre and poorer at the outskirts (this is the situation in many cities in developing countries, where shanty towns of poor families spring up around the outskirts). Where transport is of good quality but expensive, a tendency is produced for richer households to locate on the outskirts, as is more common in cities in developed countries. Needless to say, transport costs may not be the only, nor even the most important, factor in producing this trend; the historical development of the city is extremely important.

So far, it has been assumed that all jobs are located at the city centre. This is, of course, unlikely to be true. Some service employment will always be located close to the population in the suburbs; some industries will be located close to specific natural resources, or will locate at the fringe because they require large amounts of land per worker. If the accessibility of the city centre is high relative to other work-places, rents at the city centre will be high and occupations concentrated on commercial activities, which have a large workforce per unit land area. Lower accessibilities and lower rents may lead to a more mixed pattern, with more jobs decentralised to suburban locations. Such a pattern will be encouraged by improvements or reductions in fares on local or circumferential transport routes in the suburbs (although these may also improve the quality of feeder services into the radial routes to the city centre).

6.5 The practical effects of urban transport improvements

In the light of the model of the preceding section, we may now set out in brief the expected effects of various types of improvement in transport facilities:

1. *Acceleration of services or reduction in fares on radial routes.* If these affect all distance bands equally, the result is a uniform lowering in house prices (except, perhaps, in some choice peripheral sites) a tendency towards reduced density and an increase in the size of the urban area. Rents and employment at the city centre will be expected to increase. A tendency to favour outer areas rather than inner in the improvements will tend to reduce house prices and densities more in the inner areas than elsewhere (and vice versa). Of course, when the improvement affects one corridor only, house prices there will be raised rather than lowered.

2. *Replacement of graduated fares by flat sum or free public transport.* The effect here is to remove the fare element from the distance-related component of generalised cost (c_1). The result on radial routes is similar to that of (1), but favouring outer areas more than inner. However, if the system is adopted throughout the urban area, local transport – above a minimum distance, in the case of flat sum fares – will be cheapened. Nevertheless, on the assumption that city-centre journeys to work are on average longer than journeys to work in the suburbs, it may be assumed that such a policy will favour city-centre employment.

3. *Improvement in speed and frequency of local and circumferential transport in the suburbs.* The tendency produced by this is likely to be for a reduction in rents and employment at the city centre, with jobs transferring to the suburbs. Historically, it seems clear that major revolutions in the transport system can have a substantial impact on land use. The introduction of suburban railways, trams and buses first enabled work-places and residences to be separated, and encouraged ribbon development, with jobs centralised and housing located in bands alongside the major routes. Rising car ownership permits infilling of the space between the main routes, and raises speeds of local and circumferential journeys for those with a car available, whilst the radial trunk routes become congested and public transport (particularly road-based) declines. The result is job decentralisation and decline of the city centre. What may be doubted, however, is whether the long-run effects of more modest changes, such as changes in fares policies, are usually very significant. According to equation [6.4] the effect of a change in fares will be to change house prices at location d by:

$$500 \, \Delta \, c_1(p - d)$$

Now in smaller cities and towns, fares will normally account for a relatively small part of c_1. Suppose that $\Delta \, c_1 = 5p$ (e.g. when mileage-related fares are abolished). The maximum change in housing rents (close to the city centre) will be £25 d. Only if d is very large (i.e. we are dealing with a city such as London, with large-scale commuting from 10–20 miles out and considerable numbers commuting further) is the result likely to be significant in terms of density. Similarly, only when very major improvements take place in speed (for instance, construction of an underground railway line on a long congested route previously served only by buses) can significant results be looked for.

It has been suggested that a policy of standard fares throughout an urban area regardless of density may have distorting effects (e.g. Kolsen and Docwra, 1977). Similar fears may be aroused by policies which seek to equalise the quality of public transport services regardless of patronage. Presumably the fear is that developers will be encouraged to build new low-density housing, secure in the knowledge that the cost of providing them with public transport will fall on the public at large. However, to seek to prevent this by providing poorer quality and higher-priced public transport in existing low-density areas may be quite contrary to the policies suggested in previous chapters. There it is suggested that service levels and fares should be determined by a combination of price and frequency elasticities of demand and the costs of increasing capacity where needed. There seems no general reason to expect price elasticities to be lower in less dense areas, and whilst the lower volume of traffic is likely to lead to lower service frequencies, this is likely to raise the frequency elasticity of demand and prevent a proportionate reduction in services. The result of this is lower load factors and more spare capacity, so that fares may well be lower than on other routes, at any rate at certain times of day. For instance, on a route from the outer suburbs to the city centre, peak fares would be lower over the outer sections, where load factors are low, than over the inner sections where housing is of higher density and load factors are high. The result may well be to encourage construction of more low-density suburbs that are difficult and expensive to serve by public transport.

6.6 Land-use planning and public transport

We have shown in previous sections some of the ways in which public transport decisions may influence the pattern of land use in an urban area. In this section, we consider whether this means that long-run planning objectives must be allowed to overrule the requirements for efficient use of existing public transport systems as outlined in preceding chapters, or whether other methods of influencing land use may be used to offset any harmful effects of public transport decisions. Whether the effects are harmful or not is, of course, a matter of tastes, but lower densities may be considered harmful inasmuch as they:

1. Raise the cost of providing public services (including transport).
2. Raise mean trip lengths (raising the externalities produced by transport systems).
3. Raise the proportion of trips undertaken by motorised private transport (again raising mean trip lengths and externalities produced).

On the other hand, many will argue that they make for a more pleasant environment and reduce the impact of externalities by increasing separation of households from each other and from other externality producing sites (including transport systems).

Similarly, it is hard to reach an unequivocal conclusion on the external effects of job decentralisation which may reduce mean trip length but encourage a switch from public to private transport.

The theoretical ideal would be to cost all such externalities and to reflect them in prices or taxes charged to employers, households and developers. Rates, for instance, could reflect the higher costs occasioned by low-density housing; employers could pay a tax to cover the additional transport costs caused the State by their job-location decisions (such a transport tax on employment already exists in Paris and other French cities, at a higher rate for central than for suburban location). However, in view of the uncertainty regarding the effects of such charges, and the fact that the externalities are likely to vary greatly with exact location, such measures are likely to need reinforcing by planning controls. These may be used to restrict low-density development, to push development into locations where the transport system has spare capacity and to prevent encroachment on sur-rounding countryside by means of a green-belt policy (Hall, 1974). Land-use planning can also do much to make provision of good-quality public transport easier by siting facilities such as hospitals and schools near major public transport network nodes; by designing housing estates in such a way that through bus routes exist without the need for reversal or lengthy detours; and so forth (Bruce, 1977).

The conclusion we reach, then, on urban public transport policy is that only in the most major strategic decisions of network design and fares policy is it likely that land-use considerations need be taken into consideration. For day-to-day management, the type of decision rules outlined in Chapter 4 will suffice provided that the relevant planning authority is taking appropriate action to offset any harmful effects.

6.7 Freight transport, location and the environment

As shown in Chapter 3, there is a particular difficulty in pricing road freight transport which is even more acute than for passenger. The ideal tax structure would embody a different rate per mile according to the gross weight and number of axles of the vehicle. Unless the mileage run by individual vehicles is metered for taxation purposes (as is the case in Sweden), it is impossible to achieve this; the best that can be achieved is a fuel tax, plus an annual lump sum related to gross weight/number of axles. This means that costs are almost inevitably undercharged for long-haul work, even though environmental damage may typically rise less than proportionately with miles run, as a smaller proportion of miles will be in built-up areas. Thus not only does the tax system fail to reflect the variation of costs with time and space; it also fails to reflect adequately the variation with type of vehicle and length of haul.

The significance of this for rail freight transport is clear. It is in the long-haul field that rail is most likely to be in competition with road (Ch. 10), and it is here that road is most likely to be underpriced. If the rail operator is obliged to cover his overheads by price discrimination, the result is not merely to lose him traffic at the margin, but also to reduce the maximum price he can charge for non-marginal traffic. This may reduce the size of system that he can profitably sustain.

In considering the relative environmental effects of road and rail freight transport, it is clearly necessary to distinguish between a number of types of traffic, according to the extent to which it requires extra road collection and delivery:

1. Private siding to private siding traffic. This is traffic passing between mines, quarries and industrial plants which, if handled by rail, will not use the road system at all.
2. Private siding to private terminal traffic. This traffic requires road delivery at one end, though if the private terminal would be used as a warehouse/transhipment depot regardless of mode used for trunk haul, the delivery stage can be ignored in inter-modal comparisons, since it would take place in any case.
3. Private terminal to private siding traffic. The most common case of this is where agricultural produce is consolidated at a terminal for forwarding to a factory for processing; the same argument applies as for (2).
4. Traffic passing through a public goods depot at one or both ends. Obviously this will normally require additional road collection and delivery.

Where road collection and delivery is involved, it is possible that the road mileage involved will be in urban areas and will inflict higher environmental costs than would throughout road haulage. Sharp (1973) cites three examples of consignments where he believes this would be so. However, the example relies heavily on the fact that the public rail freight transport depots are sited deep in built-up areas from which road access is poor. When freight depots can be sited at main road/motorway interchanges or in the heart of the industrial areas generating most of their traffic, this would not apply, although rail would not necessarily give very great environmental benefits.

What this suggests is that the environmental benefits of using rail rather than road freight depend very heavily on the nature and location of the terminals in question. Thus if subsidies are to be used to encourage the transfer of freight from road to rail, it is likely to be best to tie these to specific terminals, rather than using blanket subsidies. Such a subsidy does, in fact, exist in Great Britain; under the 1974 Railways Act, up to 50 per cent of the cost of new private sidings, private terminals and rolling-stock may be paid by the State if sufficient environmental benefits accrue. Given the difficulty in quantifying benefits, a political judgement is required on the amount of money that it is worth spending to remove a given number of heavy goods vehicle miles from roads, according to their congestion and the numbers of persons affected by them. Although the grant does not cover rail-owned terminals, it does include private terminals owned by road hauliers, who may undertake collection and delivery work on behalf of customers.

The second point to be made is the desirability of influencing the location decisions of actual and potential rail customers, so that they can be easily joined to the rail network, or served by a rail depot. This is much more a long-term strategy, but given the importance of planning permission and the availability of suitable sites in location decisions, the relevant planning authorities may be able to exert considerable influence without having so serious an impact on the firms' costs as to make it not worth while.

6.8 Inter-urban transport and regional policy

It is sometimes argued that specific public transport facilities should be retained, or prices reduced, as part of regional policy. (The argument is heard more often in favour of road construction; for a review in this context see Dodgson, 1973.) This applies both to freight and to passenger transport (the latter particularly in the context of fast links to major conurbations). It is given as a reason for subsidising airports, rail freight rates on specific commodities, canal construction and so forth. It is therefore necessary to consider whether public transport policies are able to influence regional location in such a way as to form a worthwhile part of regional policy.

Within the UK, freight transport as a whole accounts for some 6.5 per cent of value added (in manufacturing industry, the average is higher at around 9%. Edwards, 1969; 1970). This in itself suggests that a very large reduction in transport cost would be needed to bring about even a modest reduction in the price of goods manufactured in depressed regions. It could not compensate for any significant disadvantages in respect of other factors, such as labour supply. Moreover, a general reduction in transport cost not only reduces the cost of transporting goods out of a depressed region but also that of bringing goods in. Thus, protected local markets may be lost. Similarly with passenger transport, improved communications may encourage out-migration (this has been reported in developing countries).

Where the effect is likely to be greatest is when the region specialises in a product (most likely a primary product, rather than a manufactured good) for which transport costs are a significant part of total costs (more likely, obviously, in a country with long lengths of haul). Changes in the transport infrastructure may then have a substantial impact. It is also possible in such cases to give specific subsidies for carriage of that commodity in the desired direction, thus overcoming the problem referred to above. But specific commodity subsidies also have problems – for instance, it is argued that the subsidy of the transport of wheat from the Canadian Prairies to the East Coast discourages its use for feedstocks or manufacturing in the prairies.

For this reason, production rather than transport subsidies are usually preferable (Heaver and Nelson, 1977).

6.9 Conclusion

It is interesting and reassuring to note to what extent the environmental advantages of public transport are strongest where its economics are best. Diverting scattered low-density flows of passengers or freight from private to public transport will seldom make much contribution – indeed, if load factors were very low, the environment could even be damaged. It is by attracting dense flows of traffic, particularly in urban areas, that significant environmental benefits may accrue both directly, and by avoiding the need for a major expansion of road infrastructure.

To this end, if there is a serious political commitment in favour of public transport, it is necessary to go beyond short-run subsidies to think in terms of creating and sustaining an environment in which public transport can operate efficiently and in which the rate of increase in car ownership with income will be limited by the relatively low additional benefits of higher car ownership (particularly second cars). This means influencing job locations, and housing location and density. However, whilst the provision of transport facilities is one way of influencing land use, it is likely that taxation and planning permission are more powerful tools.

This chapter has concentrated on the relationship between land use and environmental planning and public transport; naturally enough, since this is a text on public transport. But this should not be taken to imply that the author believes encouragement of public transport to be the only, or even the major, way of reducing the environmental impact of transport systems. Vehicle design, traffic management, bypassing of urban areas and reduction of the need to travel to reach appropriate facilities all have a major role (see, for instance, Sharp and Jennings, 1977). But the potential of public transport needs to be considered alongside these, and it is difficult to believe that, particularly for the urban journey to work, encouragement of the use of public transport does not have an important part to play.

Chapter 7

Urban passenger transport

7.1 The urban passenger market

The basic characteristics of the urban passenger market, set out below, are fairly obvious and well known.

1. *Use of local public transport is relatively high.* This arises from a complicated interaction of effects. In the first place, relatively high density of population makes it possible to provide a good-quality public transport compared with rural areas. This, in turn, together with the greater accessibility of facilities to pedestrians leads to lower car ownership for a given level of income (Fairhurst, 1975). There is a positive feedback effect from this to the quality of public transport provided. Furthermore, car parking is often difficult and expensive (especially in major city centres) and there may be deliberate restraints on the use of the private car to counter congestion and environmental problems. This set of relationships is illustrated diagrammatically in Fig. 7.1; clearly the degree to which it operates depends critically on the age and structure of the urban area, older, higher-density inner suburbs experiencing these effects more strongly than new, low-density suburbs or new towns (Fowkes, Pearman and Button, 1978).

2. *Demand for public transport is very heavily peaked, at the times of the journeys to and from work.* This leads to the problem of low utilisation of staff and assets discussed in Chapter 3. Table 7.1 shows the pattern of passenger traffic on: (i) BR rail services into Central London; and (ii) bus services in Bradford by time of day on a typical weekday. If anything, the problem of the peak has been getting worse, as city centres become more exclusively white collar with common hours of work, and as work and school hours move closer together. Moreover, growing use of the car for off-peak journeys, where the constraints are less severe, may make this peaking of traffic continue to strengthen.

3. *Relatively low mean trip lengths.* For instance, the mean trip length on Bradford buses is 3 km and even on London Transport railways it is only 8 km. Again, this varies greatly from place to place, and some commuter railways into capital cities stretch for 50 km or more. (Strictly, such services·

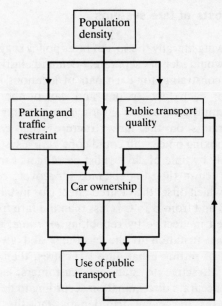

Fig. 7.1   Interrelationships between geography, car ownership and use of public transport.

Table 7.1 Peakedness of urban public transport traffic

	Peak	Off-peak	Total
BR arrivals in Central London* (000's) (1973)	449.1 (69%)	199.7 (31%)	648.8 (100%)
Bus passengers in Bradford† (1973)	53,500 (39.4%)	81,740 (60.6%)	135,240 (100%)

* For BR, the periods in question are:
    peak: 7.00–9.59
    off-peak: All other arrivals
Source: BRB.
† For Bradford, the periods are:
    peak: 7.00–9.00
    off-peak: 9.00–15.00
Source: Travers Morgan (1976).

can hardly be described as 'urban', but they are included in this chapter for convenience.)

The combination of these characteristics throws up a set of problems in terms of pricing, planning services and integration of modes, and investment appraisal which are to a considerable extent unique to urban areas. In this chapter, we consider each of these issues in turn.

7.2 Administrative costs of fare systems

The implication of following literally the sort of fares policy suggested in Chapter 4 would be that one would identify separately demand elasticities, incremental costs and capacity constraints for each pair of locations in the public transport system and for each time of day and day of the year. Obviously this is not possible simply in terms of information requirements, and there are practical constraints on the fare structures that can be implemented. No bus crew or booking office staff could cope with a system in which fares change too frequently by time of day, whilst passengers can only respond rationally to a fare structure they understand. Moreover, certain structures may afford loopholes which offset the desired effect (for instance, if the sum of the fares from A to B and from B to C is less than the fare from A to C, the latter may be rendered ineffective by rebooking *en route*; at the least, the result will be to cause irritation to the customer and give the operator a bad image). The art of setting urban fare structures, then, is to trade off simplicity, which is attractive to staff and customers, against complexity, which enables more accurate discrimination according to demand and cost conditions. The shorter the mean trip length and the more homogeneous the market, the more one is likely to come down on the side of simplicity.

Related to the choice of fare structure is the decision as to: (a) how fares are to be collected; (b) what forms of information are to be extracted from ticket sales; and indeed (c) what sort of route pattern is to be operated.

(a) If tickets are to be sold on the vehicle, there is a severe constraint on the degree of complexity that can be handled within the time available for ticket sales, especially at peak periods. If this time is exceeded, the vehicle is delayed (causing increased user and operating costs). Alternatively, the number of conductors can be increased (this is a common solution on train services on which tickets are issued on the train, where large numbers of customers may have to be dealt with in a very short time). Time available for ticket sales is obviously most severely constrained on one-man-operated buses; sample boarding times for various fare systems are given in Table 7.2. Refusal to give change is an obvious way of saving time. (West Midlands PTE claim to achieve boarding times comparable with two-man operation with their highly differentiated but no-change autofare system. However, such systems may not be popular with users, and obviously work best where most users travel regularly and know the system.) Where tickets are sold off the vehicle, as is the case for most urban rail systems, and is also possible for buses or trains (in the form of season tickets or travel cards, books of tickets available at newsagents, or by stationing booking offices or conductors at the busiest boarding points), tickets sales time is less crucial, although increased sales time still costs extra staff, whilst long queues at peak times may lead to increased user costs and loss of revenue. It is also generally the case that simpler fare structures are most suited to automation.

Table 7.2 Effect of alternative fare structures in reducing OMO boarding times and increasing cost savings from conversion (hypothetical route)

Typical configuration and fare structure (London)	Marginal boarding time (sec/passenger)	Average time spent at stop (sec)	Total journey time (sec/mile)	Increase in journey time over crew op. (%)	Cost increase over 'no fare collection' OMO (%)	Saving of original crew-operating cost (%)
Crew operation: rear platform	Different formula	7.9	320	–		–
Crew operation; front entrance, centre exit with doors	1.15	8.1	321	Negl.		Negl.
'No fare collection' OMO	1.15	8.1	321	Negl.	–	29
Flat fare; high use of seasons (no change)	2.0	11.2	334	4.5	3.5	26
Flat fare; mainly cash, with change giving	2.5	12.6	341	6.5	5.5	25
Graduated fare; high use of second stream, or high use of seasons	3.6	15.6	354	10.5	9	22
Graduated fare today	4.0	16.8	359	12	11	21

Source: Quarmby (1973).

(b) It is possible to use ticket machines which record comprehensively information on type of ticket sold for each origin/destination pair: such machines are standard equipment for major railway booking offices, but may also be used on a more limited scale for portable machines. Obviously, this involves an intricacy of equipment that is only likely with a fairly complicated fare structure; moreover, it does not record (obviously) the use of season tickets, travel cards, etc. Where ticket sales are off-vehicle, time of day of use is not recorded, and separate surveys are still needed to establish loadings on particular vehicles. At the other extreme, it may be cheaper and more reliable to collect all data on passenger movements from sample surveys, and only to extract basic revenue data from ticket sales. In this case, it does not matter how coarse the fare structure is, or indeed whether fares are charged at all.

(c) The route pattern is also important. On relatively short routes where journeys made are very homogeneous, a flat-sum and/or travel-card system obviously loses less opportunities for differentiation than on longer routes (hence the widespread use of flat-sum fares on city-centre bus services). Where mean journey length is high, traffic is sparse or vehicles of small capacity are used, the time losses from one-man operation are less significant than on city routes that are heavily used for short-distance trips.

7.3 Practical methods of fare differentiation in urban areas

There are generally five main fields for differentiation in urban fare structures: (1) time of day; (2) length of trip; (3) route or area; (4) mode or service type; (5) type of passenger; and before considering each of these areas in turn it is worth recapping on how one should seek to set fares, given alternative objectives and constraints.

If the objective were to maximise social surplus with no financial constraints, fares would only be charged at times and places where there was pressure on capacity, but the benefits of increasing capacity did not justify the costs. That is to say, fares would be charged in peak periods over heavily used (usually inner) stretches of route (peak here might include, for instance, Saturday mornings, late evening services, etc. according to local traffic characteristics).

Given the need to satisfy financial constraints, the aim is then to raise the additional revenue in the least damaging way possible. In the first place, given the shadow price on public funds, some reduction in services compared with the unconstrained situation might be called for, with fare increases where required by capacity considerations. For the rest, if the objective is social surplus maximisation,[1] fares will be raised in accordance with the following marginal condition:

$$P = \lambda \left| \frac{\partial P(Q) \cdot Q}{\partial Q} \right| \qquad\qquad [7.1]$$

where P = price;

$\bar{Q}$ = passenger mileage;

λ = shadow price of user benefits in terms of revenue.

Thus P represents the user benefit of an additional passenger mile and

$$\lambda \left| \frac{\partial P(Q) \cdot Q}{\partial Q} \right|$$

the value of revenue foregone in attracting it multiplied by the relevant shadow price (assuming space capacity; if this does not exist, a further cost term must be added). As long as P exceeds

$$\lambda \left| \frac{\partial P(Q) \cdot Q}{Q} \right|$$

it is worth lowering the price in question to attract additional traffic.

Noting that

$$\left| \frac{\partial P(Q) \cdot Q}{\partial Q} \right| = \text{marginal revenue} = P\left(1 + \frac{1}{e}\right)$$

where e is the price elasticity of demand, equation [7.1] may be rewritten:

$$P - \lambda P\left(1 + \frac{1}{e}\right) = 0 \qquad [7.2]$$

or

$$\frac{1}{\lambda} - 1 = \frac{1}{e} \qquad [7.3]$$

In other words e is a function of λ, and thus constant for all fares for a given value of the budget constraint. If there were the possibility of discriminating by route, time of day or length of journey, then – for a given level of bus mileage – fares would always be set so that elasticities of demand were equal (as long as $|e| < 1$. If no solution exists with $|e| < 1$, then the constraint cannot be met.) What this would mean in practice is seeking out market sectors with below-average elasticities and raising relative fares there (and vice versa).

It will be noted that this is a special case of the Baumol–Bradford Condition (Baumol and Bradford, 1970) that the prices of any two goods should be set so that:

$$\frac{P_1 - MC_1}{P_1} \bigg/ \frac{P_2 - MC_2}{P_2} = \frac{1}{e_1} \bigg/ \frac{1}{e_2} \qquad [7.4]$$

where MC_1 and MC_2 are the relevant marginal costs.

If $MC_1 = MC_2 = 0$, this reduces to:

$$\frac{1}{e_1} = \frac{1}{e_2} \qquad\qquad [7.5]$$

In practice, discussions with operators suggest that they frequently look at trip length distributions and raise fares most where demand is 'strongest' in terms of absolute volume. For bus operators, this is typically in the short- to middle-distance range (e.g. Fig. 7.2) leading to a strongly tapered fare structure. There is no *a priori* reason to suppose that this is where, for a given fare level, demand elasticities are lowest, although in practice evidence suggests that this may well be true, at any rate of the middle-distance trips.

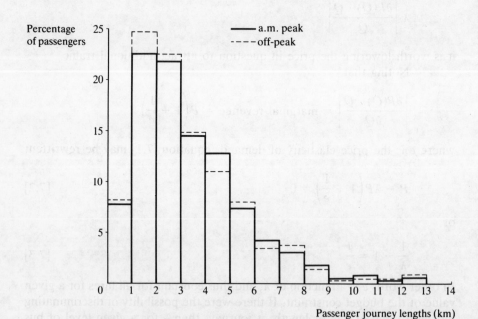

Fig. 7.2   Distribution of passenger journey lengths on Bradford buses in 1973 (*Source:* Travers Morgan, 1976).

Given that differing demand elasticities are the basis for differentiation in the fare charged, what practical methods are there of discriminating in terms of the four fields distinguished above?

Time of day

Given the evidence below that peak elasticities are in general much lower than off-peak elasticities, there is a clear case for differentiation by time of day. At one extreme, it might be possible to have a completely separate tariff for peak and off-peak trips. Theoretically, this might be highly desirable since the entire structure with respect to, for instance, length of trip, could then be varied. For instance, it might be desirable deliberately to damp down carryings of highly elastic short trips in the peak by encouraging diversion to walking, in order to save providing capacity that is very badly utilised in terms of length of time occupied, but in the off-peak a low minimum fare to encourage such trips is desirable.

In practice, a completely separate fare structure is only likely to be possible with off-vehicle ticket sales. Elsewhere, a flat-sum peak surcharge is the most that has usually been tried (the flat-sum nature of this will in any case have the desired effect of discouraging very short trips). From the point of view of public relations, it is perhaps better to talk of an off-peak discount than a peak surcharge. Such a discount may be generally applied, or it may be confined to particularly elastic sectors of the market (day return fares, longer trips, shoppers' excursion fares to specific destinations, evening or Sunday excursions, etc.). Free or half-fare passes for retired persons are a case in point; they may simultaneously generate many extra trips whilst redistributing income in a desired fashion. The case for providing such passes rather than higher pensions rests on the fact that whilst the former requires little diversion of real resources from other users, being largely a way of raising load factors, the latter, if spent on goods and services in general, does.

A particularly simple way of giving an off-peak discount to longer trips, if these are judged to be the most elastic on existing fare scales, is simply to ignore the upper part of the tariff in off-peak periods, and to charge all journeys above a certain distance at the rate for that distance. Well marketed, such a discount may generate extra longer-distance shopping and leisure travel.

Length of trip

There is seldom any justification for urban public transport fares to be at a constant rate per mile regardless of trip length. In the peak, heavy costs may be incurred in offsetting overcrowding on the short inner sections of routes, and road congestion lengthens journey times there too, so that a doubling of mean trip lengths is unlikely to double costs. Particularly for suburban rail services faced with a narrow 'needle' peak, it is unlikely that trains will be able to make more than one loaded trip during the true peak, so that the extra costs of longer trip lengths may be confined to fuel and wear and tear costs (although it is true that most railways provide higher-quality stock and lower degrees of overcrowding on longer routes). In the off-peak, when spare capacity is available anyway, the issue turns solely on relative demand elasticities (except, perhaps for a low flat-sum boarding charge to reflect the costs of delaying the bus). There seems no reason to suppose that the elasticity of demand for trips of x miles at a fare of y pence is the same as that for trips of $2x$ miles at $2y$ pence. Generally, then, one can see an *a priori* case in favour of a fare structure that tapers with trip length; the degree of the taper is an empirical matter to be determined by the variation of demand elasticities with trip length and fare.

Route or area
Generally, there has been a long-standing trend towards standardisation of fare structures and levels by route and areas. This has its attractions in that it is more readily understood by staff and consumers; anyone preparing to make a trip with which he is not familiar will be able to predict the fare reasonably accurately, and so forth. However, it does remove one potential area of price discrimination; demand elasticities may vary with income and car ownership of the area in question. The justification for subsidies on other grounds (for instance, distributive or to discourage use of the car) will also vary between routes and areas.

However, differentiation between routes and areas does have equity considerations. Whilst it is hard to justify the view that equity requires complete uniformity of fares, use of price discrimination to charge high fares where there is heavy captive traffic to cross-subsidise routes and areas of light traffic may well be thought objectionable, especially as the latter areas may well be more affluent than the former.

Mode or quality of service
Where services giving different degrees of speed, comfort or reliability operate between the same pair of points (e.g. rail and bus, express and stopping bus), the difference in quality of service may lead to a difference in demand elasticities and hence in the optimal fare to charge.

Now so far in this chapter we have completely ignored cross-elasticities of demand. This is never strictly valid; some passengers may substitute off-peak trips for peak trips or long trips for short trips when relative prices change (the phenomenon of passengers getting off a stage early and walking the final stretch after a fares increase is particularly well documented). But when considering the relative fares on parallel services (e.g. rail and bus over the same route) knowledge of cross-elasticities of demand is crucial, since the major effect of changing relative fares may be to shift passengers from one service to the other. It is necessary to extend our above formula to take this into account.

The objective of the exercise is to raise fares in such a way that the loss of social surplus per pound raised is minimised. At the margin, the expression for this ratio when price is raised, given two modes (i and j) is:

$$\frac{(P_i - C_i)\dfrac{\partial Q_i}{\partial P_i} + (P_j - C_j)\dfrac{\partial Q_j}{\partial P_i}}{Q_i + (P_i - C_i)\dfrac{\partial Q_i}{\partial P_i} + (P_j - C_j)\dfrac{\partial Q_j}{\partial P_i}} = \frac{S_i}{R_i} \qquad [7.6]$$

where P_i = fare by mode i;

Q_i = traffic by mode i;

C_i = marginal cost by mode i (which is zero except when up against a capacity constraint);

S_i = change in social surplus from a one-unit rise in P_i;

R_i = change in revenue from a one-unit rise in P_i.

To see this, note that the difference between willingness to pay (price) and marginal cost on a marginal unit of traffic gained or lost is equal to the change in social surplus. Raising P_i changes traffic volumes on both modes. The effect on profitability of a one-unit rise in P_i is equal to the extra revenue on mode $i(Q_i + P_i(\partial Q_i/\partial P_i))$ plus the extra revenue on mode $j(P_j(\partial Q_j/\partial P_i))$ less the net rise in costs:

$$C_j \frac{\partial Q_j}{\partial P_i} + C_i \frac{\partial Q_i}{\partial P_i}$$

The latter term is, of course, negative. An identical expression may be written for raising the price of mode j, and the marginal conditions will then require:

$$\frac{S_i}{R_i} = \frac{S_j}{R_j} \tag{7.7}$$

Note that this may be written:

$$\frac{S_i}{Q_i + S_i} = \frac{S_j}{Q_j + S_j} \tag{7.8}$$

This can only hold if:

$$\frac{S_i}{Q_i} = \frac{S_j}{Q_j} \tag{7.9}$$

Or in full:

$$\frac{(P_i - C_i) \dfrac{\partial Q_i}{\partial P_i} + (P_j - C_j) \dfrac{\partial Q_j}{\partial P_i}}{Q_i} = \frac{(P_j - C_j) \dfrac{\partial Q_j}{\partial P_j} + (P_i - C_i) \dfrac{\partial Q_i}{\partial P_j}}{Q_j} \tag{7.10}$$

This may be rewritten:

$$\frac{P_i - C_i}{P_i} \left(e_{ii} - \frac{P_i Q_i}{P_j Q_j} e_{ij} \right) = \frac{P_j - C_j}{P_j} \left(e_{jj} - \frac{P_j Q_j}{P_i Q_i} e_{ji} \right) \tag{7.11}$$

where e_{ii}, e_{jj} = own-price elasticities of demand;

e_{ij}, e_{ji} = cross-price elasticities of demand of i with respect to j and vice versa.

It will be noted that whenever there is space capacity, $C_i = C_j = 0$ and the above formula reduces to:

$$e_{ii} - \frac{P_i Q_i}{P_j Q_j} e_{ij} = e_{jj} - \frac{P_j Q_j}{P_i Q_i} e_{ji} \tag{7.12}$$

If $e_{ij} = e_{ji} = 0$, the result is simply to require that $e_{ii} = e_{jj}$, as found above.

As an example, consider a route on which bus and rail are available as substitutes. Suppose that the own-price elasticity for rail is −0.4 and for bus −0.8. Let both cross-price elasticities equal 0.1. Ignoring the cross-price elasticity, and assuming spare capacity on both modes, one would increase the price on rail relative to bus until the two elasticities were equal. However, taking account of the full formula, if at existing prices bus had three times the revenue of rail, equation [7.12] would be satisfied and there would be no case for a rise in the rail price.

Type of passenger

The problem with discriminating by type of passenger is that the category into which any individual passenger falls must be readily identifiable. Reference has already been made to the most common form of discrimination – reduced fares for retired persons. This, as with half-fare for children, is most often an act of social policy rather than discrimination according to demand elasticities. It is also possible to discriminate in favour of families, local inhabitants (common on the Continent in tourist areas) or women (subject to anti-sex discrimination legislation!). The approach is one that has been taken much further in inter-urban than in urban transport, and will be further discussed in Chapter 8.

7.4   Choice of fares structures – a numerical illustration

In this section, a grossly simplified model of an urban bus service is used to illustrate the issues involved in choosing between alternative fares structures. The model considers six types of passenger trip – three lengths (1, 2 and 3 miles) and two time periods (peak and off-peak). Peak trips are assumed to have a constant generalised cost elasticity of −0.6 and off-peak of −1.3. Generalised cost comprises the money value of waiting time (which is a function of headways) in-vehicle time plus fare (which comprises a boarding charge plus a constant rate per mile). Walking time is ignored, since alterations in the route system are not in question; so, more seriously, is switching between trip lengths and times of day in response to price differentials, and the external costs of switching between modes. The objective is taken to be maximisation of the sum of consumers' plus producers' surpluses, and is shown as the 'social surplus index'.

Costs are taken to be dependent on peak and off-peak headways; these headways are subject to a minimum defined by a capacity constraint. It is assumed that charging flat-sum fares will reduce costs by 25 per cent by permitting one-man operation; charging zero fares will reduce costs by 29 per cent compared with full differentiation. A complete specification of the equations used is given in the Appendix. Table 7.3 presents some selected results.

The overall best result (line 1) involves flat-sum fares (5p off-peak, 20p peak). A considerable reduction in the deficit may be achieved for

Table 7.3 Some selected results from the model of alternative fares structures

Line no.	Off-peak freq.	Peak freq.	Off-peak fare		Peak fare		Social surplus index	Financial deficit (£/day)
			a	b	a	b		
1	3	6	5	0	20	0	100	310
2	4	8	10	0	10	0	97.2	709
3	3	5	5	0	25	0	99.8	147
4	4	7	15	0	15	0	94.1	513
5	3	6	5	0	5	5	94.7	668
6	3	6	5	5	5	5	89.7	620
7	2	4	5	0	35	0	95.5	−110

negligible loss of social benefit by raising the peak fare to 25p and cutting the frequency to five per hour (line 3).

If it is required to charge the same fare peak and off-peak, then the best result involves a flat-sum fare of 10p (line 2). This policy involves higher service frequencies and an enormous increase in the financial deficit. Raising this flat-sum fare to 15p involves a substantial loss of social surplus and only succeeds in reducing the deficit to £513 per day.

Finally, the best differentiated fare scheme (line 5) is inferior to the flat-sum scheme (line 1) in terms both of social surplus and deficit. Adding the constraint that peak fares should equal off-peak (line 6) makes matters still worse. This unattractiveness of differentiated fares schemes may be the result of the extremely coarse fare structures and trip length distribution assumed, but it is interesting that even with a severe financial constraint, the best procedure remains a flat-sum fare, with an increase in the peak fare (line 7). Certainly, these results suggest that flat-sum fares schemes should be looked at seriously in practical situations, although there would obviously be great opposition to such steep rises in short-distance peak fares. Moreover, it should be noted that a relaxation of the assumption that differentiated fares require a two-man crew would greatly change the results; in the absence of any delays in loading, one-man operation of the differentiated fare scheme in line 5 would lead to a social surplus index of 101.3 (the best result) and a financial deficit of £343.

7.5 Empirical estimation of fares elasticities

Clearly, implementation of any of the decision rules discussed in this chapter requires a great deal of empirical information. Much effort has been put into estimating public transport demand elasticities in recent years, and a full survey would be beyond the scope of this chapter, but a few comments on the main approaches to the problem and the range of results produced may be appropriate at this stage.

Aggregate models may use time-series data for a single operator or cross-section for a set of operators. In practice, it is difficult to allow for all the other social and geographical factors apart from fares that influence demand levels of alternative operators; moreover, there is a substantial identification problem (high fares may be caused by low passenger demand, a supply side relationship, as well as being the cause of it). Thus time-series data has usually been ·preferred. (The identification problem still exists, but may be diminished by varying lags in reactions). Smith and McIntosh (1973) report the results of estimating a log-linear equation relating number of passenger trips made to the mean real fare per passenger, vehicle mileage operated (an index of service frequency) a time trend and seasonal dummies, for a sample of British municipal operators. This work has been extended to include a larger sample (with some National Bus Company subsidiaries) and estimated in ratio form (ratio of traffic in period i year t to traffic in the equivalent period in the previous year as a log-linear function of the ratios of the other variables) in order to eliminate the trend and seasonal effects (Collings, Rigby and Welsby, 1976). The results suggest that real fares elasticities in the UK typically lie in the range −0.2 to −0.4. This is broadly consistent with findings for other European and American cities (Baum, 1973; Kemp, 1973). Thus, although there is no particular reason why similar elasticities should be found for cities with greatly different characteristics, findings outside the general range, −0.1 to −0.5, are rare.

Similar work undertaken within London Transport bus services suggests a mean value of around −0.3, with a lower value (perhaps −0.2) for work trips and a higher value at weekends. The effect on passenger mileage of fare increases appears much greater – perhaps −0.5 (Fairhurst and Morris, 1975). In other words, a fares increase reduces mean trip lengths. For rail, assuming bus fares increase in proportion, the elasticity appears much lower (perhaps −0.1). This compares with figures of −0.12 for the Paris Metro (ECMT, 1971) and −0.19 and −0.32 for work trips and shopping trips respectively, in Boston (Kraft and Domencich, 1972). It also appeared in London that a 1 per cent rise in rail fares, unmatched by a change in bus fares, caused approximately 0.25 per cent of rail traffic to transfer to bus.

At the disaggregate level, studies of the reactions of individuals have most commonly been associated with fares experiments, such as free fares (Rome), or particular concessions made available to certain groups. Experimental situations obviously can at best produce evidence on short-run elasticities, but such studies do not generally contradict the evidence given above.

Overall, then, it appears that the elasticity of demand for urban public transport is low, particularly for the journey to work. For off-peak journeys, elasticity is rather higher (shopping trips or leisure trips may switch destinations or be suppressed entirely, whereas any such reactions for work trips would be very much long term). Elasticity also appears lower for rail than bus (at least for London Transport. Where mean trips lengths are longer and road transport more competitive, there is evidence of peak rail elasticities which are much higher.) No clear evidence is available with respect to journey length, although with existing graduated fares structures it has been suggested that price elasticities are higher for very short trips (where walking is an obvious alternative) and for long trips (where fares become more significant relative to journey time as a determinant of travel behaviour) than for middle-distance trips.

What evidence is there that reduced fares may have beneficial external effects by reducing the use of the private car? In Boston, the elasticity of car use with respect to transit fares was estimated at 0.14; recent work for London produced a figure of 0.06 for peak periods, the only period for which statistically significant results were obtained (Lewis, 1977). Fares experiments are rather more difficult to interpret since they only reflect a very short-run reaction, but the Rome free fares experiment is estimated to have reduced road traffic in the morning peak by 5 per cent and in the evening peak by some 15 per cent. Whilst these figures may sound unimpressive, it should be remembered that on overloaded urban roads even a small reduction in traffic may have a substantial impact on speeds.

7.6 Some empirical evidence on alternative fares systems

There are few well-documented studies of the effects of alternative fares systems, for the simple reason that it would be politically and socially difficult to introduce an entirely new structure, other than on the basis of a general reduction in fares. Complete revisions occasionally take place, particularly in association with one-man operation or automation, but most decisions are of a marginal nature. This does not mean that the above discussion is irrelevant; on the contrary, the most common problem facing the public transport operator today is how to raise additional revenue whilst doing the least possible harm to the business, and this is precisely the question addressed above.

Webster (1976) undertook a comparative analysis of flat-sum and graduated fares systems, using London data (but ignoring possible interactions with rail services). The conclusions were similar to those of section 5.4 above. If there were no operating cost savings from the introduction of flat fares, then for any given budget constraint, a greater amount of traffic could be attracted with graduated fares than with flat. However, if substantial operating cost savings resulted from the introduction of flat fares, greater traffic resulted from the flat fare if considerable subsidies were provided. If the undertaking was required to break even, the flat fare would again be so high that considerable traffic would be lost in comparison with a graduated fare scheme. These results are interesting, particularly when it is remembered that those cities in Western Europe and North America where flat fares are the norm usually do have much greater proportions of costs covered by subsidies than in Britain, where graduated fares prevail.

A number of studies have sought to estimate the effect of complete abolition of urban public transport fares. For instance, the study in Boston referred to above (Kraft and Domencich, 1972) estimated the financial cost of this as \$75.3 m. p.a. in 1966/67. The bulk of this cost, however, is a transfer of income from taxpayer to passenger. Only \$8.4 m. additional operating expenditure would be required for the extra traffic, and this would be partly offset by a saving in fare collection costs of \$3.5 m. On a simple cost–benefit basis, then, the abolition of fares would be justified by \$4.9 m. worth of benefits in terms of generated transit usage, and relief of congestion and the environment. The case would be strengthened if the funds would be raised in such a way as to make the redistribution of income progressive. However, this argument ignores political and institutional constraints on tax levels, and the possible distorting effect of taxes. The former is probably the real stumbling block.

Similar results have been obtained using the CRISTAL model for London (Tanner and Lynam, 1973) and the SELNEC model for Manchester (Hill, 1973). Zero fares for Central London were found to reduce peak car traffic by 5 per cent if; implemented for Central and Inner London, car traffic would be reduced by 10 per cent. Considerable net benefits were found to accrue to generated public transport trips and from the relief of congestion. These benefits were not found to be very sensitive to the construction of Ringway 1 and new radial roads. However, to make buses free whilst retaining existing prices on rail produced serious net disbenefits, by diverting large numbers of trips from the mode with low marginal costs (rail) to bus. The Manchester study concluded that not only would there be net benefits, but if financed from a progressive income tax, the effect on income distribution would be desirable. If financed from rate revenue, however, the effect would probably be harmful, although rate rebates may have affected the latter conclusion; certainly, a more recent study by Grey suggests that it does not hold for London (Grey, 1975).

The major innovation that has taken place in recent years is the wide spread introduction of travel cards; weekly or monthly tickets which give free travel within a defined area. These tickets have two main effects. The first is that for passengers who make long journeys (longer-distance commuters), a large number of journeys (non-car owners who use public transport for work and also make many leisure trips, or workers who go home to lunch) or journeys involving interchange (for which the fare per mile in most systems is abnormally high), the cost of travel by public transport is reduced. The second is that, having bought the ticket, the marginal money cost of extra travel by public transport is zero. Assuming that the major purchasers of the tickets will be those who commute by public transport, additional trips generated may be largely in the off-peak, when low load factors mean that marginal cost is also virtually zero. Other advantages are accelerated loading (particularly with one-man operation) and convenience for the user (avoidance of the need to find the exact fare has been given as a reason for purchase by 40% of cardholders on the West Midlands PTE no-change system). On the other hand, there will usually be some loss of revenue, and there may be generation of costly additional peak trips. West Midlands data suggest a loss of revenue of some £0.8 m. p.a. at 1975 prices from the cardholders, with some generation of traffic and diversion from the car (particularly for joint bus/rail tickets) (Percival, 1977). The *Carte Orange* system of tickets covering specific sets of zones throughout the Paris area appears to have attracted an increase in traffic of some 10 per cent of which 6.3 per cent was newly generated, 2.9 per cent diverted from foot, 0.6 per cent from car and 0.3 per cent from two wheeled vehicles. The biggest increase was on Paris buses.

Two recent studies which attempt to calculate fares which maximise social surplus are of interest, although they both contain extremely crude assumptions concerning operating costs. The first considers the optimum relationship between bus and rail fares for the Bay Area of San Francisco, under the assumption that overall, a fixed proportion of costs must be paid out of revenue (Train, 1977). The results show that as long as there is spare capacity on both modes, rail fares should be slightly higher than bus, and any cross-subsidisation would be from rail to bus. When facing a capacity constraint, however, the lower marginal cost of rail justifies a bus fare nearly twice the level of the rail fare, with cross-subsidisation of rail by bus. The distributive implications, and the effect on the level of private transport are not considered.

A study of an integrated fares policy for transport in Greater London goes beyond this in considering the interaction between the level of private car traffic and the level of public transport fares, and between peak and off-peak, although the latter elasticities are largely guesswork (Glaister and Lewis, 1977). Even with very low cross-elasticities (0.064 for car with respect to rail fares and 0.004 with respect to bus fares), it is found that the marginal social cost of car use in London is so far above the marginal private cost that substantial reductions in rail and bus fares below marginal costs are justified.

However, it should not be thought that the kind of arguments put forward in this chapter dominate recent studies of pricing policies. As an example of an alternative approach, the *Bradford Bus Study* may be cited (Travers Morgan, 1976). This argued in favour of basing fares on average cost, both by route and by time of day, with the allocation of joint costs between times of day based on a 'basic service' approach (i.e. the costs of buses which run all day being allocated proportionately between time periods, whilst those of buses running only in the peak being allocated to the peak). A 'civic' subsidy would be given to pay for a basic level of service, and this would be deducted before calculating fares and determining service levels.

Apart from offering no clear guidance on what combination of fares and service levels to operate on each route, this approach appears to have enormous shortcomings. There is no mechanism for marginal adjustment of fares and service levels to achieve any clearly defined objective. Off-peak fares would tend to be highest where load factors were low (and marginal cost zero), but low where load factors were high. If extended to a wider range of time periods, the same logic might well justify surcharges on fares in the evenings and on Sundays, yet these are times when even a basic level of service may well have ample spare capacity and when price elasticities of demand may be relatively high. None the less, the approach may have the superficial appearance of being more equitable than that outlined in this chapter, and may as a result command political support.

7.7 Planning urban services

Chapter 4 offered some decision-rules on the level of service to provide under various objectives and constraints. The application of these rules depends upon being able to forecast the effect on traffic and revenue of alterations in the level and quality of service provided, and it is to these issues that we now turn.

A sensible starting point is to look at the results of market research studies as to what passengers and potential passengers regard as important constituents of public transport quality of service. Results of such surveys need careful interpretation; they are apt to be specific to the circumstances of the traveller interviewed, and it is hard to distinguish between items that are important in general and items that are important in a particular situation, because it is with respect to them that a particular service falls down. The better studies (Hensher, McLeod and Stanley, 1975; Stopher, Spear and Sucher, 1974; Gustafson, Curd and Golob, 1971) try to get round this by separating out 'importance' and 'satisfaction' scores; each respondent is asked to score (usually on a scale of one to seven) certain attributes on the basis of their underlying importance, and their satisfaction with the existing journey.

For urban services, there is a fair degree of agreement on the following list of attributes, in order of importance, other than fares:

1. Journey time.
2. Ease of access to the system.
3. Ability to arrive at the destination at the planned time.
4. Probability of getting a seat.
5. Number of changes.
6. Freedom from weather (when walking, waiting and changing).
7. Cleanliness, noise, ventilation.

Now such a checklist is useful in considering what attributes should be taken into account when planning services, but by itself it tells us nothing about the willingness of passengers to trade off one attribute against another. What we need ideally is knowledge of the utility function of passengers over these attributes, following the goods – characteristics approach to consumer demand of Lancaster (Lancaster, 1966). In practice, the most common approach is to use a linear approximation – the concept of generalised cost (i.e. the sum of fare, walking, waiting and in-vehicle time, the last three being valued at appropriate money values) – and it is worth looking at the above list to see how far a conventional measure of generalised cost might cover it. Item (1) is clearly covered, as is (2) to the extent that it is measured by walking time. Items (5) and (6) are also partly covered, to the extent that they are measured by walking and waiting time, although the generalised cost measure says nothing about the circumstances in which the walking and waiting take place. An interchange penalty is often added to reflect the inconvenience of changing between services. Items (4) and (7) are in no way measured in conventional studies. Consideration of item (3) is somewhat more tricky.

Ability to arrive at the destination at the planned time depends both on the timetable operated and on the reliability with which the service runs. Consider first a frequent service with a constant headway (H minutes) such that passengers arrive randomly. Mean waiting time will clearly be $\frac{1}{2}H$ minutes. However, to be absolutely certain of reaching his destination at the desired time, the passenger will have to arrive at the stop H minutes in advance of the latest departure time that will get him to his destination on time. To be 95 per cent certain, he must allow $0.95H$ minutes and so on. But suppose the service is not entirely reliable. For instance, suppose that, in practice, it runs at a set of headways given by $H_1, H_2 \cdots H_n$. If the passenger has no knowledge of which headway he will arrive in, his expected waiting time will now be the sum over i of the expected waiting time in the ith headway time, times the probability that he arrives during that headway, i.e.

$$\sum_i \left[(\tfrac{1}{2}H_i) \left(\frac{H_i}{\sum H_i} \right) \right] = \tfrac{1}{2} \frac{\sum H_i^2}{\sum H_i}$$

The more irregular the service, the greater the excess of this over $\frac{1}{2}$H. A corresponding increase occurs in the time he must allow for any particular degree of certainty of reaching his destination on time.

The greater the headway of the service, the bigger the proportion of passengers who will arrive to catch a particular trip – above about 15 minutes headway, this probably applies to most passengers. Thus for longer headway trips, waiting-time algorithms are usually used, based on empirical observations at bus stops or railway stations. For instance, the *Bradford Bus Study*, obtained the result (in minutes):

Waiting time = 1.47 + 0.26 headway   [7.13]

(Travers Morgan, 1976). For Manchester, the relationship has been estimated as:

Waiting time = 1.7 + 0.28 headway   [7.14]

(Seddon and Day, 1974).

However, simply to look at actual waiting time does not adequately take account of the disadvantage to passengers of a high headway service. Whenever a journey is required to end or begin at a specific time, there is the risk of a further period of 'idle' time, equal on average to one-half of the headway less actual waiting time (Starkie, 1971). This time may not be completely wasted – it may be spent shopping, window-gazing or reading the newspaper at the work-place. But it is time the passenger would have preferred to spend in another place.

When low-frequency services are unreliable, the problem is compounded again. For instance, if the passenger wishes to be 95 per cent certain of arriving on time and there is a 10 per cent probability that a particular service will not run, he has got to catch an earlier service, and incur a further H minutes of idle time. Variability of in-vehicle time can similarly lead to a passenger needing to catch an earlier service than would otherwise be necessary. Finally, in the absence of guaranteed connections, the need to change vehicles will mean that the entire procedure must be repeated for the second service.

Two important omissions from the conventional generalised cost measure arise from this discussion. Firstly, there is the importance of reliability – indeed, this may be so strong as to make it desirable to hold crews and vehicles in reserve to cover for breakdowns and delayed vehicles rather than trying to achieve maximum utilisation of resources (Bly, 1976). Secondly, there is the question of idle time. Although in principle it could be introduced in the same way as waiting times, evidence is lacking on the proportion of journeys to which it applies and on the valuation that should be placed on it. Subject to these important qualifications, we shall proceed in the next section to use generalised cost as an appropriate measure of service quality.

7.8 Choice of technique

It is tempting to think of the issue of choice of technique, in urban public transport, largely in terms of the 'rail versus road' issue. Although this is an important aspect, there are far more than just these two options to consider. Rail services may vary from high-speed services running many miles between stops to tram-cars with stops every few hundred yards. Buses may be express or stopping, large capacity (including articulated) or small, running on reserved busways or lanes or sharing track with cars and lorries. However, in what follows, a single rail option (for a conventional service with halts at 2-mile intervals, averaging 30 mph including stops) is compared with three types of bus service, average 30 mph (which would clearly require express operation and probably reserved track), 20 mph and 10 mph. Services are compared for a 10-mile corridor operating 18 hours per day with 2 hours' peak in each direction on weekdays. (This example is based heavily on Mackie, 1977, to which reference should be made for a fuller exposition.)

User costs for these services may be expected to vary as follows. Walking times will be highest for rail and express bus; ordinary bus services reduce this item by offering a greater variety of stopping points. But in view of the difficulty of generalising this item, it is omitted in what follows. Waiting times will depend on headways (in the following, the *Bradford Bus Study* waiting-time algorithm is used). In-vehicle time depends, of course, on speed. The total of waiting and in-vehicle time, assuming a value of time of 40p per hour for in-vehicle time and 90p per hour for waiting time, is calculated for an average $7\frac{1}{2}$-mile journey, assuming that 50 per cent of all journeys are in the peak.

To this sum must be added operating costs. These are derived using the *Bradford Bus Study* data for bus, and the rough estimates derived in Chapter 3 for diesel multiple-unit rail. When these are added in, the results (excluding infrastructure costs) are shown in Fig. 7.3. With respect to operating cost, for any given level of service, the higher the volume of traffic, and the higher the proportion of traffic that is in the peak, the more favourable is the comparison for rail. Alternatively, the extra volume on rail may be catered for by improving service levels, reducing the reduction in unit operating costs achieved, but also reducing waiting times on the mode for which these are usually longest. It is also true that longer journeys obviously favour a faster mode (rail or express bus) since the penalty of longer walking and waiting times becomes a smaller portion of total travel time (for instance, an increase in walking and waiting times of six minutes – assuming this carries twice the weight of in vehicle time – will be offset by an increase in speed from 10 to 30 mph when trips are 3 miles long, but from 10 to 20 mph when the journey is 4 miles long).

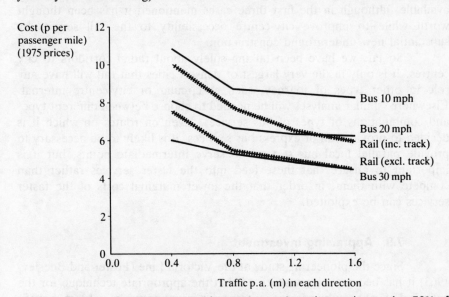

Fig. 7.3   Bus and rail total (operating and user) costs (assuming 50% of traffic in the peak). (*Source:* Mackie, 1977.)

Although circumstances vary greatly, some tentative general conclusions may be drawn from Fig. 7.3. If track costs can be ignored, because both road and rail infrastructure of the required capacity would be provided in any case for other traffic, rail services may be worth providing at even relatively low corridor flows of 400,000 passengers p.a. At the other extreme, if rail track costs are wholly specific to the service in question, very high flows may be required to justify a rail service unless road congestion makes it impossible to operate an express bus service at 20 mph (which will, of course, very often be the case). This sensitivity with respect to bus operating speeds is only partly because of the effects on users; bus operating costs also vary significantly with speed.

So far the discussion has assumed the infrastructure for both modes already to be in existence. If this is not the case, the issue becomes one of investment appraisal. Rail infrastructure is likely to be somewhat more expensive to build than busways, but has other advantages, such as the relative ease with which it may be placed underground. Where good-quality infrastructure exists for one mode but not for the other, it will naturally be difficult to justify investing in new infrastructure, although where the physical circumstances permit, the possibility of converting infrastructure from one use to another should also be borne in mind. The importance of historical accident is heavily apparent, here. The cases (outside London) in Britain where heavy investment in urban rail facilities has been thought worth while (Tyne and Wear Metro, Liverpool 'Link and Loop', Glasgow Clyderail and, on a smaller scale, the Birmingham Longbridge–Four Oaks line) have all been cases where a substantial amount of the rail infrastructure was already available, although in the first three cases mentioned it has been thought worth while to improve city-centre accessibility to the rail service by substantial new underground construction.

So far, we have been talking solely about radial corridors to city centres. It is only in the very largest or densest cities that rail will have any role in other types of journey, such as circular or city-centre internal. Elsewhere, similar analyses will be needed to choose between different types and combinations of types of bus services. Even on routes on which it is decided to provide rail or express bus services, it is likely to be necessary to provide parallel local bus services to serve intermediate points, but it is important to ensure that these feed into the faster services rather than compete with them, in order that the lower marginal costs of the faster services can be exploited.

7.9   Appraising investment

Since the pioneering study of the Victoria Line (Foster and Beesley, 1963) it has become widely accepted that the appropriate technique for the appraisal of urban public passenger transport investment is social cost–benefit analysis. Such an appraisal will take into account, in addition to costs and revenues to operators, benefits to existing and new users of the model in question (in terms of a reduction in generalised cost of journeys made) and benefits to remaining road users (from a reduction in congestion and road accidents). Clearly, such an exercise requires assumptions to be made about pricing policies – in other words, investment appraisal cannot be divorced from the framework of objectives and constraints within which the operator is required to work. Indeed, it appears that the increase in fares on London Transport in general, necessary to finance the operating deficit on the

Victoria Line under the break-even constraint then applied to London Transport as a whole, substantially reduced the net social benefits of the Victoria Line from the level forecast in the original article (Beesley and Foster, 1965). There are two morals to this. Firstly, it is desirable to consider social costs and benefits when determining fares policies as well as investments. But, secondly, when investing, it is necessary to take a realistic view of the financial constraints under which the operator will be working in future years.

The set of benefits with respect to which most difficulties are met in such a study is that relating to the effect on remaining road users. A variety of techniques have been used try to deal with this; for instance, in Britain the so-called Appendix J method (Cmnd 3686, 1968). This requires use of a mode-split model (usually a simple diversion curve relating the proportion of trips on each mode to the ratio of journey times or generalised costs by the two modes) to predict how many trips will be diverted from private to public transport by the investment, a junction-delay formula, plus knowledge of how many overloaded junctions are affected to predict the effect of this reduction in traffic on road journey times, and subsequent iteration between the two. The general layout of the model is shown in Fig. 7.4.

In London applications, the normal assumptions are that the delay per vehicle per junction in minutes (D) is given by the formula:

$$D = 67.5 \frac{x(1 + x)}{1 - 2x} \qquad [7.15]$$

where

$$x = \frac{\text{traffic flow}}{\text{capacity}} - 1 \quad (\text{i.e. } \% \text{ overload})$$

In other words, if a junction with a capacity of 2,000 passenger car units per hour has a 10 per cent overload, the delay per vehicle will be 9.28 minutes. One extra vehicle will increase the delay to 9.34 minutes. Thus, one extra vehicle will lead to a total of more than two hours of delay to subsequent vehicles taken together per hour for which the junction remains overloaded. For Central London, it was assumed that two junctions per mile would have a 10 per cent overload; in the so-called 'glue-pot ring', one junction per mile a 5 per cent overload. It can readily be appreciated how even modest diversions from the private car could lead to large social benefits being recorded.

More recently, several misgivings have been voiced about the Appendix J method, culminating in its official withdrawal in 1977. In part, these refer to its internal workings (the accuracy of the mode-split and junction-delay formulae, for instance) but other problems are wider ranging. In a heavily congested area, if sufficient trips are removed from certain junctions for them to be noticeably less prone to delay, it is likely that there will be other trips which will find it advantageous to reroute via these junctions, offsetting part of the reduction in delay at those junctions, but at the same time reducing delay elsewhere. Partly, this is a question of transfer

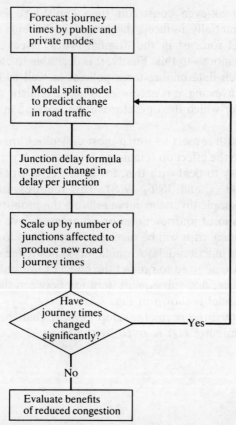

Fig. 7.4 Stages in measuring and evaluating benefits from reduced road congesting resulting from a public transport improvement.

of benefits, but the absolute magnitude may be affected as well. Even worse problems arise if the effect is great enough to lead some trips to change destinations or time of travel. Such changes can only adequately be modelled in the context of a large-scale transportation study (for a discussion of such models see, for instance, Jones, 1977).

It is also the case that public transport improvements are not the only way to relieve traffic congestion, and other approaches should be compared for their cost-effectiveness – for instance, parking restraint or road pricing (see DOE, 1976, Vol. 2, Paper 3). However, a realistic view is needed of the chances of overcoming the political and administrative problems of such approaches.

7.10   Conclusion

The urban public transport market is not amenable to the naïve application of economic theory – marginal or average cost pricing, service level decisions based on profitability, etc. The administrative cost of having a sufficiently complicated pricing system for such an approach to work, together with the presence of joint costs and indivisibilities, makes such an approach impracticable even if externalities are ignored. But this does not mean that economic theory is irrelevant to decision-taking in this field. What is necessary is that decisions be taken on a systems basis, looking at the interactions between modes, service levels, fare systems and traffic. The main economic technique used will be that of appraisal of alternative plans, in the light of the objectives and constraints to which the undertaking is working. Naturally, it is not worth undertaking a full systems analysis for every revision – there are times when short-cut methods will have to be used, and indeed their absence would lead to a heavily centralised approach to decision-taking which is bound to make response to changes in the market slow. It is just this that makes it so essential to find a way of disaggregating overall objectives and constraints in a way that is meaningful for day-to-day management. But such day-to-day decisions need a clear framework of corporate planning with respect to issues such as fare structures and investment. It is in this field that the greatest scope lies for the application of economics and management science within urban public transport operators.

Note

1. Alternatively, if the aim were to maximise passenger mileage, in addition to some service adjustments as specified above, one would raise fares so that equation [7.16] below was satisfied:

$$\frac{\partial Q}{\partial P} + \lambda \frac{\partial [P \cdot Q(P, B)]}{\partial P} = 0 \qquad [7.16]$$

Here λ is the shadow price of passenger miles in terms of revenue. The derivative $[\partial P \cdot Q(P, B)]/\partial P$ may be rewritten as $Q + P(\partial Q/\partial P)$ to give:

$$\frac{\partial Q}{\partial P} + \lambda \left[Q + P \frac{\partial Q}{\partial P} \right] = 0 \qquad [7.17]$$

Or:

$$\lambda = -\frac{\dfrac{\partial Q}{\partial P}}{\left[Q + P \dfrac{\partial Q}{\partial P} \right]} \qquad [7.18]$$

Any possibility of differentiation now would require fares to be set so that

$$\frac{\dfrac{\partial Q}{\partial P}}{\left[Q + P \dfrac{\partial Q}{\partial P} \right]}$$

takes the same value for each sector of the market.

Suppose that for trip types i and j, we set:

$$\frac{\frac{\partial Q_i}{\partial P_i}}{Q_i + P_i \frac{\partial Q_i}{\partial P_i}} = \frac{\frac{\partial Q_j}{\partial P_j}}{Q_j + P_j \frac{\partial Q_j}{\partial P_j}}$$

In other words:

$$(P_j - P_i) = \frac{\left(\frac{\partial Q_i}{\partial P_i} Q_j - \frac{\partial Q_j}{\partial P_j} Q_i\right)}{\frac{\partial Q_i}{\partial P_i}\frac{\partial Q_j}{\partial P_j}} \qquad [7.19]$$

Appendix

Choice of Fares Structure – A Simple Model

The model referred to in Section 7.4 consists of the following sets of equations:

1. Equations expressing generalised cost (pence) for peak journeys of 1, 2 and 3 miles (CP1, CP2, CP3) and off-peak journeys of the same lengths (CO1, CO2, CO3) as a function of peak and off-peak frequencies (PF, OF) and peak and off-peak fares. Fares consist of a boarding charge (PPO in the peak, OPO off-peak) and a charge per mile (PP1 and OP1 respectively).

$$CP1 = 1.7 \times 0.5 \times \left(1.47 + 0.26 \frac{60}{PF}\right) + PPO + PP1 + \left(0.5 \times \frac{1}{6}\right)$$

$$CP2 = 1.7 \times 0.5 \times \left(1.47 + 0.26 \frac{60}{PF}\right) + PPO + 2PP1 + \left(0.5 \times \frac{2}{6}\right)$$

$$CP3 = 1.7 \times 0.5 \times \left(1.47 + 0.26 \frac{60}{PF}\right) + PPO + 3PP1 + \left(0.5 \times \frac{3}{6}\right)$$

$$CO1 = 1.7 \times 0.5 \times \left(1.47 + 0.26 \frac{60}{OF}\right) + OPO + OP1 + \left(0.5 \times \frac{1}{6}\right)$$

$$CO2 = 1.7 \times 0.5 \times \left(1.47 + 0.26 \frac{60}{OF}\right) + OPO + 2OP1 + \left(0.5 \times \frac{2}{6}\right)$$

$$CO3 = 1.7 \times 0.5 \times \left(1.47 + 0.26 \frac{60}{OF}\right) + OPO + 3OP1 + \left(0.5 \times \frac{3}{6}\right)$$

2. Equations expressing demand for the six categories of traffic as a function of generalised cost:

$$QP1 = 4,000 \, CP1^{-0.6}$$
$$QP2 = 8,000 \, CP2^{-0.6}$$

$$QP3 = 8,000 \, CP1^{-0.6}$$
$$QO1 = 16,000 \, CO1^{-1.3}$$
$$QO2 = 32,000 \, CO2^{-1.3}$$
$$QO3 = 32,000 \, CO3^{-1.3}$$

3. A cost function for the bus operator as a function of peak and off-peak frequencies.

$$C = 152 \cdot PF + 130 \cdot OF$$

Costs are then reduced by 25 per cent if fares are flat-sum, and by 29 per cent if the service is free.

The model then calculates revenue, cost and user benefits in the usual fashion for any specified set of fares and service levels.

Chapter 8

Inter-urban passenger transport

8.1 The inter-urban passenger market

In considering the characteristics of the inter-urban passenger market, it may be helpful to look at some data for one country, Great Britain. Table 8.1 shows mode split for journeys of more than 25 miles. Whilst, as in all sectors, the private car dominates, rail has more than twice as many journeys as all other public modes combined. Scheduled and unscheduled (i.e. private, excursions and tours) bus and coach have roughly equal numbers of trips, whilst the number of trips by air is very small (naturally, these trips tend to be far longer than those by other modes). This pattern is probably fairly typical for Western Europe, although in large countries such as the United States, Canada and Australia, air plays a far more important role and rail a small one.

Table 8.2 shows the journey purpose for rail trips. Nearly half of all rail trips over 25 miles are to or from work. These are predominantly

Table 8.1 Mode split for journeys of more than 25 miles in Great Britain, 1977–78

(% of trips)

Transport	percentage
BR	15.3
Scheduled bus and coach	3.4
Other bus and coach	3.3
Car driver	49.3
Car passenger	24.3
Air	0.1
Other	4.3
	100

No. of trips recorded: 57,539

Source: DTp (1979).

Table 8.2 Journey purpose for rail travellers on trips
25 miles in Great Britain, 1977–78

(% of trips)

Purpose	*percentage*
Commuting	47.9
In course of work	9.7
Shopping and personal business	8.7
Holiday	3.4
Sport and entertainment	3.4
Visits to friends and relatives	18.6
Pleasure	8.1
	100

Source: DTp (1979).

long-distance commuters into London, and are not considered further in this chapter. Of the remainder, less than one-fifth of trips are on business, although on some longer-distance trunk routes this figure rises to one-half; the most common journey purpose is visiting friends and relatives, followed by shopping and personal business and pleasure.

The distinction between business and leisure travel is an important one. For instance, results of a survey of potential inter-city travellers carried out by BR showed the following factors taking top priority (Table 8.3). It is, of course, subject to the usual difficulties in interpretation of this kind of survey, but the differences between the sectors are considerable. Business travel takes place in working time, is typically regarded as essential to the

Table 8.3 Priorities amongst inter-city travellers

	% of travellers listing first	
	Business	*Other*
Price	17	18
Speed	31	18
Frequency	7	6
Comfort	10	24
Convenience	29	19
Other factors	6	15

N.B: The sample was not random, being stratified by choice of newspaper to over-represent the more mobile sections of the community.
Source: Freeman Allen (1968).

dertaking involved (although there is some scope for cutting down on business travel by reorganising management structure and by greater use of telecommunications if transport costs are seen as excessive) and tends to be carried out by the better-paid members of the community, travelling on expenses. In this situation, journey-time savings may have a very high value and comfort and convenience (including the ability to work *en route*) are also likely to be important (Hensher, 1977).

On the other hand, leisure travel covers a multitude of journey purposes (Table 8.2). Whilst there may be strong social or moral pressure for some of these trips to take place, few of them can be regarded as 'essential' in the sense that the journey to work or to the local shops is. In this area, the public transport operator is not just competing against other modes of transport, but also against all other possible forms of discretionary spending of money and time that the consumer might enjoy (television, gardening, consumer durables, etc.). For that reason, we expect demand to be much more elastic in this sector than in urban or business travel. Moreover, the factors which 'sell' transport in comparison with other goods are not confined to the characteristics of the journey itself; the quality of the destination in terms of entertainment, comfort of accommodation and price is also important. This leads transport operators in this field to become increasingly involved in providing 'package' deals, including such items as accommodation, admittance to places of interest or entertainment, guided tours.

Generally, one expects the value passengers place on time savings to be much less for leisure than for business travel, although there is some evidence (e.g. Watson, 1974, on the Edinburgh–Glasgow route), that it may be higher for certain types of inter-urban than for urban leisure-time trips. On the other hand Mansfield's work (Mansfield, 1969) on motorists' trips to national park areas, indicates a value of time if anything below 25 per cent of the wage rate (the 'norm' used in urban transportation studies). Much inter-urban demand modelling does not directly use the concept of a time value, as will be seen in the following section.

8.2 Determinants of inter-urban passenger demand

In the urban field, although 'direct demand' models (which forecast the number of trips from A to B by a specific mode in a single equation) are used, the more orthodox approach is the sequential demand model, which first forecasts the number of trips originating and terminating in each zone, then how these are linked to provide an origin/destination matrix and finally modal split. Although some inter-urban studies have taken the latter approach (e.g. OECD, 1977), there are two reasons why direct demand models are often preferred in this field.

1. *Data limitations.* A full-scale urban transportation study will involve several thousand home interviews. Not only is this, in itself, beyond the budget of most inter-urban public transport operators – particularly when the modelling work is specific to a particular route or area – but because

of the relative infrequency of inter-urban relative to urban trips, a much larger sample may be needed to obtain observations on a sufficiently large number of trips. This is a particular problem in modelling trip generation; for the distribution and mode-split stages, interviews of travellers *en route* may suffice. But interviewing car travellers *en route* is difficult and expensive; also one public transport operator is unlikely to obtain permission to interview travellers on the vehicle of another operator. Thus, except when a government body undertakes a comprehensive and expensive survey in the way that is normal in the urban sector, modelling work in the inter-urban field is usually severely limited by the scope and quality of the data available. The models discussed below can be estimated on the basis of ticket sales data, provided that sufficient detail is recorded.

2. *Elasticity of travel demand.* The usual urban trip-generating models assume that the number of trips generated by a particular zone is determined solely by the socio-economic characteristics of the inhabitants of that zone. Provided that walking and cycle trips are included, this may be reasonable, particularly for work trips (the most important factor in urban transportation studies), which will be explained by the active labour force resident in that zone. Similarly, the number of work trips terminating in a zone will be explained by the number of jobs located there. Any feedback from the transport system on to number of work trips originating and terminating in a zone will be by the roundabout method of influencing population density and land use in the zone.

No such simple model is likely to work for inter-urban travel. There is a fair amount of evidence that destination and frequency in inter-urban travel do depend on the quality of the transport system provided (Evans, 1969; Mansfield, 1969). Thus, inter-urban demand models tend to allow explicitly for transport improvements to generate additional travel. Whilst this is not impossible within the sequential framework, and many inter-urban models do suffer from a certain weakness in not representing directly competition between alternative destinations (number of trips from *i* to *j* is taken to be independent of number of trips from *i* to *k*), or even alternative modes, the lack of a simple way of forecasting numbers of originating and terminating trips does reduce the advantage of the sequential approach.

Most inter-urban travel demand models are elaborations of the basic gravity model principle, which states that:

$$T_{ij} = \frac{\alpha P_i^{\beta_1} P_j^{\beta_2}}{d_{ij}^{\beta_3}} \qquad [8.1]$$

where T_{ij} = number of trips from *i* to *j*;
P_i = population of *i*;
P_j = population of *j*;
d_{ij} = distance (or other measure of impedance) from *i* to *j*; α, β_1, β_2 and β_3 are parameters, to be estimated.

It is frequently assumed that $\beta_1 = 1$, so that the dependent variable takes the form of 'trips per head'. Further socio-economic variables may be added (for instance, the income distribution and age structure of P_j may be introduced directly), and other measures of attraction introduced (measures which reflect the importance of the destination as a business and tourist centre, for instance). The resulting model may be estimated by log-linear multiple regression analysis. If attention is focused on the 'impedance' parameter, β_3, the problem may be much simplified by working in first differences of logs, so that P_i and P_j are approximately constant, and the equation reduces to:

$$\Delta \log T_{ij} = \log \alpha - \beta_3 \Delta \log d_{ij} \qquad [8.2]$$

Obviously, such a model can only be estimated on data where the measure of impedance is something other than distance (e.g. journey time) and has changed significantly (for instance, Evans, 1969, estimated such an equation on data from British main lines before and after electrification).

The choice of measure of impedance is a matter causing considerable difficulty in such work. Ideally, one would wish to introduce several measures – journey time, price, frequency of service and possibly distance itself (although, rationally, one might expect distance to have no effect independent of time and price; in practice social ties between towns have often developed historically on the basis of distance, rather than on the characteristics of present-day transport services). Yet they are likely to be too closely correlated for their coefficients to be well identified. One solution would make use of the concept of generalised cost (i.e. valuing time in money terms and adding this to the fare), but this would require better evidence on the value of time for inter-urban travel than is currently available.

Tyler and Hassard (1973) get round this problem by using price and speed as measures of impedance. This procedure may be justified as follows. To estimate the model:

$$Q = \alpha D^{\beta} P^{\gamma} T^{\delta} \qquad [8.3]$$

where Q = volume of trips;

       D = distance;

       P = price;

       T = journey time

(plus other explanatory variables not listed here).

One may make use of the relationships:

$$T = \frac{D}{S} \qquad \text{where} \quad S = \text{speed} \qquad [8.4]$$

and

$$P = aD^b \qquad [8.5]$$

Substituting [8.4] and [8.5] into [8.3] gives:

$$Q = kP^{\beta + b\gamma + \delta}S^{-\delta} \qquad [8.6]$$

Thus the journey time elasticity can be identified in equation [8.6] (it is the negative of the coefficient on speed), but the price elasticity cannot (unless β is assumed $= 0$).

A further problem is posed by the question: 'What is meant by time, or speed, in equation [8.3]?' Is it purely in-vehicle time, and if so, is it by the fastest service, the mean time of all services, or the mean of the fastest services? Tyler and Hassard resolve this issue by combining in-vehicle time and frequency of service to answer the question: 'Suppose that passengers wish to arrive at their destination at random times during selected hours, what is the mean length of time in advance of their desired arrival time that they would have to set out?' If services ran at equal headways and speeds, this would, of course, again be in-vehicle time plus half the headway. However, the justification for the formula in this context is not that people arrive at departure terminals randomly, but that they wish to arrive at their destinations at random times. Obviously this is not entirely true, and strictly speaking, more weight should be given to services at the particular times when most people wish to travel. Other models have used mean journey time and frequency as separate variables (Williams, 1976). In either case, one has to beware of possible simultaneous equations bias from a supply side relationship between frequency and volume.

Finally, journey time should include access and egress times to and from terminals. In the absence of knowledge as to the exact patterns of origins and destinations within cities, and feeder modes used, Tyler and Hassard simply adopt a weighting procedure for population, attaching less weight to population the further it is situated from the terminal.

So far, the models referred to have been 'mode-specific'; that is to say they are calibrated on data solely from one mode, and predict solely for the designated mode. Since Quandt and Baumol (1966) formulated the concept, there has been considerable interest in 'abstract-mode' models, which pool the data for a number of modes, each of which is represented solely as a bundle of characteristics. In the original formulation, the characteristics of each mode are measured relative to that of the best mode for the characteristic in question (with the curious result that, for instance, rail may be compared to air in terms of speed and to coach in terms of price when, overall, it is car that is the strongest competitor) (Lave, 1972). However, this problem is largely a matter of exact formulation and does not arise when only two modes are present. More serious is the fact that two modes with identical quantified characteristics will be represented as identical within the model, and equal flows forecast. This makes it crucial to find a way of measuring comfort and convenience, since there is ample evidence that car, and to a lesser extent rail, will be preferred to other modes even when times and prices are equal. Nevertheless, the abstract-mode approach is the only one that can be used when the introduction of completely new modes is contemplated. For then, no historical data exist for estimation of a mode-specific model for the new mode (although it may be sufficiently similar to an existing mode in comfort and convenience for a model for the existing mode to be used).

The discussion in this section has concentrated on simple direct-demand models, since these are most frequently used in practice by operators, and most of the small amount of published information in the UK relates to such models. However, it should not be assumed that sequential models (and particularly mode-split models) do not have a valuable role to play in inter-urban demand forecasting, particularly in large-scale studies. A discussion of such models is, however, beyond the scope of this book; the reader is referred to Jones (1977) and Quandt (1970) for further information.

8.3 Some empirical results

The study of the results of electrification (Evans, 1969), already referred to, found a journey-time elasticity of -1.4 for rail services, although this may have been biased upwards by the simultaneous introduction of additional reduced-fare bargains, better rolling-stock and surrounding publicity. He found that, whilst air traffic was halved, little diversion occurred from the car, and much of the additional traffic was newly generated. It should be noted that he was concerned with journeys of 100–200 miles in length (see below).

Tyler and Hassard (1973) used cross-section data for rail flows from 64 towns and cities to and from London. Their explanatory variables were: average fare paid, speed (including a measure of frequency as described above), car speed and characteristics of the town in question. Resulting elasticities are given in Table 8.4. This gives a similar journey-time elasticity to that of Evans. More recent time-series work suggests that these elasticities are too high, at any rate for short-run forecasting, and that figures of around -0.9 for journey time and -0.75 for fares are more likely.

Finally, with respect to BR, reference will be made to some work on shorter, less important inter-urban and cross-country routes (Williams, 1976). This work found generally that elasticities with respect to fare and speed or journey time were both greater than 1 in absolute terms, and that with respect to service frequency greater than 0.5. There was also a major difference in the amount of traffic according to whether interchange between services was necessary, and a significant difference according to the quality of the rolling-stock provided. Again, care has to be exercised in interpretation regarding the direction of causation (a frequent high-quality through service may be the result of a high level of traffic, as well as the cause of it), but in many cases, the quality of service given between secondary stations is largely the result of historical accident as to whether they happen to lie on a common main line.

Comparable results for air and coach have not been published. The predominance of business travel for air would lead one to expect journey time

Table 8.4 Estimated rail travel elasticities for Great Britain

Variable	Elasticity	t value
Average rail fare	−1.19	9.85
Rail speed	1.4	5.30
	(at 60 mph)*	
Car speed	−0.84	1.89
Population	0.77	10.19
% no family households	1.62	3.93
% retired	−1.18	3.68
Hotel beds/1,000 residents	0.19	2.52
% employed in posts and telecommunications	0.49	2.92
% employed in rail transport	0.19	2.57
% employed in air and sea transport	0.10	1.89

Source: Tyler and Hassard (1973).
* Speed was introduced in the form (1−1/s), which allowed for a declining elasticity as speeds rose. This was judged to be realistic on *a priori* grounds, although a constant elasticity model gave as good a fit.

to be of predominant importance, and so it seems: a simple linear mode-split equation for business travel gave the result (Leake, 1971):

$$P_R = 0.94 - 0.146[(L_R - L_A) + 1.5(N_R - N_A)] \qquad [8.7]$$
$$r = -0.9968$$

where P_R = proportion using rail;

L_R, L_A = line haul times for rail, air (hours);

N_R, N_A = access times for rail, air (hours)

This suggests that domestic air travel would all but disappear on any route for which rail could give comparable overall times; rail would have to be three hours slower before air captured half the market (but note the extra weight given to access times). Obviously, a simple linear relationship does not capture all the important factors; for instance, the ability conveniently to make a round trip in a day, which may give added weight to time savings in particular circumstances. For coach, the predominance of low-income leisure travellers leads one to expect low journey time and high fare elasticities, but this *a priori* expectation does not appear to have been tested in published work.

A number of studies of inter-city travel demand in the United States have been undertaken, but none seem to have produced very reliable results. The best version of the Quandt–Baumol, abstract-mode model, based on cross-section data for car, bus and air, was as follows:

$$\text{Log} \quad T_{ij}^k = -28.73 + 0.88 \log P_i + 0.88 \log P_j$$
$$(6.75) \qquad (5.47)$$

$$-0.57 \log C_{ij}^b - 2.34 \log C_{ij}^k$$
$$(-0.99) \qquad (-4.54)$$

$$-1.20 \log H_{ij}^b - 1.75 \log H_{ij}^k$$
$$(-1.23) \qquad (-4.59)$$

$$+ 0.44 \log F_{ij}^k + 5.82 \log \left(\frac{P_i Y_i + P_j Y_j}{P_i + P_j} \right) \qquad [8.8]$$

$R^2 = 0.88 \qquad F = 36.09$

+ values given in brackets beneath the coefficients

where T_{ij}^k = trips from i to j by mode k;

P_i, P_j = population of i, j;

Y_i, Y_j = income per head of i, j;

C_{ij}^b = lowest fare, from i to j;

C_{ij}^k = relative fare by mode k compared with lowest;

H_{ij}^b = lowest journey time from i to j;

H_{ij}^k = relative journey time by mode k compared with lowest;

F_{ij}^k = relative frequency of mode k compared with a hypothetical frequency for car of 96 departures per day.

It appears from these results that price elasticities (both own-price and cross-price with the best mode) and journey time elasticities are all very high. The income elasticity of demand, at 5.82, is enormous. Only the frequency elasticity at 0.44 is moderate.

Clearly, it is not possible to produce separate elasticities for different modes with the abstract-mode model. Using a similar model, but with separate equations for each mode, and calibrating on time-series data, Lave (1972) produced the elasticities shown in Table 8.5. This shows very high

Table 8.5 Elasticities of inter-city travel demand in the United States

	Income per head	Scheduled air speed	Own speed	Bus fare	Own fare
Air	2.774	–	0.043	0.802	−1.582
Rail	1.123	−0.701	−2.488	−0.834	−1.442
Bus	0.163	0.624	−1.482	–	−0.484
Car	0.563	−1.165	4.548	0.050	0.414

Source: Lave (1972).

own-price and income elasticities for air and rail, but much lower for bus. Many of the remaining elasticities have the wrong sign, and, as the author warns, the results are subject to severe statistical problems – particularly multicollinearity.

It is worth noting in passing that some European rail systems report lower price elasticities than those suggested above for British and the United States. Perhaps this is a consequence of lower rail fares and less competition (for instance, motoring taxes are generally much higher on the continent of Europe).

8.4   Determinants of access times in inter-urban transport

The previous section has stressed the importance of overall journey times in inter-urban transport. A recent study (OECD, 1977) examined the distribution of access times to the main inter-city road, rail and air networks in Western Europe (Fig. 8.1). It will be seen that, on average, road access times are less than rail, and both of these are substantially less than air. Obviously, there will be some circumstances in which this does not apply, particularly for interlining air passengers (for instance, passengers changing from domestic to international flights), whose destination egress time for the domestic trip may be zero, as opposed to an hour or more for rail and road. (A large proportion of passengers on the shorter British domestic air routes are, in fact, interlining at Heathrow, London.)

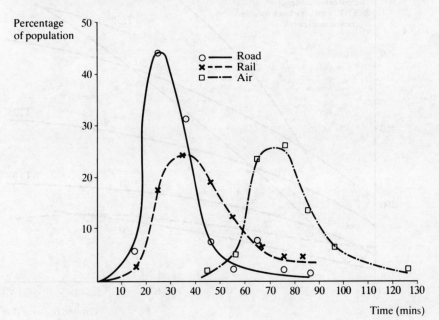

Fig. 8.1 Distribution   of   access–egress   times   by   mode (*Source:* OECD, 1977).

The consequences of this for the mean door-to-door journey speed on the three modes are illustrated in Fig. 8.2 (which also takes account of the need for long-distance car drivers to take occasional breaks). Rail with a mean commercial speed of 100 km/hour is not competitive with car; by raising the commercial speed to 140 km/hour, car can be beaten above 200 km. Air rivals car above 250 km, and rivals 140 km/hour rail service above 275 km. Since only a very small proportion of the total time of an inter-city air trip is spent in the aircraft at cruising speed, it is reducing access times that offers the main hope of making air more competitive. This could certainly be achieved by VTOL (vertical take off and landing) or STOL (short take-off and landing) aircraft flying between inner-city sites, but studies suggest both that such aircraft would be considerably more expensive to operate than conventional aircraft, and that suitable inner-city sites could not be found without great damage to the environment (Peaker, 1974). Perhaps the biggest potential improvement for domestic air services lies in faster ground transport access services.

The part of the city in which the origin and destination zones are located may also be important. Consider passengers travelling from a city,

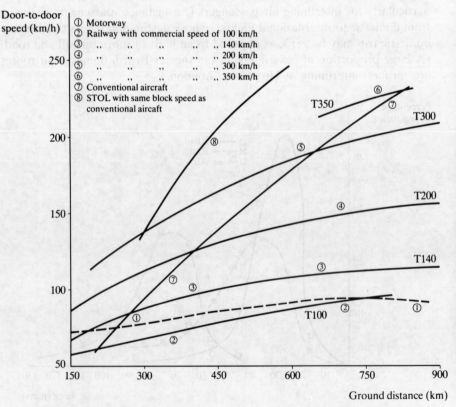

Fig. 8.2 Door-to-door speed based on ground distance for various means of transport (*Source:* OECD, 1977).

with centre C, to a point D which is a mile distant. C and D are linked by rail and motorway; C has a system of ring roads interlaced by radials (Fig. 8.3) (Evans, 1968). Suppose the passenger is starting from any point, P, and wishes to minimise his journey time. Let rail mean speed be V_1, motorway V_2, ring road V_3 and radial road V_4. We assume:

$$V_1 > V_2 > V_3 > V_4$$

Let the distance PC $= r$, and let $k = \theta/360$, where θ is the angle PCD. Thus journey time by rail is:

$$\frac{a}{V_1} + \frac{r}{V_4}$$

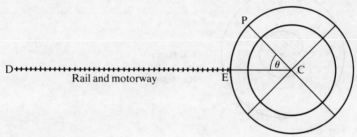

Fig. 8.3

Assuming the motorist takes a ring road to the motorway, journey time by car is:

$$\frac{k2\pi r}{V_3} + \frac{a - r}{V_2}$$

(If it were faster for the motorist to take a radial to the city centre, given our assumptions, rail would inevitably be faster overall.) For any set of parameter values, the value of k at which overall journey times by the two modes are equal is given by:

$$k = \frac{aV_2V_3V_4 + rV_1V_2V_3 - V_1V_3V_4(a - r)}{2\pi rV_1V_2V_4} \qquad [8.9]$$

Differentiating with respect to r and simplifying gives:

$$\frac{dk}{dr} = \frac{aV_3(V_1 - V_2)}{2\pi r^2 V_1V_2} > 0 \quad (\text{since } V_1 > V_2) \qquad [8.10]$$

The relationship [8.9] can be used to divide any city into areas from which rail and car respectively, will be faster; equation [8.10] tells us that the boundary will not be a straight line, but will take the shape shown in Fig. 8.4. If at some value of r, k reaches $\frac{1}{2}$ (i.e. θ reaches 180°) the rail zone will not extend to higher values of r (Fig. 8.5). By assumption $V_1 > V_2$, so that there will always be some points around the city centre from which rail is quicker.

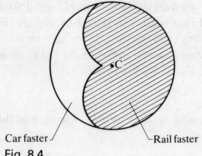

Car faster   Rail faster

Fig. 8.4

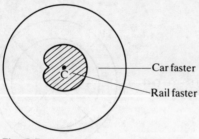

Car faster

Rail faster

Fig. 8.5

A number of important points for road–rail competition emerge from this simple model. Firstly, obviously, the greater the distance a, the larger the zone from which rail is quicker. Secondly, the more centralised the population of the city, and the faster radial urban transport, the more favourable it is to rail transport. On the other hand, urban sprawl and improvement of ring roads tend to favour the use of the car for inter-urban transport (and, to a limited extent, coach, where the additional costs of serving a larger number of pick-up points in the city are not so great as for rail). This is one factor which makes it more difficult for rail to compete in this market in North America than in Western Europe. The problem may be combated by the railway by introducing park and ride stations at locations such as E in Fig. 8.3, at the expense of some reduction in rail city-centre-to-city-centre average speeds. A more radical alternative which would favour rail is the development of so-called linear conurbations along the line of the trunk railway, each conurbation being served by more than one station. It has been suggested that this is taking place along the London–Bletchley–Coventry–Birmingham–Wolverhampton main line (Griffiths, 1974).

One point to stress is the importance to rail of good access to its terminals, whether by car, urban rail or bus. In addition, whenever insufficient traffic is available for a through inter-urban service, the quality of feeder services and the achievement of good connections will be very important. This is one aspect of the interdependence between different parts of the rail network, as discussed above; it also suggests a reason for giving railway operators the right to run (or provide by sub-contracting) feeder bus services, when these provide a more cost-effective way of providing feeder services.

8.5 Pricing policies

The discussion of Chapter 4 showed that the relationship between fares and service levels is a complex one, and that it is necessary to choose simultaneously that combination of the two which best meets the objectives set. It is convenient to approach the issue of fares policies for inter-urban transport in two stages:

(a) Fares policy for a given service level; and
(b) Adjustments to service levels and their implications for fares.

Regarding the first stage, the picture is much as for urban transport (section 7.3). One will try to segment the market and charge different fares to each segment in order either to equate the elasticity of demand in all segments (social surplus maximisation) or to fulfil equation [7.9] (passenger mileage maximisation). If there are still more passengers at particular times of day than accommodation available, the fare will be raised further. Given our assumption of demand elasticities rising as price rises, a social surplus maximising fares policy is thus likely to lead to higher peak price elasticities of demand than off-peak, whereas the reverse is the normally observed case.

In stage (b), additional services will be provided or subtracted (or train/vehicle size increased or decreased) by comparing the benefits (social surplus or passenger miles generated) with the incremental cost. For longer-distance inter-city trips, the marginal cost per seat mile of providing additional morning and evening peak services need not be prohibitive, since asset utilisation of several hundred miles per day is possible on a single round trip (in other words, not only is the daily peak less severe in inter-urban transport than in urban, but also its incremental costs are less, relative to average cost). It will also be necessary at this stage to reconsider off-peak services; if extra peak services are provided, the additional cost of enhancing off-peak services may be very low, and this may provide further benefits. In any case in which such service adjustments remove or impose binding capacity constraints, there will again be implications for fares policy.

What does make inter-urban fares structures very different from urban, however, is that in the inter-urban market, it is much less important for fares structures to be simple than in the urban market. The additional costs of providing booking offices to issue tickets in advance are much less relative to the total cost of the service and to the benefits to be obtained by finer discrimination, whilst – where vehicles are one-man operated – the time taken for the driver to issue the ticket is a much less significant part of total journey time. Both of these points are obviously more significant the longer the journey.

However, simplicity does still have one major advantage, particularly for the large number of inter-urban travellers (especially leisure travellers) who travel infrequently and over a wide variety of routes. Market research shows that such travellers rarely enquire in advance of travelling what the fare will be, but make their travel decisions on the basis of their expectations. The more complicated the tariff, the more likely it is that their expectations will prove to be false. There is a clear marketing advantage in being able to advertise 'Inter-city travel for only 3p per mile' or some such simple formula. Booking-office and administrative costs are also reduced: booking offices only need a mileage chart and a ready reckoner, instead of a complete fares book which has to be revised every time fares change. In practice, most of the world's railways, with the exception of Britain, operate on such a system, although often with a tapering charge per mile as journey length increases. Sometimes, a degree of differentiation by route is achieved by using 'notional' mileages to compile some of the fares, rather than the true distances.

Supposing that it is decided that the advantages of discrimination outweigh any such disadvantages, what are the dimensions within which discrimination may take place? Ideally, the three most important dimensions would be time of travel (i.e. anticipated load factor on the service in question), journey purpose and person characteristics (income and/or socio-economic group). Now whilst the former is possible (within limits imposed by the desire to avoid undue complication) the latter two are not. One has, then, to seek for other variables, which may reflect journey purpose and personal characteristics, as well as, perhaps, providing some evidence of differing elasticities in their own right. The main factors are:

(a) Time/day of travel (see Table 8.6).
(b) Time/day of return journey (leisure trips tend to take place across weekends; business trips within weeks).
(c) Quality of service (for the reasons explained above, fast, convenient services are likely to attract a higher proportion of business travellers out of total trips than slow, inconvenient ones).
(d) Quality of competition (obviously one expects strong competition to lead to high price and service elasticities).
(e) Type of person travelling (a limited degree of discrimination is possible by age (students, children, pensioners) and – where permitted by the absence of sex discrimination legislation – sex).
(f) Number and characteristics of persons travelling together (e.g. family groups, including children).

Fares will vary from being highest for a middle-aged man travelling alone in the peak by a luxury service and returning the same week, to lowest for a student, retired person or family group travelling together by a slow off-peak service and returning after the weekend. This is the logic behind the range of day, weekend and period return fares, family tickets, student and pensioner reductions and special off-peak bargains that many inter-urban operators provide. There are many difficult trade-offs to be made. Is a simple time of day/week/year tariff an adequate discriminator, bearing in mind its ease of comprehension, or do conditions relating to the length of stay away need to be added? (CTCC, 1977). To what extent should one disaggregate

Table 8.6 Distribution of journey purpose for Leeds/Newcastle to
London passengers

(sample of working days only)
(%)

Time	Business	Visiting friends and relatives	Holiday	Shopping	Education	Other
7.00 to 7.59	78	5	7	3	4	4
8.00 to 8.59	60	10	9	5	7	9
9.00 to 9.59	50	16	12	2	10	10
10.00 to 10.59	54	20	9	1	6	11
11.00 to 11.59	48	19	11	1	9	12
12.00 to 12.59	45	27	7	1	9	12
13.00 to 13.59	51	22	4	0	11	13
14.00 to 14.59	59	26	3	0	3	9
15.00 to 15.59	62	16	4	0	7	11
16.00 to 16.59	62	20	3	0	6	9
17.00 to 17.59	64	14	5	0	7	9
All	58	15	10	1	7	9

Source: Moss and Leake (1976).

origins and destinations into groups according to the above characteristics for which different tariffs will be levied? (No one could set separately every individual fare for a complicated network; for BR, for instance, with over 2,000 passenger stations, this would require literally millions of separate decisions.) Is it desirable to operate a two-tier system of first and second-class accommodation (which tends to reduce mean load factors) or of fast and slow services (bearing in mind that slow services may well cost more to operate than fast, given their effect on staff and asset utilisation) at different fares, as a way of improving discrimination? A particular problem is posed by the cheap day return fare. It is generally believed that day trips are the most elastic portion of the leisure market (for a given fare) since the fare makes up a much larger part of the total cost of the visit than for a longer trip. On the other hand, inter-modal competition may be less acute over longer distances than for other trips (at some distances, day return trips by coach and even car are scarcely feasible) and, moreover, there is a risk that day return tickets may be extensively used by business travellers. In part, this risk can be avoided by restrictions on the times and days on which day return tickets are valid.

Little has been said in this discussion on the relationship between fares and costs. Obviously, on those services on which the capacity constraint is binding, in the long run, the marginal cost of expanding capacity will have some influence on fares. But so, too, will demand elasticities; it is quite possible that a high-quality inter-urban rail service may have lower marginal costs but higher peak fares than a low-quality one, for instance. In the practical world in which public transport operates, no very clearcut relationship between prices and average or marginal costs can be expected. Most fares decisions are less a question of weighing up revenue against cost than of weighing up the extra traffic (and benefits) a particular promotion will achieve against the loss of revenue from existing passengers diverting to the lower fare (often termed revenue 'dilution').

We have so far assumed that the operator in question is free to pursue price discrimination without statutory constraint. There are two reasons why it is sometimes argued that such constraint should be imposed. The first is one of fairness between passengers. The second is the argument of 'unfair competition'.

Consider an operator who is charging all passengers a common price, which is in excess of marginal cost. If he is allowed to discriminate, he may increase the profitability of his services by reducing price in the elastic segments of his market. Assuming that his budget constraint is unchanged, these profits will be ploughed back in further price reductions or service improvements. In these circumstances, price discrimination leads to a Pareto improvement in welfare, and it would seem an excessive concern with equity to deny these benefits to passengers.

However, if the objective of the operator is social surplus maximisation, he will go further than this. He will not only lower price in the elastic segment of the market, but also raise it in the inelastic, and he may use the proceeds to finance still further reductions elsewhere. It is this redistribution of benefits that some writers have wished to curb, although a blanket ban on using discrimination in this way assumes that the distributive effect is always harmful and always so serious as to outweigh the benefits of the change. In practice, it may be that those who suffer higher fares are the better off, and that one would welcome the redistribution (although often they will be travelling on business, and the ultimate incidence of their fare is hard to trace). A more pragmatic approach would judge each case on its merits. But it is very difficult for an outside body to do this, since it needs to know what alternative policy would be practised in the absence of discrimination, and this is far from straightforward (many services might not exist at all in the absence of discrimination; in this case, obviously all passengers benefit from the practice).

The argument of unfair competition is often based on the crude evidence that some passengers are being carried at below average cost. From the point of view of allocation efficiency, this is irrelevant as long as marginal cost is being covered. For an outside body to ascertain the latter is again not easy. Moreover, there may be cause for concern if the operator is purely covering short-run marginal cost, in pursuit of his immediate budgetary and other objectives. Competitors may be driven out of the industry, when in fact the low prices of the surviving operator may be short-lived. Even this is only serious from the point of view of the customer if re-entry is difficult or expensive. Moreover, most discrimination may not be of this kind; as we have shown in Chapter 4, it is very possible for marginal cost to be very low (or even zero) for much of the day, even in the long run. Detecting the case where this is not so would again be exceedingly difficult for an outside body. Thus, whilst there may be some justifiable grounds for concern at discrimination, it is hard to see how any regulatory body could distinguish these from the cases in which it is beneficial.

8.6 Investment appraisal

Investment in inter-urban passenger transport may take place for any of a variety of reasons. The first, and generally most frequent, motive is the replacement of worn-out assets. Secondly, the aim may be to improve the quality of service. Very often, investment of this type is associated with replacement of existing life-expired assets, since it is then that the net cost of introducing improved equipment is lowest. The outlay can be divided into two parts – expenditure that would be necessary for like-for-like replacement, and expenditure that is caused by the 'betterment' element in the replacement. Thirdly, investment may be of a cost-reducing nature. Again, this is often associated with replacement of out-worn assets – indeed, except when it is physically impossible to retain an asset in service, or where it would be unsafe to do so, all replacement investment must be justified by a combination of cost reduction and quality improvement. (Whilst this may partly arise simply as a result of rising operating costs and declining comfort and reliability with age, evidence suggests that this is often not the whole reason for replacement; the desire for an improved or different version of the asset is often important. Nash, 1976.) Fourthly, investment may be designed to expand capacity on an existing service. Fifthly, and somewhat exceptionally, investment may be designed to enter a completely fresh market. In practice, of course, many investments will be designed to serve many of these functions simultaneously. For instance, resignalling a stretch of railway may replace life-expired equipment with modern signalling that is cheaper to operate, permits faster and more reliable train services and increases the capacity. A new short-haul airliner may offer faster services, lower costs per seat mile and an increased capacity. Nevertheless, the distinction is still of some value in examining the problems of investment appraisal.

In an undertaking operating purely commercially, replacement investment must be subjected to a two-part appraisal. Firstly, it must be decided whether the project suggested offers the most profitable way of providing the service in question, rather than investing in an alternative asset or renovating existing equipment. Only when this is done may the second, and more fundamental, question of whether the service is worth continuing at all, be accurately tackled. In view of the problems discussed in Chapter 4 in examining the profitability of individual services in a network, this stage is unlikely to be straightforward, particularly in the case of rail services. The interdependence of costs and revenue between services means that profitability must be considered in terms of searching for that package of services which together give the best results. Furthermore, when a service does not appear to have an indefinite future, it may still be worth investing a certain amount in it, to keep it running until other more major renewals are required.

When the objectives of the organisation are not purely commercial, the same two questions remain important, but the criteria by which the answers will be judged differ. If the undertaking is under an absolute obligation to continue the service in question, investment decisions become simply a question of finding the best way to do so (although political uncertainty about the long-term future of the service may remain, and may lead to a neglect of investment which would otherwise be desirable). Otherwise, it must judge the long-term future of the service according to whatever criterion – be it passenger miles per £ spent, social surplus or whatever – is implied by its objectives. It is worth noting that in each case, investment appraisal requires knowledge of the future shadow price attached to such benefits in order to translate them into money terms, as well as the rate of discount.

The only forms of investment which do not necessarily involve a substantial replacement element are investment in increased capacity and investment to enter totally new markets. Here, the necessity for the former obviously gives rise to consideration of alternatives in terms of adjustments to pricing policies (these are also obviously bound up with the issue of the scale of replacement of existing assets), whilst the decision to enter a new market is very much one of corporate strategy. In other words, there are virtually no forms of investment which it is possible to evaluate in isolation from the general corporate strategy of the organisation concerned; corporate planning and investment decisions are intimately bound up with each other. The importance of this point is directly related to the life of the assets and the degree of interdependence within the organisation involved – it is thus more true for a railway, for instance, than for a bus company.

Interdependence of investment decisions does not depend solely on the issue of the long-run future of the services in question. 'Betterment' for a particular service may often release assets that are not life-expired, and that can see further use on a different service, replacing older or poorer-quality assets. Railway investment often involves a whole chain or 'cascade' of such transfers. A key issue then is to find the best order for the set of transfers – which service should receive new equipment, which second-best and so forth. Cascading equipment from the most quality-sensitive services to the least means that each service can receive fresh equipment far more frequently than if they all had to wait for new equipment, and this can be an important marketing consideration where asset lives are long.

As a brief illustration of some of the points made in this section, the example of railway electrification schemes will be considered. These are replacement investments inasmuch as they necessarily involve replacing existing motive power; they will thus appear most attractive when motive power is due for renewal anyway, or where the existing motive power can be put to good use elsewhere in the system. They are likely to involve a 'betterment' element, both directly – inasmuch as electric services are cleaner and more reliable – and indirectly. Electrification tends to reduce the marginal cost both of improving frequencies and of improving performance compared with other forms of motive power; thus it will often be worth while improving these aspects of services at the same time as electrifying a service (Clemow, 1972). In this case, it is necessary to identify the best electrification and the best diesel option for comparison, rather than simply assuming identical performance and service levels.

But electrification projects are also cost-reducing. In return for a net capital outlay on structures (less any savings on the capital cost of motive power), one experiences a reduction in fuel and maintenance costs. The capital outlay is closely related to the track miles electrified, whilst the cost savings depend largely on the train miles operated with electric traction. For instance, suppose that the net cost of electrification (annuitised) is £3,000 p.a. per track mile and the savings are 15p per train mile. There is then a crucial number of train miles which must be converted to electric traction per track mile electrified for a reduction in the sum of capital and operating costs to occur (in the example given, 20,000 train miles p.a.). The implication is, as expected, that the more densely trafficked a route, the better the case for its electrification.

But the fact that routes are not self-contained again causes problems for appraisal (BR/DTp, 1979). Electrification of short, densely trafficked sections of track means *either* that all trains proceeding further have to change motive power at the boundary (delaying services, and worsening utilisation of locomotives and crew by the insertions of more frequent layovers between workings) *or* longer-distance services are still worked with diesel motive power. Extensions to an existing electrified system eliminate such difficulties, and may be worth while at lower densities. Correspondingly, a widespread electrification programme may be better justified than its individual components, taken in isolation. If scope exists for expanding traffic or concentrating existing traffic on a smaller number of track miles (by track or route rationalisation) this will also improve the case for electrification. Again, the importance of long-term corporate strategy in judging individual projects is clear.

8.7 Investment decisions and comparability between modes

So far, we have considered investment solely from the point of view of a single organisation pursuing its own objectives. There are two reasons why one needs to look at investment in public transport from a wider perspective than this. Firstly, projects put forward by one operator (or mode) may have beneficial or harmful effects on other operators. Secondly, even when projects are technically independent, they are still competing for a common pool of investment funds, and it is desirable to find a way of comparing marginal projects in different sectors of the transport industry, to aid in allocating investment funds between them.

The first of these problems occurs in two contexts, one static and the other dynamic. Firstly, in purely static terms, an investment in one mode of transport may divert traffic from another mode. Indeed, in a competitive market, it is often designed to do just that. If price on the mode from which the traffic was attracted equalled marginal social cost, this would be no cause for concern, even if the diversion had a financial effect on the other operator (unless the financial consequences led to distorting price or service level changes). But this is rarely the case. At the other extreme, if the loss of traffic is unmatched by any cost-saving measures (as may be the case, particularly if the operator is under an obligation to provide a particular level of service), then the loss of revenue to him is entirely a social cost of the project. If it is subsequently recovered from remaining users in the form of higher fares, there may be additional losses of consumers' surplus. In intermediate circumstances, the operator may offset part of the loss of revenue by service level changes, so that the social costs of the move are partly an increase in deficit and partly a reduced service to continuing passengers.

But the particular project under consideration may only be one stage in the dynamics of competition between the two operators. The second operator may retaliate with an investment designed to win back the traffic. The first operator may introduce further improvements . . . and so on.

Now some will argue that, far from being a problem, this is exactly how the competitive process benefits consumers. As long as both operators take a realistic view of their long-term prospects, allowing for likely retaliation, this may be the case. But if the market shares which the two operators believe they can secure in the long run add up to more than 100 per cent of the market, then there is a serious risk of over-investment; where intense competition is to be found only on certain routes, this will be at the expense of quality of service elsewhere. Such a situation is alleged to have occurred in Britain, where motorway construction, rail and air service improvements have often occurred in parallel on a particular route, whilst others have received none of these facilities.

One way of minimising this problem is to ensure that potentially competing services by different modes are provided by a single operator. This, of course, presumes that the spur to efficiency and innovation provided by additional competition is not worth these costs. (Competition from private transport would, of course, continue.) An alternative is to subject the relevant investment plans by all the organisations concerned to scrutiny by an external body (presumably the relevant government department). This is apt to cause delay, and loss of morale to the operator whose plans are rejected in order to protect a competitor. Much the same problem may occur within a single organisation if the potentially competing services are run by separate divisions with much independence, and headquarters acts as mediator between them.

Even where such interdependence of projects does not exist, the problem of allocating investment funds between modes and between operators, remains. The required information for this may appear obvious. It is to obtain from each operator (or investing authority, in the case of roads), an investment plan for alternative levels of the investment budget, together with evaluations of the marginal projects added to or subtracted from the plan. These could then be compared, and budgets adjusted until the marginal returns in each sector were equalised. The foundations of such an approach exist in West Germany, where a five-year co-ordinated transport infrastructure investment plan is prepared.

There are two problems here. Firstly, the evaluations by different operators may have used incompatible assumptions and, more fundamentally, have been undertaken with respect to different objectives. For instance, whilst most public transport appraisals will have been purely of financial effects, some may have used cost–benefit analysis, as typically will road investment appraisals. The introduction of further criteria such as passenger-mileage maximisation may add to the variety. There is no reason why these alternative criteria should lead to comparable results (Harrison and Mackie, 1973), so it will be necessary to rework the appraisals on a comparable basis. But more serious still is the problem that intangibles pose for the appraisal. For instance, the Leitch report (Leitch, 1977) has proposed a framework for a multiple-criterion comparison of road schemes, taking account of a multitude of physical, environmental and economic effects of the scheme according to the incidence group involved. Applying such criteria to a wide range of projects from different modes and operators might be extremely difficult, especially given the emphasis on pairwise comparisons of disaggregate information. None the less, it seems doubtful whether any simple cost–benefit or other criterion could do justice to the range of effects needing consideration in strategic decisions such as the allocation of investment budgets.

8.8 Conclusion

The evidence presented in this chapter suggests that the inter-urban passenger transport market is characterised by much higher demand elasticities with respect to price and quality of service than is the urban market. This is associated generally with a high degree of competition between modes – public versus private and, where permitted, between public transport modes. Access times are very significant determinants of the competitiveness of the various public transport modes, and these depend upon land-use patterns and the quality of local transport. The question of the terms of competition and the funds provided for investment are key public decisions, but by no means easy to resolve given the widespread departures from marginal cost pricing and the variety of objectives pursued in this sector. Price discrimination has a major part to play in satisfying budgetary requirements with the least loss of traffic or benefits. The role of corporate planning, in providing the setting for internal ranking of investment projects and for comparability studies between modes, is of great importance, particularly for rail transport, where investments are long-lived and interdependence between them is strong.

Chapter 9

Rural transport

9.1 The rural transport problem

The provision of public transport in rural areas has always been a problem, and in Britain even at the peak of public transport operation directly after the Second World War, there were many small communities that did not provide sufficient traffic to sustain a regular service. But a number of factors have combined to make the problem more acute in recent years:

1. Rising real costs of provision, making higher traffic, fares or subsidies necessary to sustain services.
2. Growth in car ownership, leading to a reduction in public transport patronage and increasing the size of community necessary to provide a given amount of public transport traffic (particularly at evenings and weekends).
3. The decline in the proportion of settlements having facilities such as shops, post offices and public houses, making the need for transport greater.
4. The increased concentration of public services such as schools, hospitals and local government offices on large villages and towns, with the same effect.
5. The decline in population and jobs in many areas.
6. Ageing population, and increased road traffic hazards, which mean that walking and cycling cannot play as large a role as in the past.

To some extent, of course, these trends represent people escaping from dependence on public transport, by car ownership or relocation. But for those left, including many in car-owning households who do not have cars available, a greater need for public transport is combined with declining services. This problem is not confined to rural areas, but it is here that it is most acute.

9.2 Defining the need

In other sectors of the public transport passenger market, the prime concern has been the price and quality of the services provided. In this sector, services are so sparse that concern is more as to whether they exist at all. The first requirement regarding quality is that it should be possible to make the sort of trip needed within the constraints imposed by opening hours of the facilities visited and family life. The types of trip and the sort of constraints involved may be summarised as set out below:

1. *Journey to work*.   Public transport never has been a dominant mode of transport for the journey to work in rural areas, except for commuting into towns from adjacent areas. People in rural areas have tended to live close to their work and to walk or cycle (Moseley *et al.*, 1977). The difficulties experienced by wives and children in finding jobs to which they are able to travel may be a cause of the low activity rates and high emigration of young workers found in rural areas, and the exceptionally high levels of car ownership found for given income levels in rural areas are clearly associated with a high dependence now on the car for the journey to work (Rhys and Buxton, 1974).

2. *Shopping and personal business*.   The basic requirement here is for a service into the nearest small town or shopping centre at a time when housewives are free from other family responsibilities, with a return service after a suitable interval. Obviously, access to a range of shopping centres, increasing variety and allowing a trade-off between range of facilities and journey time and cost, is a benefit, as is a variety of services allowing for different lengths of stay. In general, shopping services are the easiest to maintain, since they are needed outside the urban and school service peak, and they can attract a reasonably high proportion of local housewives (including some from car-owning households) to a common destination at the same time, either daily or on market days.

3. *School journeys*.   These services also will attract a high proportion of the relevant population to the same destination at the same time, although they suffer from a severe peaking problem.

4. *Health services*.   According to the surveys of Moseley *et al.* (1977), journeys to doctors and hospitals provide some of the most serious problems for non-car-owning rural residents. Such journeys need to be made at (relatively) infrequent and irregular intervals, and at times which often do not correspond with those for shopping trips. The main mitigating factor is the high degree of voluntary assistance given by car owners, but reliance on this lacks the reliability and independence given by a scheduled public transport service, as well as imposing costs on the car-owning members of the community.

5. *Entertainment*.   Journeys to places of entertainment pose some of the greatest problems for those dependent on public transport, being concentrated on evenings and weekends, when members of car-owning households are more likely to have the car available than during the day, and when penalty rates of pay are involved for public transport staff. The biggest dissatisfaction with the lack of services appears to be felt by teenagers, who wish to be independent of their parents at these times.

6. *Social*.   Catering for social trips by public transport again causes great problems, because of the dispersed nature of the destinations of such

Table 9.1 A suggested 'needs' table

Person Type	Job type					Facility type (non-work)											
	1	2	3	4	5	1	2	3	4	5	6	7	8	9	10	11	12
1. Dependent children (0–9)						8*	20	3†	4*	4*			3†	1*	1*		1
2. Non-dependent children (10–15)								3†	4	4	27	13	1	1	1		1
3. Students									4	4		20	1	1	1	20	1
4. Working adults: prof./managerial	40									5			1	1	2		1
5. Working adults: other non-manual		40								5			1	1	2		1
6. Working adults: Male skilled and semi-skilled			40							4			1	1	2		1
7. Working adults: male unskilled				40						4			1	1	2		1
8. Working adults: female manual					40					6			1	1	2		1
9. Women with dependent children						16		3†	8	8			3†	1	2		1
10. Women without dependent children						16		1	5	8			1	2	2		2
11. Retired persons						12		2	8	6			2	2	2		1

Note: The factors express needs in terms of trips (return journeys × 2) per nominal month.

*Requirement wholly attributable to needs of supervising adult/dependent child.

†Requirement partly attributable to needs of supervising adult (in the case of dependent children) or needs of dependent child (in the case of supervising adult).

Source: *WYTCONSULT* (1978).

KEY

Job type
1. Professional managerial jobs (male and female)
2. Other non-manual jobs (male and female)
3. Male skilled and semi-skilled manual jobs
4. Male unskilled manual jobs
5. Female manual jobs

Facility type (non-work)
1. Local shops
2. Primary school
3. Doctor's surgery
4. Post office
5. Shopping centre
6. Middle school
7. Upper school
8. Health centre or small hospital
9. Social Security office
10. Major shopping centre
11. Higher education college
12. Major hospital

trips. A comprehensive service enabling any settlement to be reached from any other cannot usually survive in rural areas, and reliance has to be placed on lifts or flexible-routed public transport services; more often, the trips simply are not made at all.

How can planners assess the value of a public transport service serving one or more of these needs? Clearly revenue earned is very much a lower limit; passengers might often pay much more than existing fares rather than forgo the use of the service, and moreover the tendency of users of these services to come from very low income groups must be borne in mind when using their willingness to pay for a service as an indication of its social value. On the other hand, where utilisation is low, there is little point in raising fares to exploit this willingness to pay, unless the price elasticity of demand is very low. Otherwise, benefits of the service will be cut with no reduction in real resource cost. It may also be that inhabitants value a particular service even when they do not use it, as a standby facility for themselves, or because it relieves them of the responsibility of driving others around. Use of a subscription system for services may recover part, but not all, of this benefit as revenue to the operator (LGORU, 1976).

It has been suggested that one way of judging the benefit of any particular service is by compiling a table showing the accessibility needs of each person type, perhaps with some needs being given a higher weighting than others. An example of a comprehensive needs table (developed as part of a study of urban accessibility), is given in Table 9.1. Whilst, it would be prohibitively expensive to provide public transport services to fulfil all the needs of all persons in rural areas, the weighted sum of the needs fulfilled could be used as a way of comparing services and ranking them for support (Coles, 1978).

9.3 Service quality

When examining rural transport, consideration of quality of service comes second to consideration of whether a service exists at all. However, the two considerations overlap. A village may have an occasional bus service, but for some residents (especially elderly) the walk to the bus stop may be so long as to make using it very uncomfortable or impossible. It may be timed in such a way that mothers cannot use it to go shopping without arranging for someone else to look after their children before or after school or without a long, and perhaps uncomfortable, wait for a return service. Whether or not the service is deemed to be fulfilling the need in question is a matter of fine judgement. Given the inevitably low frequency of rural services, it is the exact times and routes of operation that are crucial. Reliability, too, is more important on low-frequency routes.

The result is that it is difficult to measure changes in service quality in terms of the traditional user benefit variables. In an urban network, offering high frequencies and the ability (perhaps with a change of bus) to reach a large variety of destinations, it is reasonable to calibrate a demand function, and then to measure the effect of changes in the walking, waiting and in-vehicle times to reach alternative destinations in terms of consumers' surplus. In rural areas, many destinations will be impossible to reach; for others, it is the inconvenience of adjusting one's schedule to the bus times, and the enforced idle time at the destination waiting for a suitable return service that are crucial. It is not at all clear how these could be measured or valued.

9.4 Service types

Given the need to survive in areas which do not provide sufficient traffic to support a conventional public transport service, it is in rural areas that unconventional ways of cutting costs may have most to offer. Perhaps the most important ways in which costs may be reduced are the following:

1. Flexibility regarding times and routes, so that a complete service does not need to be offered regardless of whether there is traffic available or not.
2. Use of a smaller vehicle, althought the cost saving from this is modest (Ch. 3) and when larger vehicles which are required for peak duties on the same or other routes, are available, it is cheaper to use these off-peak at very low load factors than to buy an additional vehicle for off-peak work. Small vehicles may permit better routeing and faster journey time on country roads.
3. Use of part-time or voluntary labour. Problems here are those of obtaining and organising a sufficient pool of reliable part-time or voluntary labour which is suitably qualified, especially when additional licences to the normal car licence are required, and industrial relations and unemployment problems with existing bus staff when the service is replacing a current one.
4. Combining provision of rural passenger transport with other services. This is perhaps the most common and most promising way of reducing costs, but it requires some degree of compromise between the various aims of the service in routeing and timing.

Table 9.2 lists some of the services which use one or more of these approaches.

Amongst the ways in which the first element may be introduced are by dial-a-ride operation (but many of those needing to use such a service do not have access to a telephone, and would need to book in advance verbally or by post); or by introducing a more limited degree of flexibility in the routeing of scheduled services in the form of diversions on request to settlements off the main route (which poses obvious problems for timing such services). Where traffic levels are very low, such services may be most cheaply provided by shared taxis (in the United Kingdom, legal provisions currently limit this to prearranged sharing or sharing where only one person pays the fare); if this is combined with voluntary labour, it becomes more the organised giving of lifts (with often the volunteer driver needing to make the

Table 9.2 Properties of unconventional bus services

	1 Flexible routeing timing	2 Small vehicle	3 Part-time or voluntary labour	4 Multiple purpose
Shared taxi	√	√	?	–
Organised lifts	√	√	√	?
Dial-a-ride	√	√	?	–
Flexible scheduled buses	√	?	–	–
Community buses	?	?	√	–
Post-buses	–	?	?	√
Inter-urban services	–	–	–	√
Recreational services	–	–	–	√

√ Denotes that the service always embodies the features in question;
? That it may do.
For a description of such services in the United Kingdom see TRRL (1977).

journey for his own purposes, anyway). Lifts of one kind or another often provide the major method of transport to rural non-car owners (DOE, 1971); the aim of organising them is to increase dependability and coverage and – if permitted – by introducing a system of pricing, even at a low level, to provide an added incentive to lift-giving and to relieve the user of some of the stigma attached to dependence on charity. A scheme which combines volunteer labour with use of a larger vehicle and scheduled services is the community bus scheme first introduced in Norfolk (see TRRL, 1977, Papers 9 and 10).

Amongst the most common ways of providing rural passenger services in combination with other transport needs is the introduction of stops on services that are basically inter-urban in nature. This is easier to do on bus and coach services, where virtually no additional infrastructure is required and the addition of lightly used request stops adds little to journey time, than on rail. Post-buses are common in many countries, and have recently begun to develop in Great Britain. It has been suggested that there are many other publicly owned or financed vehicles which could carry passengers at relatively low marginal cost – school buses, hospital cars and vans carrying stores – and at least one service combining the carriage of passengers and local and health authority mail and stores, the Border Courier, is operating (Acton, 1980). In some cases, sufficient recreational traffic to the rural area can be attracted to play a major part in financing services, although this is likely to be very seasonal and very peaked. Perhaps the most well-known service of this type in Great Britain is the Dalesrail service between West Yorkshire and the Yorkshire Dales National Park, which has succeeded in attracting substantial numbers of visitors to the area (half of whom are car owners), and in providing a valuable service for residents in the area with only a small amount of outside financial support (Grigg and Smith, 1977). There is always some conflict between providing for the two aims of the service; also, legal and licensing constraints may often have to be removed. However, the skilful combination of such services may provide a reasonable level of accessibility to rural areas at low marginal cost. It is important also to remember the role of contract and private hire coaches; the size and location of this sector is subject to influence by public decisions – for instance, in the allocation of contracts for schools services.

9.5   Accessibility and land use

So far, we have considered only transport solutions to the rural transport problem. However, it may be argued that much of the problem arises not because of deficiencies in transport but because of deficiencies in location of housing, jobs and facilities. Indeed it is sometimes argued that provision of subsidised rural passenger transport will have the harmful effect of perpetuating mislocations, and that the better reaction is solely through seeking to influence location decisions. To argue this is to attribute a higher influence to public transport services than they probably have and to ignore the inconvenience and hardship caused in the interim. Moreover, there may well be a wish on the part of many not directly affected to retain a particular form of country life. None the less, locational influences must certainly not be overlooked.

Resolution of the difficulty by relocation may take two forms – moving people and jobs to facilities and moving facilities to people. Whilst subsidies (such as rate relief) to maintain facilities such as village shops and public houses, and tolerance of the increased operating costs of small local schools, may well have a part to play, they cannot provide all the facilities that transport to a larger village or town opens up, and are likely to be more expensive than provision of public transport in any but the larger villages. Therefore, the concept of key villages emerges. These are villages in which it is deemed worth providing such facilities, and to which future growth of population and employment will be encouraged. For remaining areas, a transport solution is still sought, perhaps based on services to the nearest key village and connecting these into the national public transport network.

When it is recognised that the problem of rural passenger transport may interact with provision of many other services to such areas, and that location decisions are partly substitutes for, and partly complementary to, provision of public passenger transport, it becomes clear where ultimate responsibility for planning and financing public transport in rural areas is likely to be most appropriately placed. It is the planning authority for the area concerned that has the relevant range of responsibility and experience. But it is important to ensure that adequate marketing of services takes place, and the operator himself may usefully play a part in both market research and selling.

9.6   Rail services in rural areas

Most railway companies throughout the world still operate rural rail services on a considerable branch line network. Such services, as illustrated in

Chapter 3, are likely to have exceptionally high specific costs per passenger mile, and – whilst they do attract additional revenue to main lines by acting as feeder services – require high levels of support. Although their presence is not, in general, the main reason why railway operators require support, it is perhaps the least cost-effective use of support. The problem is worsening as equipment ages and the high costs of renewal are faced. Yet there is extremely strong opposition to further cuts in services, and the political support for retention of services is often much higher than for rural bus services.

A number of rural railways in Britain have been subjected to cost–benefit analysis since the Cambrian Coast study of 1968 (MOT, 1968a). Six such studies were reworked by Dodgson (1977) to put them on a comparable basis in 1977 values. The result was that the measured benefits of the services were very similar, at around 5p per passenger mile. Subtracting an average fare of 3p per passenger mile, this leaves consumers' surplus and external benefits of 2p per passenger mile. This is lower than the required subsidy for many such services.

The main benefits measured in these studies are time savings, the value of journeys which would not be made at all in the absence of the rail service and the costs of providing replacement road services. A number of other benefits – comfort, reliability (especially in the face of bad weather or seasonal road congestion), 'crush' capacity and luggage space – are generally not valued. Moreover, some such lines serve as a tourist attraction and a recreational facility in their own right. Nevertheless, the level of political support for their retention remains remarkable. Dodgson suggests that this might soon wane if financial responsibility for their support were devolved to local authorities. Moreover, such an approach would place the local authority in a position to improve co-ordination between local bus and rail services.

Such an approach would clearly involve difficulties inasmuch as most local rail services cross local authority boundaries, and the allocation even of the avoidable costs of the service in question between adjacent authorities would be necessary. This could only be arbitrary, or determined by relative bargaining strength, and would thus run a high risk of distorted decision-making. Moreover, it is to ignore the fact that local rail services tend to play two roles, either of which may be predominant in any one situation. The first, that of purely local travel, is clearly one which needs integrating into the local bus network, and where the principal alternative means of provision will be the traditional bus service. The second, however, is that of long-distance travel, feeding into other services and requiring integration with them. Here, the nearest road equivalent is the express coach. In Britain long distance traffic on rural branch lines ranges from as little as 2 per cent to as much as 75 per cent of the total.

Where long-distance trips are important, the obvious substitute for rail to consider is a network of express coach services feeding into main line rail services at appropriate railheads. Rees (1975) estimates that such a network for rural Wales would not only save money compared with the rail services (costing £$\frac{1}{4}$ m. compared with £2 m.), but would also improve the service to the majority of communities by permitting more appropriate routeing not constrained by the limited coverage given by rail routes. Where the major role of such services is to provide feeders to inter-city services, it is desirable that they should be marketed as a part of the rail network, with through ticketing and good connections. In many Western European countries such services are provided by railway-owned buses, or by bus under contract to the railway company.

9.7   Conclusion

It is in rural areas that the diseconomies of the small-scale operation of public transport become most acute. It may be that there is no combination of price and service level that permits break-even, or that the combination is so bad that not merely inconvenience but acute hardship is caused. Traditionally in Britain, as in many countries, rural public transport services have been cross-subsidised from the profits made on urban and inter-urban services. In the case of rail services, adequate profits for this have long since ceased to be possible; for bus services, it may still be possible to make sufficient profits for this purpose, but at an increasingly severe price in terms of loss of traffic on the healthier routes. The long-run effects on patronage on these routes may be even more severe.

Thus the choice is between direct subsidies for conventional public transport services and attempts to fulfil the need with lower-cost unconventional services. Assessment of the relative value for money of these alternatives is not easy. Clearly, public transport subsidy has gone too far when it would be cheaper to give all passengers free tokens for the equivalent number of taxi-rides. Whether social car schemes, post-buses and so forth offer better value than conventional services in any particular circumstances is more controversial. But undoubtedly provision of rural public transport is an area which calls for marketing flair, initiative and flexibility.

Chapter 10

Public transport of freight

10.1 The market for freight transport

The demand for freight transport is, even more unequivocally than for passenger, a derived demand. It is dependent upon the level of output in the economy in question, and the location of the producers and consumers of that output. This leads one to expect a quite close relationship between ton miles of freight transported and GDP, and indeed this is so. However, it does appear that for most industrialised countries the ratio of ton miles to GDP is falling over time (Tanner, 1974). This could be due to shifts in the composition of GDP towards lighter products, changes in the degree of specialisation of plant which affect the degree to which semi-finished goods are transported or changes in the location of production relative to consumption. In fact, it is likely that all three of these factors are at work, and probably in different directions. This illustrates the need to disaggregate in order to understand the freight market.

Rather than working in terms of a single index of output, it is desirable to consider three different aspects of output: (a) tons carried; (b) length of haul; and (c) consignment size (see for instance Rao, 1978a).

Tons carried

It is this that one would expect to be most closely related to the output levels of the various sectors of the economy, and the most obvious technique for examining this is the technique of input–output analysis. Changes in the amount of freight transport per unit of GDP may be the result either of changes in the composition of final demand, or of changes in the input–output coefficients themselves over time (due to changes in technique or in industrial structure). One study of the Canadian rail freight business found changes of the latter type far more important than changes in composition (Rao, 1978b). It is important to remember that tons transported is not necessarily equivalent to tons produced; some products may be consumed at the point of production, whilst other products are transported several times at different stages of production.

Length of haul

There are two major approaches to modelling the length of haul of freight traffic. Firstly, when the product in question is homogeneous and production and consumption are tied to specific locations (as is often the case with primary products, and particularly those going for export), it may be expected that – either by central planning or by market forces – a pattern of freight flows will emerge which minimises the sum of production and transport costs. This pattern may be found by the use of mathematical programming techniques (Meyer and Straszheim, 1971, Vol. 1, Ch. 10).

Unfortunately, in an industrialised country a comparatively small part of the freight transport market is composed of such products. For manufactured goods, industries are often 'footloose' (i.e. transport costs make up such a small part of final cost that industrial location is fairly flexible and depends more on such factors as the state of the local labour market – see Luttrell, 1962) and products differentiated, so that 'cross-hauling' of the same product (i.e. simultaneous transport of the product from A to B and from B to A) is commonplace. Modelling such flows is extremely difficult, although most researchers have used some form of gravity model (Chisholm and O'Sullivan, 1973), relating the flow of goods between two areas to their population, employment or income and the cost of transporting goods between them.

Consignment size

Consignment size is an extremely important factor in competition in the freight market, since it is the economies from aggregating consignments into lorry- or trainloads that provide one of the main ways in which public transport can undercut the own-account operator. Yet it is perhaps the most difficult of the three factors to analyse. Firstly, it depends on the stage in the production and distribution process at which the consignment is taking place – raw materials to producer; intermediate goods between producers; producer to wholesaler; wholesaler to retailer and retailer to final consumer. Secondly, it depends upon the structure of the industry concerned; consignment size will be larger as a proportion of output the more the industry is concentrated into a few large plants. Thirdly, it depends upon the distribution system used – whether direct from factory to customer or via distribution depots or wholesalers (and, at the other end of the process, agricultural produce may be forwarded direct from the farm or brought together at concentration depots). Fourthly, it depends upon the size of stocks held both by the forwarder and the receiver. If they are willing to hold substantial stocks, consignments may be infrequent and large; if, on the other hand, stockholding is to be minimised, more frequent smaller consignments will be required. Thus it is at this stage of freight demand forecasting that general distribution economics come to the forefront of the picture.

It is also here that demand – supply interactions are at their most important. Of course, it is always possible for the price of transport to influence the quantity transported by its effect on the final price of the product in question. But for the majority of manufactured goods, transport costs are a sufficiently small proportion (around 10%, see Edwards, 1970) of the total cost that even a major change could be expected to have little effect on sales of the good. Transport prices are more likely to influence the location and size of plant and the general distribution pattern used, and in this way to change both length of haul and consignment size. The relationship between these factors is considered in more detail in the next section.

10.2   The demand for freight transport and distribution economics

As an example of the way in which freight rates fit into general distribution economics, consider a simple example taken from the literature of inventory control. Suppose that a given product is produced at A and consumed at B at a known, steady rate of X units per week. If it is transported in N weekly consignments of equal size, then the average stock necessary at A and B together will be X/N. The cost per unit of holding stock is equal to the sum of interest on the value of the stock (r), depreciation and/or obsolescence of the stock (d) and the costs of warehousing (w). Thus the total costs of stockholding will be $(X/N)(r + d + w)$.

The transport rate is usually related both to the number of consignments and consignment size; assume the charge is given by $fN + v(X/N)N$. In addition, the commodity is subject to interest and depreciation costs during the transit time (t). The total cost (TC) per week for this operation is given by:

$$TC = \frac{X}{N}(r + d + w) + fN + vX + (r + d)Xt \qquad [10.1]$$

If there is a single mode of transport available to the firm, then the only choice open to it is that of the number of consignments per week to ship (N), and therefore its level of stockholding. Minimising TC with respect to N:

$$\frac{\mathrm{d}TC}{\mathrm{d}N} = -X\frac{(r + d + w)}{N^2} + f = 0 \qquad [10.2]$$

(The second-order derivative will always be positive, indicating a minimum.) Solving for N gives:

$$N = \sqrt{\frac{X(r + d + w)}{f}} \qquad [10.3]$$

The number of consignments shipped per week will be greater, the higher the stockholding costs relative to the fixed charge per consignment.

Now suppose that two alternative modes of transport – road and rail – are available. Rail usually has a higher value of f and a lower value of v than does road transport. (In other words, economies of consignment size are greater for rail than for road.) Thus optimal consignment size and levels of stocks will differ according to the mode chosen. The procedure now must be to solve for the optimal value of N (number of consignments per week) for each mode, and then to calculate total cost using each mode on the basis of that number of consignments. Notice that in this comparison t, transit time, may differ between modes. In practice, however, transit time takes on much greater significance when X, the rate of consumption of the product, is a random variable. For then the firm must trade off the costs of increasing its stockholding against the costs of risking running out of stocks at B; the more quickly it can replenish its stocks, the less costly a given risk will be. (It may be possible to use a different, faster, mode for such urgent consignments from that used for regular deliveries.) Reliability of transit time is also important; for a given risk of delay, the firm must balance the cost of running out of the item against stockholding costs.

The aim of introducing this simple example has been to show how the choice of transport mode must not be considered in isolation, since it may involve simultaneous choices about the other aspects of the distribution system used by the firm. The only factor considered here is the level of stockholding, but the number and location of warehouses and distribution depots may well also be relevant.

For instance, suppose that in our example above, the flow X could be handled through more than one depot. The number of consignments per week will now equal NH (where H is the number of depots and N is the number of consignments to each). Mean consignment size will be X/NH. Because it is generally believed that there are economies of scale in depot operation, we can add a further overhead cost element related to the number of depots, oH.

What possible benefit could there be from having more than one depot? The most obvious answer is that it reduces the mean length of haul at the final distribution stage. Complete consideration of this effect requires comparison of alternative depot locations, alternative allocations of customers to depots and alternative routeings of delivery vehicles, and is well beyond the scope of this chapter (see Eilon, Watson-Gandy and Christofides, 1971). Generally, a given reduction in the area served by a single depot will have a less than proportionate effect on mean length of haul. For simplicity, however, in what follows it will be assumed that the elasticity of final distribution cost with respect to number of depots is minus unity – that is, final distribution cost is equal to $1X/H$. The total cost function now reads:

$$TC = \frac{X}{N}(r + d + w) + fNH + vX + (r + d)Xt + \frac{1X}{N} + oH \qquad [10.4]$$

We must now minimise with respect to N and H:

$$\frac{\partial TC}{\partial N} = -\frac{X}{N^2}(r + d + w) + fH = 0 \qquad [10.5]$$

Or

$$N = \frac{X(r + d + w)}{fH} \qquad [10.6]$$

and

$$\frac{\partial TC}{\partial H} = fH - \frac{lX}{H^2} + o = 0 \qquad [10.7]$$

Or

$$H = \frac{lX}{o + fN} \qquad [10.8]$$

Clearly the decisions as to the number of consignments per depot per week (N) and the number of depots (H) are interdependent; the more depots, the smaller consignment size and hence the fewer consignments per week and vice versa for given parameter values.

Consider a simple example in which $X = 10$, $r + d = 0$, $w = 1$, $l = 10$, $o = 2$. Now the equation reduces to:

$$TC = \frac{10}{N} + fNH + 10v + \frac{100}{H} + 2H \qquad [10.9]$$

Suppose that the cost parameters for road haulage are $f = 0.42$, $v = 2$. The cheapest distribution system using road haulage involves twice-weekly consignments to six depots. This achieves a total distribution cost of $63\frac{2}{3}$ units per week. Suppose that rail transport is available, at costs of $f = 2$, $v = 1$. To use rail whilst maintaining the same distribution system would raise total cost to $67\frac{2}{3}$ units. (This is because, with a consignment size of only $\frac{5}{6}$ units, road haulage is cheaper.) However, by reducing the number of depots to five and reducing consignment frequency to weekly, so that consignment size is raised to 2 units, use of rail transport can cut total distribution cost to 60 units (Table 10.1).

Table 10.1 Breakdown of distribution costs for example in text

(costs in £ per week)

Mode	Road	Rail	Rail
No. of depots	6	6	5
Consignments per week	2	2	1
Fixed cost of depots (£ per week)	1,200	1,200	1,000
Storage cost (£ per week)	500	500	1,000
Local distribution cost (£ per week)	1,667	1,667	2,000
Trunk haulage cost	3,004	3,400	2,000
Total	6,371	6,767	6,000

In some cases, choice of mode may even be linked to the location of the production plant itself (apart from the obvious fact that to use rail or water without transhipment requires location alongside such facilities). For instance a plant, inputs for which arrive by rail transport, may be best located close to the market for the product, whereas one fed by road may be best located close to the raw materials.

Because of varying implications for total distribution cost, as well as because of differences in the rate of consumption (X) between commodities, the factors determining choice of mode of transport may be expected to vary between commodities. The simplest distinction is that between bulk commodities and general merchandise.

Bulk commodities, such as coal, oil, cement, earths and stone

These are generally moving between a limited number of extractive and manufacturing plants (the major exception is materials for the building and construction industry, which may be delivered direct to the site). There, large volumes, low unit values and generally relatively predictable consumption patterns make them suitable for transport by one of the modes relying on scale economies (rail, pipeline, water). Transit times are typically not very significant; reliability may be more so, but price may be expected to be the main determinant of mode choice.

General merchandise

This category covers a wide range of manufactured goods which may be moving between factories, from factories to warehouses and distribution depots or from any of these to the final consumer. Generally, only road haulage can perform the latter. With respect to the first two types of movement, unit values may be high, and for certain types of consumer goods, depreciation and/or obsolescence may be a problem. Thus there is more emphasis in this market on fast reliable delivery of relatively small consignments. (Security and freedom from damage may also be important.) It is correspondingly much more difficult for modes other than road haulage to compete in this market.

10.3 The role of railways in freight transport

The traditional pattern of rail freight movement consists of the following processes:
   (a) Collection and delivery by road.
   (b) Transhipment between road and rail vehicles.
   (c) Trip working between depot and marshalling yard.
   (d) Marshalling.
   (e) Trunk haul.
   Of these elements, (a) (b) and (c) may occur twice in any one transit; (d) may occur more than twice if it is impossible to make up a full trainload at the marshalling yard serving the point of origin for that serving the point of

destination. There is no reason why the time or cost involved in these processes should be related to length of haul; only with respect to (e) will there be a direct relationship. Suppose that the average time involved in each process is as follows: two hours each for (a)–(d) and one hour per 30 miles for (e). On a journey on which (a)–(d) are experienced twice, there will be an overhead time of 16 hours; in magnitude this will outweigh the time spent on the trunk haul for anything less than a 480-mile trip. Overnight transits, much valued in the general merchandise business, will be completely impossible. The categorisation of costs may be somewhat similar – the example of a wagon of coal in Table 10.2 is quoted from the Beeching Report (BRB, 1963). An illustration of the relative profitability of traffic according to terminal conditions was given for a sample week in 1961 (Table 10.3). By

Table 10.2 Comparison of wagonload and trainload costs

(cost per 16-ton wagon in £)

	Wagonload	Trainload
1. Terminals, trip-working documentation	4.8	1.4
2. Provision of wagon	4.6	1.6
3. Marshalling	1.05	–
4. Trunk hall	3.45	4.65
	13.9	7.65

Source: BRB (1963).

Table 10.3 Terminal conditions of mineral and general merchandise freight

(excluding less than wagonload)

Terminal conditions	Tons	%	Receipts	%	Direct costs	%	Margin
Road–road	26,800	2	145,300	7	214,000	9	−68,000
Road–station	17,600	1	64,400	3	91,700	4	−27,300
Road–dock	25,400	1	61,600	3	91,900	4	−30,300
Road–siding	111,500	7	299,900	13	376,000	17	−76,100
Station–station	30,200	2	66,300	3	91,800	4	−25,500
Station–dock	29,600	2	65,000	3	72,500	3	−7,500
Dock–dock	5,400		3,900		9,500		−5,600
Station–siding	246,600	14	369,500	16	379,600	17	−10,100
Siding–dock	256,300	15	190,500	8	200,900	9	−10,400
Siding–siding	946,000	56	986,500	44	746,200	33	+240,300

Source: BRB (1963), p. 36. Data refer to week ending 23 April 1961.

contrast, a road vehicle – even if it is on average slower and more expensive on the trunk haul part of the journey – may offer both quicker and cheaper transits over any length of haul less than several hundred miles.

In practice, the situation may be even worse than this regarding a traditional rail freight operation. For at each stage in the journey, the rail consignment may be delayed awaiting a vehicle or train with spare capacity. Moreover, the normal operating procedure of a mixed traffic railway is to give priority to passenger services, so that in the face of any operating difficulties, freight services are most liable to delay. The consequence of these two factors is not just to lengthen transit times, but to introduce a considerable degree of variability. For instance, if a particular service operates daily, a missed connection will add a day to transit time. When the fact that traditionally railways have not even had an information system that enables them to locate consignments *en route* (other than by literally sending a shunter to search in the yards) is taken into account, it is easy to see why the principal complaint of consignors against traditional rail freight services is one of quality of service.

To some extent, trade-off between costs and quality of service is open to the railway, depending on its operating practices. Consider a simple example. Suppose that on a certain route from A to B, terminal and marshalling costs are proportional to the number of wagons forwarded (N). (This is not strictly true. There may be economies of scale. Also marshalling costs depend on the number of cuts – i.e. the number of groups of wagons requiring separate sorting – as well as the number of wagons.) Movement costs are proportional to the number of trains run (T). (Again, this may not be true; utilisation may rise with frequency of service, and some costs do depend on train weight.) A third category of costs (in part borne by the operator in terms of wagon turn-round, part by the shipper in terms of quality of service) is proportional to the delay the wagons experience waiting for a train forward from A to B. Assume a steady flow of wagons at rate N per week. If there are T trains from A to B per week, on average the delay will be $\frac{1}{2} 1/T$ weeks (half the headway) per wagon. Thus we may write the following expression for total cost (TC):

$$TC = aN + bT + \frac{c}{2} \cdot \frac{N}{T}$$
[10.10]

To discover the relationship between cost and volume we need to know what determines T. This is where the operator has the choice of policy.

1. *Suppose operators wait until a full trainload accumulates*

If wagons accumulate at a rate of N per week, and the capacity of a train is K, then $T = N/K$.

$$TC = aN + \frac{b}{K}N + \frac{c}{2}K$$
[10.11]

This gives the following expressions for average (AC) and marginal (MC) cost:

$$AC = a + \frac{b}{K} + \frac{cK}{2N} \qquad [10.12]$$

$$MC = a + \frac{b}{K} \qquad [10.13]$$

i.e.

$$\frac{MC}{AC} = \frac{a + b/K}{a + b/K + cK/2N} \qquad [10.14]$$

$$\left(N.B. \quad \frac{MC}{AC} = \frac{\mathrm{d}TC}{\mathrm{d}T} \cdot \frac{N}{TC} = \text{elasticity of cost with respect to output.} \right)$$

Thus the more important delay costs are relative to other costs, the greater the economies of scale. But the operator here is not following an optimal policy unless delay is of no importance. It may be worth operating a more frequent service in order to reduce total cost to himself and his customers (assuming changes in the latter may be reflected in the charge he levies).

2. *Suppose operators choose the frequency which minimises total cost.*

From equation [10.10]:

$$\frac{\mathrm{d}TC}{\mathrm{d}T} = b - \frac{c}{2} \cdot \frac{N}{T^2} \qquad [10.15]$$

$$\frac{\mathrm{d}^2TC}{\mathrm{d}T^2} = \frac{cN}{T^3} > 0 \qquad [10.16]$$

Therefore TC is at a minimum when $\mathrm{d}TC/\mathrm{d}T = 0$. Therefore

$$T = \sqrt{\frac{cN}{2b}} \quad \left(\text{subject to the constraint } T \geq \frac{N}{K} \right) \qquad [10.17]$$

$$TC = aN + b\sqrt{\frac{cN}{2b}} + \frac{c}{2} N \sqrt{\frac{2b}{cN}} \qquad [10.18]$$

which simplifies to:

$$TC = aN + \sqrt{2bcN} \qquad [10.19]$$

$$AC = a + \sqrt{\frac{2bc}{N}} \qquad [10.20]$$

$$MC = a + \frac{1}{2} \sqrt{\frac{2bc}{N}} \qquad [10.21]$$

$$\frac{MC}{AC} = \frac{a + \frac{1}{2}\sqrt{2bc/N}}{a + \sqrt{2bc/N}} \qquad [10.22]$$

The more important other costs are relative to wagon-related costs, the greater scale economies (as a tends to 0, cost elasticity tends to 0.5). This operating arrangement is the best solution in the face of steady demand, but given the more realistic situation of random fluctuations in demand, no guaranteed transit time can be given (transit time will itself be a random variable). It is this which has served to give railways a bad name for reliability. The only way of guaranteeing arrival times in this situation is to timetable freight trains like passenger trains and to run them, however much traffic is forthcoming on the day in question. The total cost function would then be:

$$TC = aN + bT + \frac{c}{2} \cdot \frac{N}{T} \qquad [10.23]$$

up to the capacity of the timetabled service, i.e.

$$AC = a + \frac{bT}{N} + \frac{c}{2} \cdot \frac{1}{T} \qquad [10.24]$$

$$MC = a + \frac{c}{2T} \qquad [10.25]$$

$$\frac{MC}{AC} = \frac{a + c/2T}{a + b \cdot T/N + c/2T} \qquad [10.26]$$

Scale economies are now more significant, the greater train-related costs are relative to other costs.

As soon as capacity is reached a problem emerges. One can either:

1. *Duplicate the service.* This will be costly if the duplicate service is lightly loaded; it will also raise the expected value of the marginal cost of an extra wagonload, since one will have to take into account the probability of an extra train being required due to the presence of the wagon.
2. *Delay the traffic.* If a small number of vehicles is involved, this will be the cheapest way out, but quality of service will fall below the promised standard.
3. *Refuse traffic.* This requires a reservation system, so that traffic is only accepted up to the capacity of the train concerned. With such a system one could offer two qualities of service: first class with guaranteed transit time and second class at a lower rate making use of spare capacity.

What can be done to improve quality of service *and* reduce operating cost simultaneously? It is clear that raising linehaul speeds (whilst helpful in terms of improving staff, locomotive and track utilisation, particularly where track is shared with express passenger services) only solves a minor part of the problem. The heart of the matter lies in stages (a) to (d). The cost and quality of rail freight services will be improved if one or more of these stages can be eliminated.

(a) Road collection and delivery at one or both ends can be eliminated by linking the customer's plant and/or distribution depot directly to the rail network by means of a private siding. (In fact, in Great Britain, the role of the railway-owned transhipment terminal has been greatly reduced; by 1976, 98% of rail freight originated and 88% terminated at privately owned sidings or terminals.)

(b) Transhipment may also be eliminated by private sidings; alternatively, it may be considerably simplified by containerisation, piggyback operation (where the entire road trailer travels on the train) or use of dual-mode vehicles.

(c) Trip working may be eliminated if consignments can be made up to full trainloads at the terminal or siding.

(d) Marshalling may be eliminated by trainload working; it may be considerably simplified by making up trains as a series of sections for different destinations which may be transferred between connecting trains without complete remarshalling.

Finally speed, reliability and asset utilisation may be improved by implementation of a real-time computerised monitoring and information system, such as the TOPS systems, which was originated by the Southern Pacific Railway (USA) and has since been introduced by other railways including BR. This enables any authorised person with access to the system to ascertain the exact location of all rolling-stock and consignments at any point in time, and greatly benefits marshalling and train planning and asset utilisation. Timetabling guaranteed connections (as with passenger services) and introducing a space reservation system are also facilitated.

Clearly, at one extreme, the biggest opportunity for improvement will come where consignments are large enough to permit trainload working between private sidings at both ends. In these circumstances, provided there is sufficient regular traffic of the type in question to keep asset utilisation high, rail should be able to achieve a quality of service, reliability and cost superior to road haulage regardless of length of haul. However, use of trainload freight services may require the customer to increase his average stockholding and to use a different distribution network in terms of size and location of depots from that best for road haulage, as illustrated above.

Where individual consignments do not permit trainload working, but the overall volume of traffic on a route does, there are two choices. If locations can be provided with private sidings, stages (a) to (d) can be reduced to a single trip working and marshalling stage. Otherwise, consignments may be taken by road to a single concentration depot, where full trainloads may be made up. In either case, a fixed element in the cost per consignment will remain (its size depending on the length of the trip or road working, and on whether traffic characteristics permit efficient utilisation of assets involved in this stage); this can only be compensated for by length of haul.

In the absence of sufficient volume to provide a regular through train between a pair of points, additional marshalling time and cost will be involved. This may be slight, if flows are large enough for trains to comprise simply two or three sections to be dropped or transferred *en route*, or large if complete remarshalling at one or more intermediate points is involved. In other words, wagonload rail freight operations are subject to two forms of economies of scale – with respect to consignment size and with respect to the overall size of flow on a route. Additionally, as with passenger traffic, there is a correlation between size of flow and quality of service in the form of frequency. Frequency can be increased for a given size of flow, but at the expense of raising costs.

The consequence is that for each combination of terminal conditions at origin and destination, and size of overall flow, there is a different break-even length of haul above which rail becomes cheaper than road haulage. For instance, Johnson and Garnett (1971) suggest that on average for Freightliner container services this lies at about 150 miles (Fig. 10.1). (In practice, shorter distance traffic may be worth sending by rail if collection and delivery costs are below average. This is the case with much maritime traffic, where ports are closely served by terminals. On the other hand, for low-density commodities the break-even distance may be much greater, since road trailers usually offer a larger cubic capacity than the containers. Warner and Joy, 1971.) However, given that rail has to recover the difference between marginal and average cost by charging a surplus over marginal cost where circumstances permit (as discussed in Ch. 5), rail charges for length of haul above 150 miles will be based not on rail cost but on road costs, as is shown in Fig. 10.2.

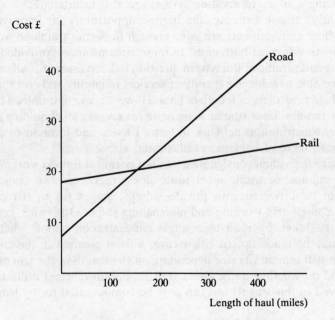

Fig. 10.1 Direct costs of sending containers by road and rail (*Source:* Johnson and Garnett, 1971).

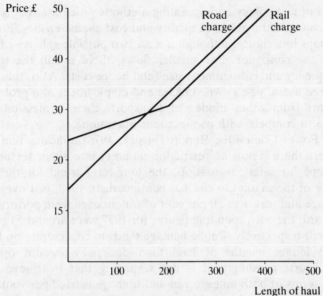

Fig. 10.2 Charge for sending containers by road and rail (*Source:* Johnson and Garnett, 1971).

The importance of this last point should be stressed. A railway which is required to operate commercial rail services in the face of competition can do this most successfully if it bases its prices not on its own costs but on those of its competitors (adjusted to allow for any costs imposed on the customer by differences in quality of service, consignment size and stockholding, provision of rolling-stock or specialised facilities, etc.) (see Ch. 5). The role of the railway costing officers is then to provide 'acceptance criteria'; rules which determine what traffic is financially acceptable. These may not even be stipulated in money terms; they may relate solely to physical characteristics of the traffic. Where a particular aspect of the railway freight business has spare capacity, a different criterion will apply for short-run acceptance of traffic than for long term; in the terminology of Chapter 3, traffic may be worth retaining in the short run as long as it covers its specific expenses; in the long run it will have to cover its specific and joint costs. Overall, a route will only be worth retaining for freight in the long run if the surplus earned on freight over movement and terminal costs exceeds the track and signalling costs that could be avoided if freight services were withdrawn (Joy, 1971). However, this criterion is not as easy to apply as it may sound; interdependence of different routes and different types of traffic means that it can only be accurately applied in the light of a long-run plan for the system as a whole.

10.4   The public road haulier

The previous section showed that it is very misleading to think of rail as a single mode of freight transport; in fact, there are many different combinations of technology and operating methods which use the fixed rail, each with its own combinations of quality and cost characteristics. For road, there is perhaps less choice, although a least two possible spheres of choice are open to the consignor. For smaller flows, there is still the trade-off between frequency and consignment size (and hence cost). Also, there is the choice between use of one's own vehicles and employment of a professional haulier. Apart from other modes of transport, then, professional road hauliers have to compete with own-account operation.

The Foster Committee Report (Foster, 1978) indicates that within the UK, where there is now no restriction on entry into either sector of the market, except for safety legislation, the long-term trend for the public haulage share of the market to rise has continued. In 1962, just over 40 per cent of tonnage and just over 50 per cent of ton mileage were performed for hire and reward; the corresponding figures for 1977 were around 54 per cent and 65 per cent respectively. Public haulage tends to concentrate on heavier vehicles and longer lengths of haul than does own-account operation (Table 10.4); correspondingly, it is not surprising that it achieves better utilisation in terms of both mileage run and tonnage carried per vehicle (for instance in 1965 public haulage vehicles averaged 25,000 miles and 3,300 tons per vehicle, compared with 15,000 miles and 1,200 tons for own-account vehicles. Edwards and Bayliss, 1971.)

The preference of many firms for own-account transport is presumably largely one of quality of service – the firm has direct control of the operation, it can use the drivers partly as salesmen when making deliveries, vehicles are used for advertising, etc. (TRTA, 1959). At the same time, unless the characteristics of the traffic are such that regular employment with reasonable load factors is possible for the assets involved, the firm may pay

Table 10.4 Ton miles by vehicle unladen weight and mode of working (1977)

(000 m.)

Vehicle unladen weight (tons)		Mainly public haulage	Mainly own account
Over	*Not over*		
–	1.5	0.2	1.4
1.5	5	3.7	4.8
5	8	6.2	4.3
8	–	30.4	9.9
Unknown		0.2	0.2
All vehicles		40.7	20.6
Mean length of haul (km)		52.3	31.6

Source: Foster (1978), pp. 113–14.

dearly for this luxury; moreover, when transport is only a minor part of the firm's activities, it may not receive the attention necessary for efficient operation. Surveys have shown that the data collected by own-account operators about their transport activities are frequently inadequate (Fernando, 1971).

The advantage of the professional road haulier lies in his ability to pool traffic from alternative customers in order to obtain higher utilisation of his fleet. (Although, in countries where licensing regulations permit, as is the case in Great Britain since 1968, it is open to the own-account operator to do the same; early indications are that relatively little use is being made of this possibility. The own-account operator apparently does not consider the extra expense and loss of flexibility resulting to be worth while. See Bayliss, 1973.) This is likely to offer more scope for cost-cutting, the longer the length of haul (since it is essentially a way of reducing trunk-haul costs at the expense of additional distribution mileage and possibly transhipment), the smaller the consignment size (Bayliss and Edwards, 1970, found a strong positive relationship between consignment weight and the probability of own-account transport) and the smaller the firm, so that its opportunities for keeping a road haulage fleet fully employed are limited.

Of course few firms use a single method of transport exclusively; Bayliss and Edwards (1970) found a considerable use of public hauliers by firms operating own-account vehicles. This might be to even out fluctuations in demand or to serve some areas where traffic was too thin to justify own-account operation.

10.5   Freight transport decisions and pricing policies

The earlier sections of this chapter have proceeded on the usual assumption that customers for freight transport have perfect knowledge and take decisions on rational grounds. Obviously there are the usual reservations on this score – search costs, likelihood of satisficing rather than maximising behaviour, etc. – but there are also some particular worries concerning the structure of the freight transport industry.

First there is the question of knowledge of alternatives, which is made difficult both by the large number of competing road hauliers and by the lack of any road or rail published tariffs. One solution to this might be thought to be to require publication of tariffs (as used to be the case in Great Britain, and still is required in the United States and many European countries). However, publication without regulation to ensure that it is conformed with is likely to achieve little, as most freight will still be carried at special rates which differ from those published (this is the case, for instance, on most European railways). But if rates are enforced (as in the case of US, West German and Italian railways), much of the ability of rail-freight operators to discriminate between customers to cover overheads will be lost, whilst small road hauliers (regulation of whose rates is exceptionally difficult, given their numbers) will know exactly what price they need to undercut. Traditional railway rates structures (as still found in some countries) group commodities according to value, and charge a higher rate the higher the value. This was all very well when railways had a near monopoly, since the sensitivity of total traffic offered to transport rate is likely to be closely related to the value of the product, but where competition exists, it simply enables the competitor to cream off the high-rated high-value commodities. Cost-based tariffs, on the other hand, involve all the difficulties of cost allocation discussed in Chapter 3 if they are to cover total cost. One solution proposed by the EEC was the use of 'bracket tariffs' (upper and lower bounds) such as are found for road haulage in West Germany, but even this was considered to be unworkable and was replaced by a 'reference tariff' of no legal status and of very doubtful use.

Secondly, is the fact mentioned above that many own-account operators appear to have a very limited knowledge of what their own-account fleets cost to operate (see Fernando, 1971). The situation has probably improved over time, and some firms (e.g. Unilever) treat their road haulage fleets as separate subsidiaries who have to compete with public hauliers for traffic. Nevertheless, the suspicion remains that particular flows or consignments that would be better sent by public transport may often fail to be identified.

Thirdly, there is the problem of the treatment of transport costs in pricing policy. For many commodities, transport costs are simply absorbed into a delivered price, regardless of location, consignment size (quantity discounts, where given, are often related more to competitive position than to transport cost variations) and length of haul. There is thus no incentive to the consumer to order in an economically optimal way. Competition in speed of delivery may be one aspect of quality competition in oligopolistic markets where open price competition is ruled out. Some firms in weak market positions even give their customers a considerable measure of choice over delivery mode, whilst charging a standard delivery price regardless of mode. Where transport costs are important, they may be charged on the basis of distance from an artificial 'basing point' regardless of where the consignment actually originates. This presumably is a collusive policy designed to avoid a situation in which competing firms charge different delivered prices according to their location relative to that of the customer.

Fourthly, there have been suspicions of irrational prejudices against particular organisations, perhaps based on public image and perhaps on unhappy experiences in the past. Such prejudices almost always work against rail, since in most countries there are many alternative road hauliers but only one rail. This may indicate some merit in the traditional United States policy of trying to ensure that at least two independent railways serve every location of any importance, but in view of the above discussion of scale economies, this is likely to be a costly solution. Since many of the scale economies in rail freight transport arise in the track and signalling field, it may be thought better to allow competing operators to run services over common track, although this poses major problems of organisation and control, and may fail to exploit economies of longer trains. An alternative which certainly is feasible is for competing specialist freight forwarders, operating their own depots and road vehicles, to charter space on railway services and market it themselves. This is common in many countries (e.g. Australia) and a rising trend in Great Britain.

10.6 Conclusion

The freight transport market is an extremely heterogeneous one, and flows need to be distinguished by commodity (value/weight and bulk/weight ratio), consignment size and length of haul before anything useful can be said about modal split. But it must be recognised that these variables are themselves interdependent with mode choice; marketing public transport of freight, therefore, requires consideration of not just the price and quality of the service offered, but also the way in which it can link in to the entire distribution system of the firm. Studies which concentrate on identifying flows which are currently suitable for public transport (by road or rail) are bound to miss market opportunities which would emerge if a systems approach to distribution as a whole were taken.

Chapter 11

The future
of public transport

11.1 Introduction

In Chapter 2 of this text, we saw that the commonly painted picture of land-based public transport as a sector of the economy in universal decline is very far from the truth. Within Great Britain, it is true that bus and local rail traffic has declined as car ownership has grown, but for the rail mode this has been offset by a rapid rise in inter-city passenger carryings. In many countries, including some of the richest European countries, rising prosperity has been accompanied by rapidly rising rail passenger traffic. In the freight sphere, public transport has generally shared in the rise in total volume transported even if the fastest growth has been in own-account operation. To what extent can we expect these trends to continue in the future? In this chapter, we consider long-run trends briefly under four main headings – social and economic change, technical change, costs and productivity and the political arena.

11.2 Social and economic change

By far the most crucial variable in this, as in most economic forecasting tasks, is the rate of economic growth. It is generally agreed that this will be slower than in the 1950s and 1960s, but opinions differ as to how slow. On the passenger side, growth in real disposable income per head tends to bring with it higher car ownership, reducing the demand for local public transport. Even if economic growth does resume, one should be cautious about projecting this decline in demand relentlessly into the future. At the least there will always be a residual demand for public transport from schoolchildren, pensioners and from those who because of location or tastes find it more convenient to use public transport than to own one (or two) cars. Moreover, the arguments of previous chapters suggest that public transport has a much more positive role to play. Within existing large cities it is inconceivable that public transport could be completely supplanted for the journey to work without a major switch towards low-density decentralisation of work-places. For longer-distance journeys, growth in prosperity tends to raise the total amount of travel, and there is every reason to suppose that public transport can continue to share in this growth by providing an overall price and quality package which is attractive to many potential motorists.

Regarding freight traffic, the picture is more complex. For many railways, a handful of heavy commodities (coal, oil, iron ore, iron and steel products) form the bulk of traffic. For these railways, it is not merely the level of economic growth but also its composition that is important. For instance, in the 1960s, economic growth was combined with a massive switch from coal to oil as a main fuel, and this hit even those railways which were able to secure some oil traffic (for instance, British Rail carryings of coal and coke declined from 148 m. tons in 1964 to 87 m. tons in 1974. Over the same period, carryings of oil and petroleum products rose only from 7.4 m. tons to 18.6 m. tons). The current prospects of greater stability and long-run growth for the coal industry dramatically affect the prospects for rail carryings. Similarly, trends in the size, location and output of steelworks are crucial. (The extreme case is Belgium, where it is estimated that 75 per cent of domestic rail freight traffic is associated with the iron and steel industry.) Concentration on such products tends to make railways more susceptible to the effects of fluctuations in economic activity than is road transport, with its broadly based traffic.

Within the general merchandise field, it is only for longer distances and larger consignments that rail is able to compete (such traffics are also more favourable for public road hauliers relative to own-account operators). Trends towards increased specialisation and larger plant size tend to increase the proportion of traffic falling into this category, albeit slowly. A key factor here is the prospect for multi-modal methods (piggyback and containerisation). It is in the United States that the growth in this traffic has been strongest, although the system of regulation which holds rates for such traffic very high relative to those for bulk (and especially agricultural) commodities may have limited growth (Friedlander, 1969). In Europe, railways have developed this approach less enthusiastically; only Britain has developed a network of through overnight container trains between all major points, and here lengths of haul are so short that on most routes rail container traffic is only worth while for denser commodities or for maritime traffic.

So far in this section we have tended to assume a fairly conventional future scenario, extrapolating existing trends. Already the events of 1973 (when the price of crude oil quadrupled) have shown how severely these trends may be disrupted by natural resource shortages. The immediate cause of that crisis was political, but it illustrated the immense power possessed by producers of raw materials. Future fears centre on two factors; firstly the risk of further disruptions in supplies due to political circumstances, and secondly the long-run physical shortage of oil reserves, which is expected to lead to declining world production levels towards the end of the century. (Hubbert, 1969).

At first glance, it may be thought that this factor is one of the most hopeful for public transport. Table 1.1, in Chapter 1, shows clearly that consumption of fuel by public transport is lower per unit of output than for private. However, two limitations to this argument must be mentioned. Firstly, whilst it is true that fuel costs are only a small proportion of public passenger transport costs (see Table 11.1) they are generally untaxed or taxed at a very low rate. For the private car, the net-of-tax price of petrol is usually one-half or less of the market price. Even if motorists only perceive petrol costs in their mode-choice decisions, a 100 per cent rise in the pre-tax price of petrol may only raise the perceived cost of motoring by 50 per cent if taxation is not simultaneously raised. In freight transport, a rise in the pre-tax price of fuel may raise road costs by a lower percentage than for rail. In other words, much depends on the reaction of the government to increases in the price of fuel. A gradual increase in the price of fuel for all purposes will be of modest advantage to public transport; physical shortages, rationing or substantial increases in road taxation might produce a greater shift between modes.

Table 11.1 Composition of total cost of principal British transport operators (%) 1976

	BR	National Bus Co.	British Airways Europe	Inter-Continental	National Freight Corporation General	Parcels
Fuel	7	6*	9	18	14*	8*
Staff	67	72	45	35	20†	25†
Other	26	22	46	47	66	67

* Includes vehicle excise duty.
† Drivers only.
Source: Annual reports of nationalised industries.

The second reason why the energy situation may be a mixed blessing for public transport is as follows. Firstly, increases in energy prices appear to have an immediate and serious effect on the cost of living, stimulating wage demands. As a labour-intensive industry, public transport costs are immediately hit by this. Furthermore, the impact of energy price rises on the level of economic activity has mixed effects on public transport demand; whilst a slowdown of growth in car ownership may assist local public transport, long-distance passenger and freight public transport will be adversely affected. Certainly, the 1975 recession had very serious consequences for traffic and financial performance of railways.

Overall, then, it is not clear that the modifications to our previous scenario necessitated by the energy situation are favourable to public transport. Much depends upon the reactions of governments and the success of incomes and employment policies. Only if governments respond to the problem by strong measures to restrict private and promote public transport is the latter likely to benefit. Certainly, any public transport operator who believes that energy crises are automatically helpful to him has not learned the lesson of 1973–75.

11.3 Technical change

In examining changes in transport technology over the past two decades, it is surprising how few major changes of technique have taken place, the grounds of which were not set out many decades earlier. Despite the huge amount of research that has been undertaken, new technology such as personal rapid transit systems (where small vehicles directed by computer respond to the demands of individual users), mini-trams, monorails and hover-trains have not progressed beyond the prototype or demonstration project stage. The mainstay of land-based public transport systems remains the diesel or electric railway, bus or tram. Is this situation likely to change in the future?

A number of factors have contributed to the failure of any completely new mode of transport to make a substantial impact in the past two decades. Firstly, systems have tended to be designed to achieve much-improved performance, perhaps matching that of the car or aircraft, with little thought as to cost. Secondly, introduction of a completely new system involves high overheads in terms of the construction of new infrastructure and inflexibility. For instance, the new stretches of high-speed conventional railway under construction in France and Italy will enable train services to destinations on a large part of the existing network to be improved. Had a new technology been adopted, either a comprehensive new network would have to be built or traffic would need to change mode at the termini of the new system. Similarly, a new urban bus lane or busway may benefit services over a much wider network than could an isolated stretch of a new form of infrastructure. Thirdly, new systems have been designed for a greater degree of automation than is justified by current relative prices (Black et al., 1975). The day may come when labour costs are so high that public transport requires to operate without drivers, ticket collectors, etc. Whilst existing rail systems are capable of being operated on such a basis, it is doubtful whether bus services over shared infrastructure could be. Very high labour costs might justify replacement of bus systems by highly automated mini-trams. But such a day, if it ever comes, is still a long way off, even in the richest countries in the world.

It seems more likely, therefore, that the next two decades will continue the process of marginal, if important, improvements to existing technologies rather than the adoption of completely new ones. Many countries have plans for increasing speeds of conventional rail services, and judging from the evidence in Chapter 8, this should increase the rail long-distance market. The only major retaliation from air would be if acceptable VTOL aircraft operating from urban airports were developed and this seems unlikely. It is more likely that congestion at existing airports and rising fuel costs will hamper the growth of air transport (OECD, 1977).

Further electrification is likely to increase the reliability of rail transport and reduce costs. With respect to buses, it is hard to see major changes forthcoming. Those of most benefit in terms both of cost and service quality would be improved ticket issuing arrangements and more bus priority or reserved bus lanes.

The more significant changes in technology in recent years have been those brought about by the growing use of the computer in management information and planning systems in public transport. Firstly, in terms of short-run planning, the task of timetable preparation, vehicle and crew scheduling is an enormous one involving much manual effort. When undertaken by hand, the various tasks (Fig. 11.1) can only be worked sequentially to produce a feasible solution. Individual stages cannot be optimised, and it is certainly not feasible to produce a variety of timetable specifications for detailed testing. Timetable preparation may need to start 6–12 months before implementation. Computerisation of these processes generally enables better

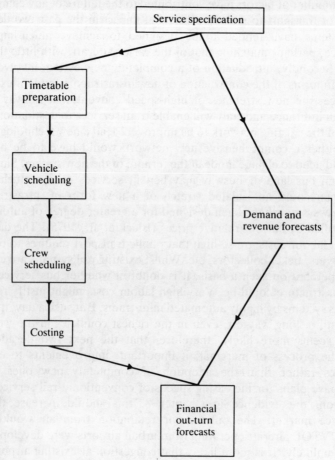

Fig. 11.1 Short-run planning in public transport.

solutions to the individual tasks to be found, saves labour and by producing quick results enables alternatives to be tested and implementation to follow more quickly after services specification. Such techniques are now in use in short-run planning for road haulage, bus (Wren, 1971) and rail (Holt, 1975) services.

Secondly has been the growth of corporate planning techniques. Whilst the use of these does not necessarily involve the use of computers the amount of data manipulation involved is such that some degree of computerisation, if not a full-scale corporate planning model such as that given by Holtgrefe for Netherlands Railways (Holtgrefe, 1975), is almost invariably involved.

Corporate planning generally involves the stages indicated in Fig. 11.2. It is particularly important for undertakings with a high degree of interdependence and where investment is of a long-term nature. Thus it is a more important function for railways, where decisions need to be taken in the context of an examination of the consequences for the company as a whole, than for road haulage and bus companies, where a more piecemeal approach may be adequate. Corporate planning usually examines a time period of 5–10 years. Since the gestation period for major new rail projects or systems reshaping may approach this length it is necessary for railways to look even further ahead at a strategic level.

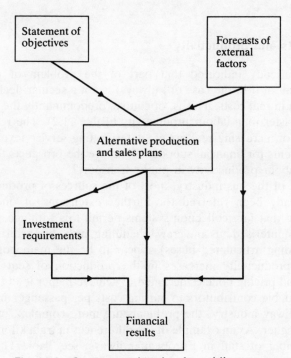

Fig. 11.2 Corporate planning in public transport.

A necessary part of improved management decision techniques has been improved information. Decision-taking by hunch does not necessarily require information, although the quality of the decisions may be improved if a manageable amount of information is available. Scientific decision-taking techniques require data, often in volumes that could never be assimilated directly by the decision-taker himself. It is perhaps in this role that the computer has played its greatest part in aiding public transport operations, whether in the analysis of specific surveys (such as those undertaken as part of the British National Bus Company's Market Analysis Project) or in day-to-day pay-roll, accounting and sales data analysis. For instance, all British Rail ticket machines at major ticket offices contain magnetic tapes which record full information of all tickets sold. This information is analysed to produce data on ticket sales and revenue by origin and destination, ticket type and time period. The result is to enable management to react swiftly to changes in ticket sales, whilst at the same time accumulating time-series data for statistical studies of rail passenger demand.

It is in these spheres that one may expect the spread of existing techniques and the development of new ones to yield the greatest benefits in future decades. However, a word of warning is necessary. Previous chapters have shown that many data concerning public transport operations, particularly cost data, require extremely careful interpretation. The need for management judgement is not removed by the use of new techniques, although it is redirected into a better informed arena.

11.4 Costs and productivity

We have already indicated that part of the problem of public transport (indeed, all of it in the case of railways) is not a secular decline in demand but growth in real costs. This is, of course, predominantly the result of wages growing faster than labour productivity (Table 11.2). The result is some combination of increasing real prices, deteriorating service levels and increased requirements for financial support. What are the prospects for the future growth of labour productivity in public transport?

In the case of the bus industry, most of the sources of productivity increase have already been referred to. Further extensions of one-man operation, provided that fare collection systems permit this with acceptable boarding times, computerised bus and crew scheduling, more bus priority and larger buses (including articulated buses) appear to be the main potential sources of future productivity increases in the production of seat miles. Growth in traffic and pricing policies designed to achieve higher load factors would be most valuable contributors to cutting costs per passenger mile.

For the railway industry, the problems are more complex, but the potential rewards higher. As an example of the differences in train kilometres produced per member of staff in European railways, see Table 11.3. Of course, these differences have a variety of causes. Traffic mix is one major

Table 11.2 Changes in public transport traffic, staff and wages, Great Britain 1967–1977

(%)

	Public road passenger transport	British BR
Traffic units*	−8.6	−5.1
Staff numbers	−13.1	−15.2
Traffic units per man	+5.2	+11.9
Real average earnings	+39.2†	+36.1
Staff cost per traffic unit	+32.3	+21.6

* Passenger miles plus freight ton miles.
† National Bus Company only (Source: Annual Reports).
Source: DTp (1979).
Comparable data is not available for road freight transport.

Table 11.3 Weighted train miles per member of staff for European railways*

(000 s)

	1971	1977	% Change 1971–77
Britain†	0.84	0.91	+8.24
West Germany	0.62	0.62	+0.00
Italy	0.49	0.44	−11.25
Netherlands	1.23	1.31	+6.01
France	0.71	0.80	+12.75
Sweden	1.03	1.20	+16.00
Belgium	0.57	0.58	+1.93
Denmark	0.70	0.81	+16.18
Norway	0.73	0.84	+14.77

* To allow for the lower staff requirements in the passenger sector, passenger train km have been given a weight of 0.45 as against 1 for freight and parcels train km.
† BR figures exclude staff of the subsidiary company British Rail Engineering Limited. If allowance is made for use of BREL staff on heavy maintenance work, British figures for train miles per man would be reduced by some 15%.
Source: Nash (1981)

factor. (Freight trains generally require more terminals and marshalling and shunting staff than passenger. High-frequency regular-interval services permit better utilisation than spasmodic rural services.) Quality of the infrastructure is another – modern electrified main line with colour light signalling requires fewer staff. Nevertheless, a recent study concluded that part of the difference between railways was due to different manning levels (especially the number of staff on a freight train, which in Britain is usually three, as opposed to two or one in some cases elsewhere). Other factors may of course be changed over time by new investment (electrification, signalling, sliding-door stock, automated ticket issuing and collection equipment) and in many cases will inevitably change over time as life-expired equipment is replaced in modern form. Similarly, changes in traffic mix are in part deliberate policy to concentrate in those areas in which labour productivity is highest (the most spectacular change in this respect being that in the BR freight business, from one where 31 per cent of traffic was conveyed in full trainloads in 1968 to 80 per cent in 1977). Between them factors such as these account for very large differences between countries (Netherlands Railways, with a predominantly regular-interval electrified passenger service achieving twice the train kilometres per man of BR) and have permitted some railways (France, Sweden, Denmark) to enjoy very rapid rates of growth in productivity. Again, such increases are most often achieved where traffic is growing rapidly enough to absorb much of the displaced labour. (BR/University of Leeds, 1980).

With road haulage, there is no obvious reason why trends in productivity should differ between the public haulier and own-account sectors, except that public hauliers tend to do more long-haul work and to be in a better position to make use of heavier lorries than own-account operators. The trend to larger vehicles, and the possibility of raising of maximum weight limits, may benefit public hauliers most; on the other hand, greater restrictions on drivers' hours could cause them more difficulties than own-account operators.

One of the greatest problems facing all transport operators in raising productivity is that of industrial relations. In an era of relatively high unemployment, almost any change in working practices is seen as a threat to job security. Even where operators have given no-redundancy guarantees, absorbing displaced labour through natural wastage and/or growth in output, change is resisted as a threat to stability and bargaining power. Particularly in those sectors of the industry in which the labour force is on a long-term downward trend, management discretion is very heavily restricted. Industrial relations lie outside the scope of this text and the current author has no advice to offer on this difficult problem. But the degree to which any of the subject-matter of this text can be applied in practice will depend critically on the success with which management secures the co-operation of unions and workforce in working towards agreed long-term objectives. In other words, planning must take place within the realistic context of what is or may be negotiable; it is no use leaving industrial relations problems to be resolved at the point of implementation. Moreover, confrontation policies are commercially dangerous in an industry where a key quality variable is that of reliability. Private transport offers a high degree of reliability, with the possibility of using public transport as a standby. It is more difficult for firms and individuals who place their reliance on public transport to make short-term switches to private.

11.5   The political arena

The importance of central and local government decisions to the future of public transport will have become apparent at many stages in this text. First and foremost is the critical issue of subsidies. It is clear that in almost all developed countries, public transport is heavily dependent upon subsidies, withdrawal of which would cause substantial changes to networks, frequencies and fares. Our philosophy is that there is good *a priori* justification for public transport subsidy, but that its level can only be determined with reference to other public expenditure options and the total budgetary situation. It is not just the absolute level of subsidy that is important. In Britain, in recent years, we have seen violent swings of policy for and against public transport subsidies, in connection with direct political intervention on pricing and investment decisions. Violent fluctuations in support levels produce similar violent fluctuations in fares and service levels, producing uncertainty for customers and staff alike. Whilst it is a natural part of the political process that changes in government bring changes in the priority given to public transport, it would be helpful if politicians could be convinced of the need to set realistic targets for gradual change over a number of years, with a high level of commitment to future short-run expenditure plans.

The other main way in which politicians affect the future of public transport is in influencing the competitive situation between modes. The level of taxation of road vehicles, quality of the trunk road system, and the degree of competition permitted between modes are particularly important for railways; for instance, the very high level of rail passenger traffic in France must surely be partly the result of high petrol taxes, motorway tolls and near absence of bus and coach competition. For buses and suburban railways, patterns of land use, parking and traffic restraint and bus priorities, are important variables.

The risk is that the absence of immediate dramatic effects from such policies will lead to their neglect, to the long-term peril of local public transport.

11.6   Conclusion

In this chapter, we have commented in brief on the way in which future trends in the economy, new techniques, costs and political attitudes may affect public transport. Our conclusion is that public transport will remain an important industry, with growth in some spheres balancing decline in others. It is also an industry which has a great deal to offer in terms of quality of life, permitting energy-efficient, low-pollution mass transport. But it is important to examine this claim within the context of what the industry realistically can achieve. That is what we have sought to do in this text.

Abbreviations

AASHO	American Association of State Highway Officials
BR	British Rail
BRB	British Railways Board
CIE	Córas Iompair Eireann (Irish State Transport)
CIPFA	Chartered Institute of Public Finance and Accountancy
CTCC	Central Transport Consultative Committee
DOE	Department of the Environment
DTp	Department of Transport
ECMT	European Conference of Ministers of Transport
EEC	European Economic Community
GDP	Gross Domestic Product
LGORU	Local Government Operational Research Unit
MOT	Ministry of Transport
OECD	Organisation for Economic Co-operation and Development
OMO	One-man operated
PTE	Passenger Transport Executive
SCPR	Social and Community Planning Research
SELNEC	South East Lancashire North East Cheshire
TOPS	Total Operations Processing System
TRRL	Transport and Road Research Laboratory
TRTA	Traders' Road Transport Association
VED	Vehicle Excise Duty

References

Acton, P. (1980) 'Successful first year for Border Courier', *Transport*, May/June.

Allen, G. Freeman (1968) 'British Rail Inter-City: the next steps', *Modern Railways*.

American Association of State Highway Officials (1962) *Special Report 61-E*, Highways Research Board, Washington.

Batty, J. M., P. Hall and D. N. M. Starkie (1973) 'The impact of fares free public transport upon urban land use and activity patterns' in *Symposium on Public Transport Fare Structure*, TRRL, Supplementary Report 37 UC, Crowthorne.

Baum, H. (1973) 'Free public transport', *Journal of Transport Economics and Policy*, Vol. 7.

Baumol, W. J., and D. F. Bradford (1970) 'Optimal departures from marginal cost pricing', *American Economic Review*.

Baumol, W. J., and W. E. Oates (1971) 'Use of standards and prices for protection of the environment', *Swedish Journal of Economics*.

Bayliss, B. T. (1973) *The Road Haulage Industry Since 1968*, DOE, London.

Bayliss, B. T. (1979) 'Transport in the European communities', *Journal of Transport Economics and Policy*, Vol. 13.

Bayliss, B. T., and S. J. Edwards (1970) *Industrial Demand for Transport*, MOT, London.

Beesley, M. E. (1971) 'Economic criteria for the maintenance, modification or creation of public transport services which may not necessarily be profitable', *4th International Symposium on Theory and Practice in Transport Economics*, ECMT, The Hague.

Beesley, M. E. (1973) 'Regulation of taxis', *Economic Journal*, Vol. 83.

Beesley, M. E. (1974) *Economic Criteria for the Maintenance, Modification or Creation of Public Urban and Suburban Transport Services which may not necessarily be profitable*, ECMT Round Table 24, Paris.

Beesley, M. E., and C. D. Foster (1965) 'The Victoria Line: social benefit and finances', *Journal of the Royal Statistical Society*, Series A, Vol. 128.

Black, I., *et al.* (1975) *Advanced Urban Transport*, Saxon House, London.

Bly, P. H. (1976) *Depleted Bus Services: the effect of rescheduling*, TRRL Report 699, Crowthorne.

Bonavia, M. R. (1971) *The Organisation of British Railways*, Ian Allan, Shepperton.

Bonsall, P. W. (1981) 'Car sharing in the United Kingdom', *Journal of Transport Economics and Policy*, Vol. 15.

British Railways Board/Department of Transport (1979) *Review of Main Line Electrification – Interim Report*, HMSO, London.

British Railways Board/University of Leeds (1980) *A Comparative Study of European Rail Performance*, BRB, London.

British Railways Board (1963) *The Reshaping of British Railways*, BRB, London.

British Railways Board (1976) *Strategic Planning Studies – environmental and social impact study*, BRB, London.

British Railway Board (1978) *Measuring Cost and Profitability in British Rail*, BRB, London.

Bruce, D. M. (1977) 'Buses in newly designed housing areas', *Proceedings of the Planning and Transport Research and Computation Ltd. Summer Annual Meeting*, University of Warwick.

Central Transport Consultative Committee (1977) *Report on British Rail Fares Policy*, CTCC, London.

Chapman, P. (1975) *Fuel's Paradise*, Penguin, Harmondsworth.

Chartered Institute of Public Finance and Accountancy (1974) *Passenger Transport Operations*, CIPFA, London.

Chisholm, M. (1959) 'Economies of scale in road goods transport', *Oxford Economic Papers*.

Chisholm, M., and P. O'Sullivan (1973) *Freight Flows and Spatial Aspects of the British Economy*, Cambridge University Press, Cambridge.

Clemow, C. J. (1972) 'Planning for Railway Electrification', *Proceedings of the Institute of Electrical Engineers*, Vol. 119.

Cmnd 3686 (1968) *Transport in London*, HMSO, London.

Cmnd 4483 (1970) *Report on the London Taxicab Trade*, HMSO, London.

Cole, H. S. D., *et al.* (1973) *Thinking About the Future*, Chatto and Windus, London.

Coles, O. B. (1978) 'Accessibility goals and the optimisation of rural bus services', *Tenth Annual Seminar on Public Transport Operations Research*, University of Leeds.

Collings, J. J., D. Rigby and J. K. Welsby (1976) *Passenger Response to Bus Fares: some evidence*, DOE, Economic and Statistical Notes No. 24, London.

Dalvi, M. Q., and C. A. Nash (1977) 'The redistributive impact of road investment' in P. Bonsall, M. Q. Dalvi and P. J. Hills, Eds, *Urban Transportation Planning*, Abacus Press, Tunbridge Wells.

Dawson, R. F. F., and P. Vass (1974) *Vehicle Operating Costs in 1973*, TRRL Report, LR661, Crowthorne.

Department of Employment (1979) *Family Expenditure Survey 1978*, HMSO, London.

Department of the Environment (1971) *Studies of Rural Transport in Devon and West Suffolk*, HMSO, London.

Department of the Environment (1973) *Report of the Urban Motorways Project Team to the Urban Motorways Committee*, HMSO, London.

Department of the Environment (1975) *National Travel Survey 1972/3*, HMSO, London.

Department of the Environment (1976) *Transport Policy: a consultation document*, HMSO, London.

Department of Transport (1979) *Transport Statistics: Great Britain 1968–78*, HMSO, London.

Dodgson, J. S. (1973) 'External effects in road investment', *Journal of Transport Economics and Policy*.

Dodgson, J. S. (1977) 'Cost–benefit analysis, government policy and the British railway network', *Transportation*, June.

Dyos, H. J., and D. H. Aldcroft (1969) *British Transport*, Leicester University Press, Leicester.

Edwards, S. L. (1969) 'Transport costs in the wholesale trades', *Journal of Transport Economics and Policy*, Vol. 3.

Edwards, S. L. (1970) 'Transport costs in British industry', *Journal of Transport Economics and Policy*, Vol. 4.

Edwards, S. L., and B. T. Bayliss (1971) *Operating Costs in Road Freight Transport*, DOE, London.

Eilon, S., C. D. T. Watson-Gandy and N. Christofides (1971) *Distribution Management*, Griffin, London.

European Conference of Ministers of Transport (1971) *Determination of Elasticities of Demand for the Various Means of Urban Passenger Transport*, 13th Round Table on Transport Economics, ECMT, Paris.

Evans, A. W. (1968) *A Study of Inter City Travel Between London, the West Midlands and the North West of England*, University of Birmingham, Birmingham.

Evans, A. W. (1969) 'Inter city travel and the LM electrification', *Journal of Transport Economics and Policy*, Vol. 3.

Evans, A. (1973) *The Economics of Residential Location*, Macmillan, London.

Fairhurst, M. H. (1975) 'The influence of public transport on car ownership', *Journal of Transport Economics and Policy*, Vol. 19.

Fairhurst, M. H., and P. J. Morris (1975) *Variations in the Demand for Bus and Rail Travel up to 1974*, London Transport Economic Research Report R210, London.

Fernando, G. W. (1971) 'The use of own-account operators' accounting information for quantity licensing', unpublished M.Phil Thesis, Leeds University.

Foster, C. D., Chairman (1978) *Report of the Independent Inquiry into Road Haulage Operators' Licensing*, HMSO, London.

Foster, C. D., and M. E. Beesley (1963) 'Estimating the social benefits of constructing an underground railway in London', *Journal of the Royal Statistical Society*, Series A, Vol. 126.

Foster, C. D., and S. Joy (1967) 'Railway track costs in Britain' in *Development of Railway Traffic Engineering*, Institution of Civil Engineers, London.

Fowkes, A. S., A. D. Pearman and K. J. Button (1978) 'The sensitivity of car ownership of households in West Yorkshire to household accessibility', *Proceedings of the Planning and Transportation Research and Computation Ltd. Summer Annual Meeting*, University of Warwick.

Fowler, D. (1979) 'Financial analysis of railway operations', *Chartered Institute of Transport Journal*, May.

Friedlander, A. F. (1969) *The Dilemma of Freight Transport Regulation*, Brookings Institution, Washington.

Ghosh, D., D. Lees and W. Seal (1975) 'Optimal motorway speed and some valuations of time and life', *Manchester School*.

Glaister, S., and J. J. Collings (1978) 'Theory and practice of maximising passenger miles', *Journal of Transport Economics and Policy*, Vol. 12.

Glaister, S., and D. Lewis (1977) 'An integrated fares policy for London', paper presented to the Centre for Environmental Studies Urban Economics Conference, Keele University.

Grey, A. (1975) *Urban Fares Policy*, Saxon House, Farnborough.

Griffiths, A. (1974) 'Rail passenger transport and regional development', paper presented to the Regional Studies Association Conference, London.

Grigg, A. O., and P. G. Smith (1977) *An Opinion Survey of the Yorkshire Dales Rail Service in 1975*, TRRL Report 769, Crowthorne.

Gustafson, R. L., H. N. Curd and T. F. Golob (1971) *User Preferences for a Demand Responsive Transportation System*, Highway Research Record 367, Highway Research Board.

Gwilliam, K. M., and P. J. Mackie (1975) *Economics and Transport Policy*, Allen and Unwin, London.

Hall, P. (1974) *The Containment of Urban England*, Allen and Unwin, London.

Hamer, N., and S. Potter (1979) *Vital Travel Statistics*, Transport 2000, London.

Harman, R. G. (1974) 'Fuel in transport', *Traffic Engineering and Control*.

Harrison, (1965) 'Some notes on road transport costs', *Bulletin of the Oxford University Institute of Economics and Statistics*, Vol. 27.

Harrison, A. J., and P. J. Mackie (1973) *The Comparability of Cost Benefit and Financial Rates of Return*, HMSO, London.

Harrison A. J., and D. Quarmby (1969) 'The value of time' in R. Layard, Ed., *Cost–Benefit Analysis*, Penguin, Harmondsworth 1972.

Heaver, T. D., and J. C. Nelson (1977) *Railway Pricing under Commercial Freedom – the Canadian experience*, University of British Columbia, Vancouver.

Hensher, D. A. (1977) *Value of Business Travel Time*, Pergamon Press, Oxford.

Hensher, D. A., P. B. McLeod and J. K. *Stanley* (1975) 'Usefulness of attitudinal measures in investigating the choice of travel mode', *International Journal of Transport Economics*, Vol. 2.

Hibbs, J. (1975) *The Bus and Coach Industry: its economics and organisation*, Dent, London.

Hill, G. J. (1973) 'A note on the redistributive effects of a zero-fare public transport policy', in *Symposium on Public Transport Fare Structure*, TRRL Supplementary Report 37 UC, Crowthorne.

Hillman, M. (1973) *Personal Mobility and Transport Policy*, Political and Economic Planning, Broadsheet 542, London.

Hoinville, G. (1971) 'Evaluating community preferences', *Environment and Planning*.

Holland, E. P., and P. L. Watson (1978) 'Traffic restraint in Singapore', *Traffic Engineering and Control*.

Holt, J. (1975) 'The planning of train services using computer methods', *Rail International*.

Holtgrefe, A. A. I. (1975) *An Optimising Medium-Term Planning Model for the Netherlands Railways*, Rotterdam University Press, Rotterdam.

Hubbert, M. King (1969) 'Energy resources' in National Academy of Sciences National Research Council, *Resources and Man*, W. H. Freeman, San Francisco.

Johnson, K. M. and H. C. Garnett (1971) *The Economics of Containerisation*, Allen and Unwin, London.

Johnston, J. (1960) *Statistical Cost Analysis*, McGraw-Hill, New York.

Johnston, J. (1963) *Econometric Methods*, McGraw-Hill, New York.

Jones, I. S. (1977) *Urban Transport Appraisal*, Macmillan, London.

Joy, S. (1971) 'Pricing and investment in railway freight services', *Journal of Transport Economics and Policy*, Vol. 5.

Kain, J. F., J. R. Meyer and M. Wohl (1965) *The Urban Transportation Problem*, Harvard University Press, Cambridge, Mass.

Keeler, T. E. (1974) 'Railroad costs, returns to scale and excess capacity', *Review of Economics and Statistics*.

Kemp, M. A. (1973) 'Reduced fare and fare free urban transit services – some case studies', in *Symposium on Public Transport Fare Structure*, TRRL Supplementary Report 37 UC, Crowthorne.

Kolsen, H., and G. Docwra (1977) 'Resource allocation, price theory and policy' in D. A. Hensher, Ed, *Urban Transport Economics,* Cambridge University Press, Cambridge.

Kraft, G., and T. A. Domencich (1972) 'Free transit', in M. Edel and J. Rothenburg, Eds, *Readings in Urban Economics*, Collier-Macmillan, New York.

Lancaster, K. J. (1966) 'A new approach to consumer theory', *Journal of Political Economy*.

Lave, L. B. (1972) 'The demand for inter city passenger transportation', *Journal of Regional Science*, Vol. 12.

Leake, G. R. (1971) *Inter City Modal Split in Great Britain – air versus rail*, Centre for Transport Studies, University of Leeds.

Lee, N., and I. Steedman (1970) 'Economies of scale in bus transport', *Journal of Transport Economics and Policy*.

Leitch, Sir George, Chairman (1977) *Report of the Advisory Committee on Trunk Road Assessment*, HMSO, London.

Lewis, D. (1977) 'Estimating the influence of public transport on road traffic levels in Greater London', *Journal of Transport Economics and Policy*.

Local Government Operational Research Unit (1976) *The Subscriber Bus: a new way of financial rural transport*, Manchester.

Luttrell, F. (1962) *Factory Location and Industrial Movement*, National Institute of Economic and Social Research, London.

McClenahan, J. W., and D. R. Kaye (1975) 'A method of bus route costing developed by Arthur Anderson and Co.', in *Symposium on the Costing of Bus Operations*, TRRL Report SR 180 UC, Crowthorne.

Mackett, R. L. (1977) 'A dynamic activity allocation transportation model' in P. Bonsall, M. Q. Dalvi and P. Hills, Ed., *Urban Transportation Planning*, Abacus Press, Tunbridge Wells.

Mackie, P. J. (1977) 'Costs of operating bus and rail services in urban areas', paper given at the *Symposium on Integrating Public Transport*, Newcastle University.

Mansfield, N. W. (1969) 'Recreational trip generation', *Journal of Transport Economics and Policy*, Vol. 3.

Melinek, S. J. (1974) *Methods for Determining the Optimum Level of Safety Expenditure*, Building Research Establishment Current Paper CP 88/74, DOE, London.

Meyer, J. R., *et al.* (1959) *The Economics of Competition in the Transportation Industries*, Harvard University Press, Cambridge, Mass.

Meyer, J. R., and M. R. Straszheim (1971) *Pricing and Project Evaluation*, Brookings Institution, Washington.

Miller, D. R. (1970) 'Differences among cities and firms and costs of urban bus transport', *Journal of Industrial Economics*.

Miller, J. H., and J. C. Rea (1973) *A Comparison of Cost Models*, Highway Research Record No. 435 Highways Research Board, Washington.

Ministry of Transport (1963) *Road Pricing: the technical and economic possibilities*, HMSO, London.

Ministry of Transport (1968a) *The Cambrian Coast Line*, HMSO, London.

Ministry of Transport (1968b) *Road Track Costs*, HMSO, London.

Mohring, H. (1972) 'Optimisation and scale economics in urban bus transportation', *American Economic Review*.

Moseley, M. J., *et al.* (1977) *Rural Transport and Accessibility*, University of East Anglia, Norwich.

Moss, A. J., and G. R. Leake (1976) *Modal Choice to Central Area Rail Termini – preliminary analysis*, Working Paper 86, Institute for Transport Studies, Leeds University.

Nash, C. A. (1976) 'The replacement of road transport vehicles', *Journal of Transport Economics and Policy*, Vol. 10.

Nash, C. A. (1978) 'Management objectives in bus transport', *Journal of Transport Economics and Policy*, Vol. 12.

Nash, C. A. (1981) 'Government policy and rail transport in Western Europe', *Transport Reviews*.

Organisation for Economic Co-operation and Development, *The Future of European Passenger Transport*, OECD, Paris.

Parker, G. B., and D. A. Blackledge (1975) 'The RTM method of bus operations costing developed for the Bradford Bus Study', in *Symposium on the Costing of Bus Operations*, TRRL Report SR 180 UC, Crowthorne.

Parker, P. (1978) *A Way to Run a Railway*, Haldane Memorial Lecture, Birkbeck College, London, reprinted in *Modern Railways*, May/June.

Peaker, A. (1974) 'Economics of VTOL civil aircraft', *Journal of Transport Economics and Policy*, Vol. 8.

Percival, A. J. P. (1977) 'Experience with travelcards', paper given at the *Symposium on Integrating Public Transport*, Newcastle University.

Plowden, S. P. C. (1971) 'Transportation studies examined', *Journal of Transport Economics and Policy*.

Pryke, R. (1977) 'The case against subsidies', in *A Policy for Transport*, Nuffield Foundation, Oxford.

Quandt, R., Ed. (1970) *The Demand for Travel – theory and measurement*, Heath-Lexington, Farnborough.

Quandt, R., and W. J. Baumol (1966) 'The demand for abstract modes', *Journal of Regional Science*.

Quarmby, D. A. (1973) 'Effects of alternative fares systems on operational efficiency: British experience', in *Symposium on Public Transport Fare Structure*, TRRL Supplementary Report 37 UC, Crowthorne.

Rao, P. S. (1978a) 'Forecasting demand for rail freight', *Journal of Transport Economics and Policy*, Vol. 12.

Rao, P. S. (1978b) 'The impact of structural and compositional changes on the Canadian railway industry 1958–73', *Transportation Research*, Vol. 12.

Rees, G. (1975) *A Study of Passenger Transport Needs of Rural Wales*, Welsh Council, Cardiff.

Rhys, D. G., and M. J. Buxton (1974) 'Car ownership and the rural transport problem', *Chartered Institute of Transport Journal*, July.

Seddon, P. A., and M. P. Day (1974) 'Bus passenger waiting times in Greater Manchester', *Traffic Engineering and Control*.

Sharp, C. (1973) *Living with the Lorry*, Transport Studies Unit, Leicester University.

Sharp, C., and A. Jennings (1977) *Transport and the Environment*, Leicester University Press, Leicester.

Smith, M. G., and P. T. McIntosh (1973) 'Fares elasticity and interpretation', in *Symposium on Public Transport Fare Structure*, TRRL Supplementary Report 37 UC, Crowthorne.

Social and Community Planning Research (1978) *Road Traffic and Environment*, London.

Starkie, D. N. M. (1971) 'Modal split and the value of time: a note on idle time', *Journal of Transport Economics and Policy*.

Stopher, P. R., B. D. Spear and P. O. Sucher (1974) *Towards the Development of Measures of Convenience for Travel Modes*, Transport Research Record 527, Transport Research Board.

Tanner, J. C. (1974) *Forecasts of Vehicles and Traffic in Great Britain*, TRRL Report LR 650, Crowthorne.

Tanner, J. C., and D. A. Lynam (1973) 'Benefits of reduced fares in London estimated from the CRISTAL model' in *Symposium on Public Transport Fare Structure*, TRRL Supplementary Report 37 UC, Crowthorne.

Traders Road Transport Association (1959) *Survey of 'C' Licensed Vehicles*, London.

Train, K. (1977) 'Transit prices under increasing returns to sale and a loss constraint', *Journal of Transport Economics and Policy*.

Transport and Road Research Laboratory (1977) *Symposium on Unconventional Bus Services*, TRRL Supplementary Report 336, Crowthorne.

Travers Morgan, R. (1976) *Bradford Bus Study; final report*, London.

Tyler, J., and R. Hassard (1973) 'Gravity/elasticity models for the planning of the inter urban rail passenger business', *Proceedings of the Planning and Transportation Research and Computation Ltd. Summer Annual Meeting*, University of Warwick.

Victor, P. A. (1972) *Pollution, Economy and Environment*, Allen and Unwin, London.

Wabe, J., and O. Coles (1975) 'Short and long run costs of urban buses', *Journal of Transport Economics and Policy*.

Walters, M. A., and W. M. McCleod (1956) 'A note on bankruptcy in road haulage', *Journal of Industrial Economics*, Vol. 5.

Warner, B., and S. Joy (1971) 'The economics of rail container operations in Britain', *Rail International*, April.

Watson, P. L. (1974) *The Value of Time: behavioural models of mode choice*, Lexington, Farnborough.

Webster, F. V. (1975) 'Bus travel and the next ten years', paper given at the Annual Conference of Association of Public Passenger Transport, Bournemouth.

Webster, F. V. (1976) *Fares Structure for Bus Stage Services*, TRRL Report LR 704, Crowthorne.

Webster, F. V. (1977) *Urban Passenger Transport – some trends and prospects*, TRRL Report LR 771, Crowthorne.

White, P. (1976) *Planning for Public Transport*, Hutchinson, London.

Whitley, M. (1977) 'Optimising public transport performance – the London method', paper given at the *Symposium on Integrating Public Transport*, Newcastle University.

Williams, S. R. (1976) *The Calibration of Trip Generation Models for Cross Country Railway Services on the Southern Region*, Polytechnic of Central London Transport Studies Group, Working Paper No. 5.

WYTCONSULT (1978) *West Yorkshire Transportation Study Final Report*, West Yorkshire Metropolitan County Council, Wakefield.

Wren, A. (1971) *Computers in Transport Planning and Operations*, Ian Allan, London.

Wyckoff, D. Daryl (1976) *Railway Management*, Lexington, New York.

Index